GUIDE FOR
THE CHRISTIAN ASSEMBLY

THIERRY MAERTENS – JEAN FRISQUE

GUIDE FOR THE
CHRISTIAN ASSEMBLY

REVISED EDITION

9th to 21st SUNDAYS

Notre Dame, Indiana 46556

TRANSLATED FROM THE FRENCH BY MOLAISE MEEHAN, O.S.B.

Nihil Obstat: V. Descamps
can. libr. cens.

Imprimatur: J. Thomas, *vic. gen.*
Tournai, March 28, 1970

© Copyright, 1972, Fides Publishers, Inc.
Notre Dame, Indiana

LCCCN: 72-114245

ISBN: 0-8190-0005-1

2773

Translated from the original French edition,
Guide de l'assemblée chrétienne, Casterman, 1970.
An edition of St. Andrews Abbey, Bruges.

CONTENTS

NINTH SUNDAY

A. THE WORD

I. Deuteronomy 11:18, 26-28
1st reading
1st cycle

This passage concludes the second portion of Deuteronomy (6-11). It reminds us how carefully the memory of the law ought to be preserved (v. 18, recalling Dt 6:6-9), and gives us the doctrine of the two ways, that of blessing and that of curse (vv. 16-28), one the way of obedience, the other the disobedience to the law.

Israel of course is thoroughly engaged to the way of blessing. It is a way of blessing because it is the result of God's own life communicated to his people, and for contrary reasons its opposite is a way of curse. The communication of life springs from the love God bears to his people which procures for them prosperity and success (vv. 26-27; cf. Dt 23:6; 28:8; 30:1). True, this communication seems to be always expressed in very material terms. We ought not to find this surprising. The realization that God wills good fortune for his own, and is concerned to achieve that, is an important one. Of themselves the people cannot attain it. So, the choice between obedience and disobedience is a grave one.

It is true I suppose that there is an element of ultimatum about the choice: with me, blessing; without me, chaos. Nevertheless the sharpness of the dilemma underlines effectively the importance of this choice, and it accords fully with the encounter in mutual fidelity of two free agents.*

---

*See the doctrinal theme: *obedience*, p. 18.

1

II. Deuteronomy The Bible gives us two versions of the deca-
5:12-15 logue: the present one, which belongs to the
1st reading reform of Josias, and the one in Exodus 20,
2nd cycle which comes from ancient Yahwist and Elohist
sources, but has been revised according to
the priestly tradition.

The structure and literary form of the precepts is very distinc-
tive. We are dealing with an apodictic genre, where the formula
is given in the second person (you shall not kill) and the
ensemble of precepts constitutes either a decalogue, or a dodeca-
logue, in phrases of a highly rhythmic pattern. The genre is distinct
from the usual juridical style of the Orient, where precepts are
conditional, and in the third person (if a man kills — he shall —:
the more usual formula in Israel).

In its original form the apodictic genre is quite absolute, an
expression of will (on the part of God or the legislator) which
cannot be gainsaid. So absolute is it that there is no question of
sanctions, no preoccupation with particular cases, exceptions,
or consequences.

a) The portion of the decalogue that we have in today's reading concerns *Sabbath* observance. It is the only Deuteronomic
text that deals with this observance, doubtless because at that
particular epoch no problem was posed in this area. Contrary to
the legislation in Exodus 20, here the Sabbath is linked with the
deliverance from Egypt. This is very characteristic of Deuteronomy, where there is a constant anxiety to maintain an awareness of the principal events of salvation history.

b) Our text is highly important. Rest is prescribed for each
category of people, from the head of the family right down to
the stranger. In this it does no more than reproduce the code
of the Alliance, even to the point of repeating its terms. Evidently
however, in prescribing rest, the purpose is rather to assure the
well-being of subordinates, servants, beasts, and strangers, than
that of the family head. This reflects an important social evolu-

tion that took place at the time of Deuteronomy. The small proprietors had been ousted by the city bourgeoisie, and found themselves obliged, in order to live, to hire themselves out or enslave themselves. The Law was taking precautions to ensure such slaves a minimum of dignity by prescribing one day's rest in the week.

Our notion of *servile works* has its origin in dispositions like these. True, the head of the family, and the proprietor, is forbidden to work; but the interdict is mainly concerned with work done by slaves on the property. The purpose is to ensure them a day's relief.

Such concern is characteristic both of the Law and of Deuteronomy. The text we are considering is remarkable in that it gives a religious dimension to this Sabbath social reform: "you have been yourself a slave in Egypt and God has set you free. Do likewise for your slaves by freeing them for one day of the week." What we can discern is a rereading of the Sabbath rest legislation in the light of the desert experience. On one day of the week slaves are released from work in order to proclaim the deliverance of the people from slavery in Egypt. The rest itself gets a new dimension. It is no longer mere "cessation" from work, as in the first stage. It becomes an observance which manifests the dignity of men delivered from Egypt. For this reason too there is more concern with servile works. They recall more vividly Egyptian slavery than the tasks performed by the head of the family or the proprietor.

We can regard this as the most profound of the spiritual insights brought about by Deuteronomy in the contemporary liturgy. The Yahwist document had already linked the Sabbath rest with the desert event; but it did so negatively. In Deuteronomy this cessation in Sabbath rest from servile works reflects the pride of a people who have been delivered from Egypt, and commemorate that by freeing their inferior members one day a week from work.*

* See the doctrinal theme: *Sabbath and Sunday*, p. 24.

III. 1 Kings   When God took possession in the cloud of his
8:41-43   temple (1 K 8:1-11), Solomon addressed a
1st reading   brief discourse to the people, pointing out the
3rd cycle   significance of this dedication (1 K 8:14-21).
Afterwards he made a prayer of thanksgiving.
The redaction of this that we have is altogether deuteronomic
(6th century). It has the classic structure of Jewish thanks-
givings: thanks to God for his benevolence (v. 23), commemora-
tion of the fulfillment of the promises (v. 24), a very long
epiclesis with multiple intentions (vv. 25-40), a doxology in conclusion (vv. 52-61). Verses 41-50 are a series of additions made
to the king's prayer after the exile.

The chief interest of Solomon's prayer is emphasis on the link
between all prayer and the temple, and the necessity in order to
encounter God of *mediation* through the temple. Our verses
today give us the universalist aspect of the temple. They affirm
that the temple's mediation is not confined to those who pray
within its walls. It is sufficient to turn towards the temple from
any place on earth. Even the stranger can benefit by the mediation if he turns with faith to the temple of Sion. God is the God
of all men, Jews or strangers, publicans or Pharisees.
Jewish man then had an awareness of the necessity of a mediator in order to reach God. The temple however, in that capacity,
was too localized and too material. When Jesus presents himself
as the temple of the new covenant (Jn 2:18-21) he is maintain-
ing the principle of mediation in prayer (cf. Jn 16:24-26); but,
because he takes the monopoly himself, he is freeing human
prayer from any attachment to a temple or a place (Mt 6:5-8;
Jn 4:21-23). His mediation consists in the alignment with his will
of the will of the person praying. In some way the Christian's
lips take on the very prayer of Christ himself, and of the Father's
spirit (Rm 8:26-27). The eucharistic assembly, being the body
of Christ, is an essential focus of mediation in Christian prayer.
This aspect will be emphasized according to the dimension of

Christian faith. It must be perceived as the point where "the name of the Lord resides," the accomplishment of his will, the channel of his sacrifice.

IV. Romans   Paul has just concluded his gloomy picture of
3:21-25, 28   humanity left to its own devices, and now
2nd reading   embarks on the positive section of his letter:
1st cycle   the revelation of salvation in Jesus Christ (Rm
3:21). The section is made up of kerygmatic proclamations, and of analyses and proofs. In style and content the early verses, from which today's passage is taken, are clearly a "solemn proclamation," or kerygma, which is however occasionally interrupted. We can then expect to encounter in it extremely important ideas and phrases, which are not necessarily made explicit: justice (vv. 21-28), redemption (v. 24), propitiation (v. 25), faith in works (vv. 27-28), etc.

a) God's justice is first and foremost an event ("and now" v. 21). Already in the Old Testament ("The law and the prophets" of verse 21) God's justice meant not his judgment (over "the good and the evil") but his fidelity to the covenant, and his concern that this should prove fruitful for a humanity conformed to his will, even though this should require from him mercy and pardon. In this sense God's justice (v. 21) is contrasted with his anger (Rm 1:18), which proves destructive of the covenant. "Now," that is to say in the eschatological era that has arrived, justice is definitively manifested in Jesus Christ. He is the first man to become witness of God's "justice." Thanks to this, every man who follows Jesus in surmounting the barriers of death and egoism, and he who believes in him can live by the same justice (v. 24).

b) This justice was manifested by Jesus on the cross, above all in the work of *redemption* here accomplished. It was thus that God manifested his justice to the Jews, sinners though they were, by "ransoming" them from Egyptian captivity (Dt 5-6), by "ransoming" them again from the Babylonian exile to which they were reduced by their sins (Is 41-14). Today however all this is past (vv. 25-26a). God is undertaking the ransom of man from death itself (Rm 8:23), and from sin, by offering him, through communion with the Risen Christ, the opportunity of overcoming sin (Col 1:13-14; Ep 1:7). Redemption indeed is coterminous with God's justice. It is that act of God which enables man to go beyond himself, his limitations and his alienations, his sin and his death. Once man lives with the God of Jesus Christ, he can aspire to this.

c) How has God brought about this "redemption"? In verse 25 we have Paul's answer, where he makes Christ the "instrument of propitiation." We cannot say really whether Paul is thinking explicitly of the rite at the expiation ceremony, where the high priest poured the blood of the sacrificed victim on the "propitiatory" of the ark (Lv 16:15), or whether he uses the word "propitiation" in the general sense of appeasing the wrath of God. At the risk of making God a sanguinary figure, whose desire for vengeance could be appeased only by the sight of blood, the first interpretation seems the more likely. On the day of expiation the sinner was "ransomed" because the victim's blood (a symbol of life) came directly into contact with God on the propitiatory. In some fashion an exchange of life took place: a renewal of man's life by contact with that of God. Christ is a "propitiation," not because he offers himself up to God's wrath, but because he is the propitiatory place where human blood (life) comes into permanent contact with God, even in death. Paul's idea is not that God stemmed his wrath on seeing the blood of his Son, but that the only means of demonstrating the plentitude of God's justice was the blending of human and divine life that the incarnation meant. In verse 25, blood is not a sign of death, nor of divine wrath that has been dramatically appeased. It is, as it was in the Old Testament, a sign of life, life that has been renewed by God, restored and pardoned.

d) This "redemption" or "expiation" is absolutely gratuitous. That is Paul's point when he contrasts the works of the law with *faith alone* (vv. 27-28). He is explaining how man is enabled to benefit from the manifestation of God's "justice" that we have in Christ's "propitiation."

In order to understand his view we must remember that Paul distinguishes between justification and salvation (which Judaism did not). Justification, as he sees it, is already accomplished in Jesus Christ, while salvation (and God's judgment) is reserved until the end of time (Rm 5:9). No work of the law is sufficient to gain justification: faith is the only way (v. 30; cf. Ga 2:16; Rm 4:5). For final salvation on the other hand works are necessary (Rm 8:3-4, 14-10; 2 Co 5:10; Col 3:25; cf. 1 Co 15:9-10; Ep 2:8-10). Christian life indeed is rich in works because it is a compenetration of human by divine activity. This guarantees the gratuitousness of salvation, but in a way that differs from the absolute gratuitousness of justification.

V. 2 Corinthians This is a continuation of Paul's apologia for
4:6-11 his ministry. He had been sharply criticized.
2nd reading His numerous shortcomings, as well as his
2nd cycle frequent failures, had been alleged as evidence
that he was not an apostle. He began his
apologia by describing the glory of the Christian ministry (2 Co 3:4–4:6). Now he can turn to the matter of his own shortcomings in the apostolate. He shows that not only do they not annul his titles to glory: they actually guarantee him a share in the paschal mystery of Christ.

a) The *contradiction of the apostolic life** has its roots in the fact that an apostolic power given by God coexists with the human weakness entrusted with that power. Some of Paul's antitheses may be cast in the Stoic mould, but he makes them

*See the doctrinal theme: *growth in weakness*, p. 160.

serve his purpose well. His first is a contrast between the weakness of the apostolic life and the power of God which cancels this weakness (vv. 7-11). His next is a contrast between the weakness of his apostolate and the Corinthian pretensions to power (v. 12).

b) However this contradiction is merely a dimension of a more radical contradiction that underlies all Christian life: the *death* and *resurrection* of Jesus (vv. 10, 11, 14). He, like all Christians, shares the death of Christ by his failures and his sufferings. In the success of his mission, in the life kindled in others by his ministry, he shares the resurrection.

The contradiction endured by Paul in his apostolate becomes the lot of the Church today. She is living in a world which is enamored of death, the death of God and the death of man, of demythologizing and of desacralization. Yet she has the duty of proclaiming life in these conditions. She must show the true face of God, and the true face of man in Jesus Christ, to people who believe that God is as hidden as to be altogether incapable of manifesting himself.

Indeed there are times when the picture she presents either of God's visage, or that of man, is something woefully inadequate. For instance, when she fails to champion the tortured and the humiliated. How similar to Paul's both her grandeur and her weakness! No sooner does a particular image become established than its limitations appear, and those who would change it wind up by deforming it. We keep wishing that the Church's image were as constant as that of the God she reflects, but it is only in constant movement, constant transformation, that she finds herself. We keep wishing she would be vocal, but she is silent. She is looking for an idiom that will be comprehensible to the world that is. . . . Sometimes she discovers that silence is the only form of presence possible for her.

How contradictory her image really is. Aware of sin, but proclaiming mercy; involved in the toil of human beings, but living by the presence of another; she must bear witness to the fidelity of God and yet remain precariously associated with men and women who are neither saints nor heroes.

VI. **Galatians**   At the time of writing this letter, towards
    1:1-2, 6-10   the end of the year 57, Paul had already
    2nd reading   traversed Galatia twice (Ac 16:6, 18:23). On
    3rd cycle   the first occasion he had had an enthusiastic
welcome. There was more reserve the second time. Judaizers had been propagating another gospel in the meantime (Ga 1:8-9), based more on the law than on Christ, and had called Paul's personal authority into question (Ga 5:1, 13). At the time he was unable to stay long enough to deal with the crisis, to which his audience had shown feeble resistance (Ga 1:6, 3:1, 4:17, 6:12). Consequently, when he is at leisure, he sends them a fairly harsh letter.

The exordium of the letter indicates its plan and purpose very well. He is about to vindicate his apostleship (v. 1), and the content of his gospel (v. 4).

a) The Judaizers who succeeded Paul in Galatia challenged his *apostleship*. Doubtless, for them, the only true apostles were the twelve in Jerusalem. Paul did not belong to their group, and furthermore, at least as they saw it, he had received his mandate merely from the Antioch community (Ac 13:1-3), or from Barnabas (Ac 11:25-26). Paul does not deny the human element in the shaping of his vocation, but he insists on the divine element. The proof of divine influence is the link between his ministry and Christ's resurrection (v. 1b): it was the risen Christ indeed that he had encountered on the road to Damascus (Ac 9:1-19, 22:6-16; 26:12-18; Ga 1:12-17; 1 Co 9:1, 15:8). He is here modifying the concept of the Twelve about apostleship. Their initial concept was not missionary, but juridical. They were called, they felt, to judge the tribes at the inauguration of the

Kingdom (Mt 19:28; Lk 22:30; Ac 1:15-26). Ensconced in Jerusalem, they awaited this semi-miraculous inauguration of the Kingdom, without much thought of universal apostleship. Their view was that, for membership of their group, witness to the resurrection was not of itself sufficient. One should have followed Jesus of Nazareth from the beginning of his public life (Ac 1:16-26).

However the Kingdom did not come according to the concept of the Twelve. After the resurrection it was already in being, and there was no necessity to await the Lord's return to become a member. Furthermore the judicial role of the Twelve lost its significance, and it was possible for Paul to oppose to it his own role of universal mission. There was little point in requiring that an apostle should have lived at Jesus' side: the resurrection itself was the decisive thing, the moment of inauguration for the universal Kingdom. When he links his ministry with the resurrection, Paul is setting up a new concept of apostleship. It is freed from the limitations of Jewish eschatology, connected with the task of universal mission, of revealing to men the actual presence in their midst of the Kingdom of God.

b) The term *gospel* (61 times in Saint Paul) is typically Pauline, the more so when qualified in the phrase "gospel of Christ" (v. 7). At least in the synoptics, the preaching of Jesus is concentrated exclusively on the "Kingdom of God." It is essentially theocentric and eschatological. In Saint Paul preaching is concerned with the person of Christ himself. God is always at work, but rather as the author of apocalyptic revelations that enable Paul to structure his gospel (1 Co 2:10; 2 Co 12:1; Ga 1:16; 2 Th 1:7). The object of the gospel is Christ.

In other words Paul sees God at work in his gospel. Through this gospel God's call and his grace (here: the gift of faith) are offered to mankind. So true is this that abandonment of this gospel becomes automatically loss of faith and vocation. Christ is the object of the gospel, not as content merely ("Christ preached") but as active presence (cf. Rm 1:16; 1 Co 1:18; 2

Co 5:20). Any turning away from his gospel is actually a turning away from Christ himself (v. 7).

c) Because he is the instrument of this gospel which has come from God through Christ, Paul sees himself as a *servant* (v. 10). The verbs he uses to describe his role as evangelist are typical: he has "received" a tradition (1 Co 11:23-25, 15:1), "learned" a teaching (v. 12: both are familiar terms in the schools of Jewish wisdom). But the servant has been charged with his mission above all by an "apocalypse" or "revelation" (v. 12; cf. Ep 3:1-2; Col 11:3-4), of which Christ was the object.

It is not a matter then of receiving, either from Jesus or the apostles, a tradition or a teaching. The revelation he received could only come from God. Its content had nothing to do with the terrestrial life of Jesus, or the various dispositions of Christian living (all this Paul will "receive" from the primitive communities). It concerned things that only God could reveal: the mystery of Jesus' death and resurrection, the source of divine salvation (Ga 1:1-5); and Paul's own special calling to announce this mystery to the Gentiles (v. 6). To question this latter portion of his revelation, as the Judaizers do, is to question the apocalyptic character of the gospel he preaches.

VII. Matthew
7:21-27
Gospel
1st cycle

From the time of its primitive redaction, in the pre-gospel stage, chapter 7 of the Sermon on the Mount comprised three warnings (vv. 1-2, 15, and 21), each followed by an illustration (7:3-5; 16-20 and 24-27 respectively). The warning of verse 21 ("put into practice") is illustrated by the parable of the two houses (vv. 24-27). Verses 22-23, not found in Luke's version (Lk 6:46-49), are a pointless overloading of the original text and are taken from another context.

The homogeneity of the piece depends upon the words "to do" or "put into practice." In verse 21 it is necessary "to do" the will of the Father, in verses 24 and 26 to "put into practice" "the words I have just spoken to you." Likewise the principle enunciated in verse 21 distinguishes "saying" and "doing" (theme of the parable of the two sons, Mt 21:28-30), while the parable of the two houses (vv. 24-27) stresses the opposition between "understanding" and "doing." Such contrasts seem to indicate that the structure of verse 21 "it is not . . . but it is" (cf. Mt 5:20; 18:3), and the expression "Father who is in heaven" (Mt 10:32-33; 12:50; 15:13, etc.) are a reworking of the text by Matthew himself.

The parable of the two houses is an excellent example of the catechetical preoccupations of Matthew. He tends to cull from Jesus' words everything with a practical application to living. Here we have the mentality of the primitive community, which reacted strongly against any suggestion of formalism in the Kingdom, and against a faith devoid of works (Jm 1:22-25; Mt 5:17). This practical, moralizing tendency explains the subsequent insertion of verses 22-23. To the teaching of Christ (Lk 13:26-27) Matthew gives a particular emphasis, no doubt with certain members of the primitive community in mind. These abounded in charisms, but lacked the most elementary moral "practice" (we recall the situation in Corinth, 1 Co 12-13). He is reacting against the legal formalism of certain Jewish groups and the gnostic speculations of certain pagan ones. There can be no Christian religion without involvement. For him the image of the *rock* stresses the concrete aspect of commitment.*

Christians are never weaned from the gospel. It is always there when they want it, and in its name they can speak of justice, of hunger, of peace. They do however lack the concrete analytic knowledge that enables people trained in the Marxist system to become seriously and actively involved. Among the people of God there are many prophetic voices raised in the name of the gospel (v. 22), but they shun political involvement because they

*See the doctrinal theme: *obedience*, p. 18.

are not analytically trained and their excuse is that the Church as such has nothing to do with politics. They do the Kingdom no service (v. 24). They do not build upon the rock, or understand how solid is our foundation on God our rock.

VIII. **Mark**   These echoes of the campaign waged by Jesus
      2:23-3:6   against false ideas about the Sabbath are com-
      Gospel   mon to all the synoptics. There are however
      2nd cycle   redactional differences of a fairly important
                      nature, which indicate differences of interpre-
tation. The text of Matthew doubtless represents a tradition that was close to the actual incident and the discussions it provoked. Mark was concerned, especially in adding verses 2:27 and 3:5, to relate the whole matter to an environment that was non-Jewish. In Matthew we have much local flavor, more allusions to customary Jewish polemic ("there is a greater here than the temple," or the *a fortiori* argument of Mt 12:11-12). In Mark there is a universal dimension (above all verses 2:27 and 3:4), and a stronger challenge than we find elsewhere to Jewish legislation (cf. the liberalism of 2:27 and the violence of 3:5).

Our commentary consequently will deal first with the tradition common to the synoptics, and then with the particular elements in Mark.

a) The Pharisees had found Jesus' disciples flagrantly *violating the Sabbath*. It was a violation in two essential areas: the Sabbath rest, and freedom. The first transgression was that of the disciples in "reaping" (vv. 23-25), the second that of Jesus in setting free someone who was confined by illness (vv. 1-5). In fact of course in neither case was there a violation of a legal precept strictly speaking. What the disciples transgressed was a precept of the Mischna (Sabbath 7:2, one of the thirty-nine activities forbidden by Judaism), and they had precedent for that in Scripture (verse 25; cf. Is 21:2-7). As for Jesus, he was merely pushing Deuteronomic doctrine to its logical limit. This imposed an obligation on the Jew to release slaves from all labor on the Sabbath day (verse 4; cf. Dt 5:12-15).

The ensuing polemic accordingly is completely Jewish. Is pharisaic legalism a valid method of observing the law and being aligned with the will of the Father, or is it not? When Jesus says, in Matthew 12:6, that he is greater than the temple, and in Mark 2:28, that he is master of the Sabbath, he is claiming the right, by his very mission, of querying such precisions of law. This may very well mean a desacralization as drastic as that in the case of the loaves of proposition (v. 25), when the will of the legislator is being violated.

b) Mark suppresses these items of legalistic controversy. He gives us nothing of the details in Matthew 12:5-6 or 12:11-12. He adds however two significant points: a note about Jesus' anger when confronted by the harshness of the Pharisees (v. 5); and, above all, the sentiment in verse 27: the Sabbath is made for man and not man for the Sabbath. Here we emerge from the domain of Jewish discussion on to the purely human plane (cf. Ga 3:23-29). Mark indeed gives us the whole discussion at the end of a section where Jesus, on three separate occasions, confronts the Pharisees on a similar issue: about pardon (Mk 2:5-12), about relations with sinners (Mk 2:13-17), and about fasting (Mk 2:18-22). We have come to the end of an ancient debate that was clamoring for solution.

As Mark sees it, hardness of heart (v. 5) indicates an incapacity to appreciate values that are only evident to the man who is oriented towards God (Mk 4:12, 7:17-18; cf. 8:11-13). Turned in on himself, man will tend to give the Sabbath, or the law in general, an absolute value. This is the "flesh" of Pauline theology. The man who is open to God says "yes" to the divine initiative, and is able to measure both the Sabbath and the Law. He can use them, but they can no longer use him. The Spirit has set him free from observance of "days" (cf. Ga 4:10). This is the man that Mark has in mind in verse 27.

As long as man insists on being himself the architect of his salvation, he will absolutize or sacralize what he considers to be the means towards that. He will harass and excommunicate the person who threatens his security by making these means relative. So it was with the Pharisees and the threat to the Sabbath. What could not human freedom, human liberation, lead to?

When a man accepts the gift of the Father with a "yes" without reserve, his salvation no longer depends on external means. It is based on a free encounter between divine initiative and human faith. Such a man was Jesus.

Following him, all men with the capacity to discern the nature of God's gift to them, who respond without reserve, become lords of the Sabbath too. It is desacralized, and loses all absolute value. It is merely the time when the believer, at his secret depths, comes to the free moment of encounter.

The eucharistic celebration is that moment when humanity, in the person of Christ, gives evidence of human fidelity to God in death, and when God goes to limit of giving, by raising up Jesus. When a Christian shares the Eucharist, he renews once more the experience of openness and encounter that precludes his ever again becoming a "sabbatarian."*

IX. Luke 7:1-10   The cure of the centurion's son is recounted by
     Gospel   Matthew (28:5-13), Luke and John (4:46-54).
     3rd cycle   Matthew and Luke agree in regarding the
                         miracle as a premonitory sign of the mission to
the Gentiles, a theme that we do not find in John. All three however are at one in stressing the point that the miracle was wrought at a distance.

a) While John speaks of a royal official (who could have been a Jew) the others, Matthew and Luke (v. 2), mention a centurion, unquestionably a *Gentile*.

*See the doctrinal theme: *Sabbath and Sunday*, p. 24.

Luke refers to the prohibitions for Jews about entering the house of a Gentile (v. 6; cf. Ac 11:3) and to the necessity for clear evidence of the centurion's sympathy towards Jews (v. 5; cf. Ac 10:22). Matthew does not do this. Consequently Luke is concerned, much more than Matthew or John, to stress the insurmountable barriers that divided Jews from Gentiles. His customary restraint however is in evidence, and he forbears to reproduce the violent anti-Jewish diatribe of Matthew 8:11-12.

Curiously enough Luke's account of the miracle resembles that of the cure of the Syro-Phoenician woman (an episode that he does not relate). In both cases we have a parent interceding for a child (cf. Mt 15:28), a similar phrase "in a bad state" (Lk 7:2; Mt 15:22), other people interceding (Mt 15:23; Lk 7:3), and finally the same wonderment on Jesus' part at the faith of the person concerned (Mt 15:28 and Lk 7:9).

Parallels like this between this gospel, the account of Cornelius' conversion, and the episode of the Syro-Phoenician woman, make Luke's intention clear. It is to dispose people for the Gentile mission and to justify it. As yet the Judaeo-Christian community was unready to accept it.

b) Jesus performs his miracle at a distance, by means of the *Word* only, to respect the Jewish tabu about entering the house of a Gentile. Throughout his whole career as thaumaturge there are only two such miracles (Lk 7:1-10 and Mt 15:22-28). Healings are normally accomplished by some physical contact without words, as if his body had some particular vital force, which he was not even capable of controlling always (Mk 5:30, 6:5). He usually conveys the healing power by "touching" the sick person (Mt 8:3, 8:15, 9:25, 9:29; Lk 14:4), or by "imposing hands" (Mk 6:5, 7:32, 8:23-25; Lk 4:40, 13:13). The physical gesture of itself however does not altogether indicate full responsibility for the action, and some miracle narratives make a point of showing how the healing gesture is accompanied by the word (Mt 8:3; Mk 5:41). It is the word which indicates clearly the intention of Jesus, while the physical gesture gives this its fullest expression.

In healing the centurion's servant Jesus confines himself to the word, responding thus to the centurion's own eulogy of the word's efficacity (vv. 7-9). The centurion is probably alluding to Psalm 106/107:20, where God "sends his word to heal." He is implicitly recognizing the fact that Jesus comes from God, that he has the very word of God, which is powerful and efficacious (Ps 32/33:6-9).

It is worth remembering that the rite of communion is accompanied by an affirmation of faith on the part of the faithful in the words of the centurion: "But say only the word. . . ." Christian liturgy is so emancipated from ritual and magic as to depend upon the "Word only." It was this that sustained Jesus throughout his Pasch: it is this which implicitly sustains all of us throughout the Christian pilgrimage. The very communion rite itself brings out the point, by its summons to faith, and by putting the Christian in explicit relation with Christ.*

B. DOCTRINE

1. The Theme of Obedience

The word obedience tends to grate somewhat upon modern ears: it conjures up ideas about submission and alienation, submission, that is, to an authority that imposes itself from the outside, and alienation in the sense that personal responsibility is abdicated. The religious use of the term actually heightens these associations. If God is someone who demands the obedience of his followers as a *sine qua non,* surely he deserves to be denounced as the foremost cause of human alienation, as the foremost enemy of human freedom and dignity. Thus the vocabulary of obedience is liable to cause better Christians some embarrassment, and such terminology tends to be used very cautiously in

*See the doctrinal theme: *universalism of faith,* Advent/Christmas volume, p. 263.

modern presentations of Christianity.

Yet obedience *is* a central theme of both Testaments, the New and the Old. It is so central that it is the term chosen to epitomize the whole meaning of Christ's earthly career. It is sufficient to remind ourselves of a single example from the great christological texts: "becoming as all men are, he was humbler yet, even to accepting death, death on a cross" (Ph 2:7b-8). What was true of Christ must evidently be true of the Christian. The biblical texts which stress obedience to the will of the Father are countless. To be a Christian is to do the will of the Father, as in the old covenant the believer was he who obeyed the commandments of the living God (see 1st reading and Gospel, 1st cycle).

How then are we to explain the contemporary distaste for such an essential Christian value? Could it be that Christians are in the process of distorting their very faith? Or is the distaste an indication that the concrete presentations of obedience transmitted to us by previous generations need to be revised? It must be admitted I suppose that one particular version of obedience has had its day. But, if that is so, we have all the more reason to take care that its disappearance does not bring about misunderstanding of the reality it was meant to inculcate. The damage to Christian belief would be irreparable. Consequently we must set about tracing, step by step, the development of this theme in Scripture and Tradition. Our investigation will show that contemporary notions of the theme may perhaps be closer to the gospel concept than those we have inherited from immediate predecessors.

Obedience to the living God

For pagan man in the ancient world of course obedience could only mean constraint and submission. His whole business was to adapt himself as much as possible to the order of things set irrevocably by the gods, something that governed both individual and social life. Today, by contrast, such a man will refuse obedience to the extent that he can gradually provide, by his own resources, an order of things which assures him happiness. Submission to any outside agency seems to him a source of alienation. Paradoxically though, on a closer view, his predicament is strangely similar to that of his ancient counterpart: in neither concept is there place for the mystery of freedom.

Israel's experience gives us an altogether different perspective. It is no longer a matter of adapting oneself to a fixed order, but of being faithful to the event. In the event God recognizes his people and manifests his will. Faith is free acceptance of the resign of Yahweh in history, always unexpected and unforeseeable. The Covenant is not a fixed order: it is an order of love. Abandoning ready-made securities, Israel found herself engaged in a long process of interiorization. She had to divine the deeper meaning of Yahweh's interventions in her own history. Everyone is summoned to "keep the words of God in his heart and in his soul" (Dt 11:18; 1st reading, 1st cycle). God's will is imperative, but it is manifested to people who love it. Even the Law, which reduces to precepts the fidelity required by the Covenant, is far from being a rigid structure. Each generation will develop new insights about it. As interiorization becomes more intense, the obedience of the believer no longer indicates constraint and submission; on the contrary it becomes the most authentic expression of human liberty before the living God. Yahweh does not demand a slavish acquiescence; he is seeking free collaboration from men in order to accomplish his plan of love.

The more aware Israel became of the meaning of obedience, so much more too did she begin to realize the extent of her disobedience. Disobedience indeed had begun with human origins, but, again and again, throughout history, it was to be repeated. Israel is a "rebellious household" (Ez 2:5). All are the slaves of sin, and no one obeys God. Is his plan then to be foiled? If only because of her belief in the fidelity of Yahweh, Israel could not accept this. So, she turned her gaze towards the future, looking for someone whose obedience would be perfect. He would be the Messiah, the one capable of bringing God's plan to fulfillment.

Jesus Christ our obedience

Thus, when the New Testament concentrates on the obedience of Jesus, this is a logical consequence of the hope of Israel. For the authors, the word epitomizes the meaning of the intervention by Israel's Messiah in history. "I have come down from heaven, Jesus said, not to do my will, but the will of him who sent me" (Jn 6:38). "By the obedience of one the many will be justified" (Rm 5:19). "Obedient unto death, death on a cross" (Ph 2:8). Jesus had learned "to obey throughout all his sufferings" (He 5:8). In other words, it is the obedience of Jesus which explains how, once for all, he saved the world.

In him the process of interiorization that the chosen people had begun came to its fulfillment. His obedience to the Father was a preeminently free act. The Father's will in his case never appears as a precise structure, the details of which have been minutely predetermined. On the contrary, throughout his life, he is going forward spontaneously to encounter the Father. Events lead him. The questions raised by those he meets, their acceptance of him or their rejection, gradually shed light on the meaning of his mission among men. The Father's will was, as he said, his nourishment. Nothing was allowed to obscure his insight into the divine plan to which he gave total adherence. This sovereign exercise of freedom is above all evident in his attitude to any outside force that threatened to influence his actions, or reactions. It is most breathtaking, as the fourth gospel so clearly stresses, in the moment of the Passion.

This was the obedience that delivered a humanity which had been locked in disobedience. It set up the definitive covenant of love between God and man. What is described however in biblical terms as obedience, could be just as well expressed in terms of acceptance. By obeying the Father even unto death on the cross, Jesus is accepting unreservedly the creatural condition, and simultaneously putting death itself in proper perspective. Such acceptance is the highest expression of human liberty, which is invited to respond to God's antecedent initiative in the building of universal brotherhood. It is in terms of this new covenant that man becomes capable of brotherly love without limits. He begins to see the real meaning of his existence, the purpose of his earthly sojourn. It was the obedience of Jesus that unveiled, not only the true face of God, but the true face of man as well.

Doing the will of the Father (Mt 7:21)

This theme of obedience to the Father, which is so central in the life of Jesus, is equally so in the life of the Church. All tradition argues this: the biblical texts which are so explicit on the point were invariably looked to as sources. This is indeed to be expected, in view of all that we have said about the obedience of Jesus. Yet, when we consider the history of spirituality in Western Christianity, we are struck by the fact that understanding of this gospel theme has not been constant throughout the centuries. The usual developments and changes of emphasis tended to take place, so that gradually the notion of obedience was changed. This, we believe, is the reason for the contemporary malaise about the theme.

One particular emphasis was to concentrate more on the divine initiative than on human response. The Church was the focus where the divine initiative was manifested: through her the will of the Father became known. As the Church became more clerical and institutional, manifestation of the Father's will seemed more and more the prerogative of an Authority, divinely entrusted with this charge. She would manifest it, sometimes in minute detail, and see that it was carried out. In obeying this will, clearly expressed and very frequently codified, man, who had been delivered from sin and firmly established in divine love, could become an instrument for diffusing this will throughout the universe. In this perspective certain essential Christian insights were to the forefront, but there was a very real danger that the active, dynamic, creative dimension of Christian obedience could be obscured.

In the West, from the 12th century onwards, a more balanced view, certainly one more in conformity with the doctrine of Incarnation, gained currency. In the 13th century it found in Saint Thomas its first great interpreter. Centuries of Christian experience had led the faithful to lay equal stress, in the doctrine of obedience, on human response and divine initiative. A classic formula developed: supernature elevates nature, it does not destroy it. Obedience to the Father is a movement of the will towards fidelity, an acceptance, in our modern idiom, of the actual human condition, as God has willed it. Thus understood, the Christian becomes the free man *par excellence*, the man restored to his true status by the salvific will, the man summoned to build his own future by the use of all his resources. The Church is always the channel of manifestation for the divine will, but in the manifestation everyone has a role to play. Everyone must constantly seek to discern that will; it is a mysterious reality which is always in process of revelation. It took centuries for this notion of obedience to become established generally in Christian consciousness. We had to await the second Vatican Council for an ecclesiological formula that would incorporate it, and incorporate also a new view of authority.

Preaching the obedience of the faith

Saint Paul, the great missionary, does not hesitate to involve the theme of obedience in his formulation of the Good News. It is his charge, he tells his Roman audience, "to preach the obedience of the faith" (Rm 1:5). The phrase should be properly understood, because throughout the history of mission, interpretations have varied according to the current concept of obedience.

Thus, as long as obedience was understood to be the human response to God's salvific initiative, something channeled through the Church as a precise imperative, the evangelization of pagans was seen as a summons to conversion rather than anything else. By definition the pagan was a slave of Satan, rendered incapable by sin of obeying God. Thus salvation in Jesus Christ would have to be put forward in terms of entry to the ark of salvation, the Church. Only thus could people know the will of the Father, and, under grace, put this in practice. Consequently the primary objective of missionaries was to establish everywhere centers for the diffusion of God's Word. Here, new converts could serve their apprenticeship of obedience to the Father's will.

With the advent of new ideas about obedience, there was a profound change in the concept of evangelization. Once people became conscious of the closeness of the link between God's initiative and man's response, gradually the Good News began to be seen as the fulfillment, in the case of any people, of a spiritual pilgrimage. Preaching the obedience of the faith becomes a summons to human beings to accept without reserve the human condition. More than that, it means joining such searchers in their quest, displaying a charity that knows no limits, showing how the intervention of Christ is always actual and provides the only path of liberation. This new insight has only begun to color missionary attitudes, but at the moment, very clearly, its influence is considerable in the domain of ideas, presentation and procedures.

Initiation to the obedience of faith

So fundamental is this theme in the texture of Christian life that it should become the focus of a special initiation that will be lasting. There should be a deep understanding of the relationship of dependence upon Christ, whose influence in the world is always actual. The Christian must have an awareness of this, and realize that throughout salvation history perfect obedience to the Father must always be traced to him.

Any celebration of obedience however, to be authentic, must furthermore go the length of finding expression in the texture of Christian daily life. As things are now, it is only too evident that too often we proceed as if the obedience of the faith were some sort of passive submission. Even still we act as if the priest had a monopoly in the manifestation of the will of God. Vatican II made provision for an active and responsible role on the part of every member of the people of God, but the actual role such members play tends to be slight. If we regard the obedience of faith as a sovereign expression of human liberty, our liturgical celebrations should give evidence of that. Otherwise the number of those alienated from our liturgy is liable to increase.

The whole topic indeed invites reflection, not only about the structure of liturgical worship, but also, indeed more so, about the kind of ecclesial assembly that best fulfills the legitimate needs of the people of God. In specific terms, it is only in small groupings that the faithful can have an active and responsible role, *habitually,* in the celebration of the Word. Doubtless larger groupings are necessary in order to give concrete expression to the catholicity that ought to characterize all celebrations. However, they will be properly effective only to the extent that it has been possible for participants to give personal expression to their obedience of faith in smaller groupings. This is an area where the movements of Catholic Action have already provided us with valuable lessons.

2. The Theme of Sabbath and Sunday

Until recently, Sunday observance among Christian communities still retained its sacral aura. One assisted at Mass on that day, and refrained from all manual work. By and large people knew what was allowed, and what was forbidden, though the list might vary according to locale, or one's particular allegiance. In any case breaches of Sunday observance were regarded seriously, and people felt obliged to mention them in confession. Obvious transgressors were well known, and to some extent ostracized. This was quite a wide-spread attitude, more evident naturally in country districts than in cities.

But now, we may as well admit, over the past few years there has been a radical change. Science and technology have been transforming people's secular occupations and their mental attitudes. Sunday is beginning to lose the religious meaning it used to have. True, it is a day of rest, of leisure, of escape, and continues to be a day different from other days. For the majority, that is. There are many people who work on Sundays so that others can enjoy their leisure, or do the shopping that work has obliged them to postpone to the following weekend.

At first the Church tried to oppose this devaluation of the Christian Sunday, and there were liturgical attempts to reinstate "the Lord's day," while taking full cognizance of the ambiguities that had arisen. They underestimated the evidence; a profound mutation was under way, something that could not be reversed. Very recently the Sunday obligation about sharing the Eucharist has been extended to Saturday evening. Concerning the prohibition about servile work the Church has in fact never been very insistent.

What are we to say about this development? Is it something to be deplored, or could it be the beginnings of a rediscovery of the Lord's day, along lines that have been hitherto unexplored? Should we try to reinstate the past, or concentrate upon the future? At the deepest level, what is at stake in all this matter?

The Sabbath for Yahweh, the God of the Covenant

It is not really feasible for man to express all dimensions of his being in a single mode of action. The history of civilizations shows us that life tended to be divided into periods of work and periods of celebration. The work periods are the normal thing, where individual occupations satisfy immediate needs. One must eat, be clothed, sheltered, protect oneself, organize oneself, etc. These procedures are distracting however, and indicate only indirectly the basic quest of the human being. The unusual period, the time of celebration, is precisely the one where the quest for happiness finds expression overtly. Indeed, in the traditional religions, it was only this time that counted really. Man would share the sacral world, the stable and unending reality, through some sort of liturgical procedure and thus fully realize himself. All else was secondary, one might even say insignificant. Naturally the times of work and celebration tended to be governed by the great cosmic rhythms, varying according to environment.

The origin of the Sabbath is explained by this basic need, but, as a time of celebration, it is also highly original. Whatever its prehistory be, we find it as a weekly time of celebration, characterized by cessation from all work (the root meaning of the word Sabbath is "cessation"). Work meant the activity pursued during the other days of the week. It is a sacred day: the observances connected with the celebration are important: infraction is punished by death. The original dimension however consists in the fact that what is celebrated is not, as in pagan festivals, the stable universe; but Yahweh's intervention in the major event of Jewish history, the deliverance from Egypt. This intervention had been sealed in the contract of alliance. By comparison with this, every other Sabbath significance is secondary.

The Mosaic Sabbath was destined to have two different avenues of development. On the one hand the influence of doctors and scribes would tend towards precisions about observance, even in the smallest details, and formalism would be always a danger. On the other, prophetic influence never ceased to relate the Sabbath to the order of faith. Gradually indeed the emphasis shifted from observances, which in themselves are meaningless, to the moral demands made by the covenant. Ritual was seen to be empty unless it brought about a reformation in the whole texture of one's life.

The Son of Man, Lord of the Sabbath

Jesus' attitude towards the Sabbath is revealing. We never find him putting himself outside the Law. The Sabbath is an essential precept: his observance is above reproach, but he goes to the heart of the matter. The Law belongs to the order of faith,

and Jesus' originality is seen in the fact that this was the principle
on which he lived it. Traditional interpretations, which tended to
deform it and make it a yoke of slavery, he rejected.

He has two important affirmations to make about the Sabbath
(see today's gospel, 2nd cycle). They both stem from the simple
fact that the Sabbath is really the celebration of God's liberating
intervention for his people that was sealed in the Sinai covenant.
First, the superiority of mercy to requirements of cult — he cured
the man with the withered hand on the Sabbath. Second, the
superiority of conscience to law — "The Sabbath was made for
man, not men for the Sabbath" (Mk 2:27). Really of course the
two affirmations are the same. The exercise of mercy, in fidelity to
the covenant, presupposes the sort of acceptance of the event that
only the freedom of the faith can produce. The statements throw
a singular light on the work and personality of the Messiah. To
verse 27, which we have just quoted, Jesus adds "so that the Son
of man is Lord even of the Sabbath." It is an extraordinary
phrase in that it shows the fidelity required by the covenant to
be the fidelity of a partner. God is setting man free, so that before God he can behave with perfect freedom. This is the true
nature of the covenant. But so overwhelmingly new is the insight,
by contrast with that which Israel actually had, that the Sinai
covenant itself now yields to the one Jesus is inaugurating.

In view of all this, it is easy to understand why the Sabbath
controversy was basic in the opposition that developed between
Jesus and his own people. According to Mark 3:6 it was indeed
as a result of an argument about the Sabbath that the break
came. The Pharisees and Herodians began to plot "to destroy
him." His attitude to the Sabbath is crucial. It shows how contrary to expectations messianic fulfillment is destined to be, how
completely, in the true order of love between God and man, all
formalism and particularism must be rejected. Sinful man however finds these requirements too much. If he is to become a
partner in the order of love he must acquiesce in a complete
despoliation of self and throw himself on God's mercy. Only

under these conditions too will a man find faith to see in the Lord of the Sabbath the very Son of God.

From Jewish Sabbath to the Lord's Day

For the first Christians the major event in salvation history was the Pasch of Jesus. Crucified on the eve of the Sabbath — and this year it was a solemn Sabbath, because it coincided with the Jewish Pasch, Jesus was raised up "on the third day." It was then precisely on the first day after the Sabbath that the disciples began to realize that the Messiah was living and giving his followers proof of his presence. So, they formed the habit of celebrating Christ's death and resurrection on the day after the Sabbath.

The Sabbath itself however was one of the essential precepts of the Mosaic Law. The disciples being Jews continued to observe it, but they realized at the same time that, for them, the Cross spelled the end of the Sabbath. How could this venerable institution continue to have meaning in their context. Officially, the Jewish people continued to reject its Messiah; the principal object of celebration on the Sabbath day continued to be just the liberation from Egypt. Yet abandonment of the Sabbath would mean cutting the tie with Judaism. Was this justified? Had not Jesus come to fulfill the Law and the Prophets? For primitive Christians there really was a crisis of conscience. In the event, it was the spread of Christianity to the Gentile world which led to a diminution of the Sabbath's importance. Opposition however was considerable. Even in the Pauline communities we find attempts on the part of judaizers to vindicate the primacy of the Sabbath with its ancient requirements (cf. Col 2:16; Ga 4:9-10).

Considerable time elapsed before the Sabbath was definitely supplanted by the Lord's Pasch (some Christians were still observing the Sabbath rest as late as the 5th century: cf. the 29th canon of the Council of Laodicea). But by the end of the 1st century the Christian celebration had acquired its proper name. The author of Revelation (1:10) describes as the "Lord's day" the day on which Christians had formed the habit of celebrating Christ's Pasch. It was during the bloody persecution of Domitian. This emperor wanted all imperial subjects to give him the title of Lord (*Kyrius*). For Christians this was an exclusively divine title; it was their way of affirming faith in the divinity of the Risen Lord: Jesus alone is Lord.

It was not until the 4th century that Constantine made Sunday the official day of rest: the Lord's Day for Christians, for pagans the day of the sun. Interestingly enough it was only later that the Church ratified this decision, which indicates that for Christians the connection between celebration of the Lord's Pasch and cessation from work cannot have been very firm.

Consequently between the Jewish Sabbath and the Christian Sunday there are profound differences. The events of salvation history which they celebrate are different: the "Lord's Day" is no longer connected with a Law, and as such it is not related to a weekly rest. In a very real sense it can be said that the Sunday is made for man, not man for the Sunday.

The Good News and the Lord's Day

When missionaries proclaim the Good News of salvation in Jesus Christ, they are summoning men to conversion of heart. They are calling upon them to serve God in Jesus Christ by a life lived in conformity with the Gospel, and the new commandment of limitless brotherly love. This is the spiritual web that is pleasing to the Father. The Lord's supper is celebrated and his Pasch is proclaimed. His Pasch is the major event of history, the one on which hangs the issue of the whole human adventure. It is the event by which the people of God, here and now, live, because the Risen Lord never ceases to be present with his own, and to accomplish among them the will of his Father.

The fundamental law of Christianity being one of liberty, the celebration of Christ's Pasch, so far from being matter for observance, is actually a primary need of the people of God. In the history of the Church in the West, however, elements of the

Jewish Sabbath were gradually reintroduced. Probably, in this instance as in others, the reason for the return to an Old Testament mentality was the huge influx of pagans. In any case, from the 6th century onwards, the Christian Sunday began to be a replica of the Jewish Sabbath. Every Christian was required to assist at Mass, and abstain from all "servile" work. The object of the celebration continued to be of course the living presence of Christ in his Church, but it is abundantly clear that the whole image of Christianity was affected by the developments. Religious and moral observances of the sort that Christ himself had been at pains to denounce acquired a new lease of life.

The consequences in the conduct of missionary enterprise were immediate. Prior to that the people to whom the Church directed her message had been practicing members of another religion. Conversion for them would be presented in terms of more exacting moral demands, and abandonment of their previous religious practice in favor of a new style of worship centered on the Sunday. It is questionable indeed whether this sort of presentation contributed very much to the stature of Christianity.

Henceforward the people to whom the Church will be addressing herself will tend to be less and less persons with a previous religious background. The time may very well be ripe for Christians to give the celebration of Christ's Pasch once more its proper emphasis. It should be thoroughly purged of elements that really belong to the Old Testament, or to pagan ritual.

Ought the Lord's Day to be a fixed day?

Christians formed the habit very early of celebrating the Lord's Pasch each week on the day following the Sabbath. Neither in Palestine or the Greek world was this a day of rest, recognized as a time of celebration. For followers of the Risen Lord however this was not important. The Pasch they celebrated was that by which their daily lives were lived: there was perfect continuity between rite and life. The actual presence of the Risen Lord permeated all Christian living. Each day indeed was the

Lord's day. Man however is so constituted that from time to time he feels the need to celebrate the life that animates him and gives unity to his existence.

There is nothing whatever in the New Testament that would indicate an obligation to celebrate Christ's Pasch on a fixed day of the week. Jesus left no precept about it. We can very easily see why primitive Christians formed the habit of celebrating on the day after the Sabbath, but there was no law about it. It was a situation completely different from the Sabbath itself. We know from the gospels that Jesus himself celebrated his own Pasch on the eve of the crucifixion, and that the Last Supper which is the origin of all Christian liturgy derives all its meaning from the great event of the following day. As Saint Paul was to say of every eucharistic celebration, the Supper is the proclamation of the death of Christ.

Pagan days of celebration were understood to be sacral days, by comparison with which ordinary days were insignificant. For the Jews the Sabbath was a sacral day too, but one that had repercussions on the other days. The celebration of Christ's Pasch however is altogether concerned with the daily needs of Christian life itself. The actual time of celebration is not important; what is important is that the celebration should be consciously grafted into the actual life of the people of God.

In our day Sunday tends more and more to become the weekly day of relaxation and escape. For that reason one might very well question its suitability as the established day for weekly celebration of Christ's Pasch.

TENTH SUNDAY

A. THE WORD

I. Hosea 6:3-6
1st reading
1st cycle

The prophet is describing a ceremony of expiation and penance (vv. 1-3 and 5) that the people have organized. The object is to win God's pardon, and some sort of resurrection, in the three days set aside for such ceremonies (Ez 37).

The grace dispensed by God on this occasion is compared to a rain which soaks and fertilizes parched land (Ps 71/72:6). The prophet however stresses the hollowness of the ceremony. The repentance of the people is like the dew which evaporates. That is why God is ignoring Israel (v. 4). He is not appeased by empty sacrificial ceremonies. What he requires is love (v. 6) and knowledge.

The prophet is contrasting *knowledge* of God with rites that are celebrated without faith, but also with the sort of idolatry that makes of God something that he is not and demeans him to the level of human wishes. Intellectual knowledge is of no avail unless there is a discovery of God's love as revealed to us, and a firm attachment to that love (Ho 2:21-22, 4:2).

II. Genesis 3:9-15
1st reading
2nd cycle

These verses are taken from the maledictions pronounced after the expulsion from Paradise.

a) The *maledictions* of myth are attempts to explain abnormal or puzzling phenomena: an animal who walks without paws, a painful growth, a task of great dimension . . . death. There is little point in contrasting myth with science, as if they proceeded on similar planes, as if one were simply a rough sketch of the other. Myth in fact is more existential than science, its version of reality is deeper and more universal. Consequently, even though science has in fact, and with good reason, demythologized these maledictions, it cannot be altogether substituted for myth. The religious message of the latter must be respected.

Our author here sees the development of human history as good or bad, the object of blessing or malediction (cf. Dt 28:15-19) according to religious and moral option. The secret of history in other words is in the heart of man. Malediction represents that history as built by a man who wants to be equal to God (v. 22). Blessing on the other hand characterizes history as built by a man who accepts himself as the image of God, the great single achievement of Jesus (Ga 3:13-14). In Genesis 2-8 maledictions never finally triumph. Even though they are piled one upon the other (Gn 3:14-20, 4:11-14, 6:5-7:10), blessing comes finally to redress the balance of history. Thus the opposition between the seed of the woman and that of the serpent is already foreseen in verse 15. One day humanity will be liberated from the idolatrous cults that bring alienation.

b) When man attempted to steal from God the knowledge of good and evil, when he refused that is to submit to a greater than himself in the estimation of things and persons, he introduced malediction into the world. He set up self and egoism as the divinity. Henceforward things had not the goodness that God confers, but such as man himself concedes them. *Good and evil,* life and death, become indistinguishable realities, because man who encounters them cannot, like God, pardon evil and make it good, cancel death and make it life. He is in the likeness of God, but he does not dispose of that divine life which can transform evil and death. He makes a mockery of himself. Even if he knows good and evil, life and death, without God's power of dominating these, he can be no more that a puppet swung hither and thither.

c) So *death,* which is simply the natural lot of man, begins to seem the product of God's anger. The tension for man lies not so much in the fact of dying. It is dying with the realization that there is perhaps a way of not dying, that before our birth and after our death someone always continues to be. It is just because human intelligence is able to form a concept of the eternal that death becomes more than a natural phenomenon, a chastisement. It reveals dramatically to a man the very core of his inadequacy. It restores the proper balance between God and man, which man, with this concept that he has of eternity, is always threatening to disrupt by pretensions toward self-sufficiency.

The only one who could truly know good and evil and pass from death to life was Jesus. But he triumphed over death as God, whose life no one could ever take away, and he conquered evil by the exercise of a limitless pardon.

To all men who, after Adam, come to know life and death the Eucharist offers the fruit of that tree of life that Adam (v. 22) could not cull. The spark of divine life in them enables them to make good of evil and to conquer death.

d) This view of human history presupposes the Jewish doctrine of *retribution*. If man is suddenly swung from happiness to misery the reason must be sought in the religious and moral order. Sin has destroyed the harmony of the elements, and interferes with the fruitfulness of life throughout all creation.

But another principle is equally essential in this view. For peoples who do not have yet this sense of history, or any concept of the possibility of a radical transformation, all that is is "given" from the beginning. The only reason why happiness is strangled by misery in human history is original sin itself. In the Old Testament indeed it was progress in the understanding of salvation history that led to emancipation from any concept of an original "given." It was realized that man had the opportunity to query his very origins by means of the conversion that was always open to him. There is no real fatalism in history.

III. 1 Kings 17:17-24 *1st reading 3rd cycle*   Elias has been lodged with the pagan widow of Sarepta whose resources he multiplied (1 K 17:8-16), and he restores to her her son by means of "mouth to mouth" healing. The woman believed her son's death to be due to a bad spell cast by the prophet as a punishment for some fault of which she was unaware (v. 18). She thought that this man of God had penetrated her secrets and denounced her to the Lord, who was now punishing her through her son. Her paganism led her to think of God as someone vengeful and severe. The resuscitation of her son shows that Yahweh is a God of goodness and pardon, who wills the life of the sinner, not his death (cf. Elias' prayer in v. 20).

Later Jesus, wishing to present himself in the tradition of Elias and at the same time to surpass him, will imitate this miracle (cf. Lk 7:11-16). But he performs it without any suggestion of magical gesture: the power of his Word is sufficient.

In neither case is there question as yet of resurrection in the true sense. They are mere "recoveries." Resurrection in the true sense is access to a new life, animated by the Spirit of God himself.*

IV. **Romans**
    4:18-25
    2nd reading
    1st cycle

Here Paul concludes his analysis of the link between faith and justification, beginning with the example of Abraham (cf. Rm 4:1-8, 13-17). He has already shown that Abraham was a "sinner" at the time of his justification. He was called to be the father of a multitude before he was circumcised, before he had observed the works of the law, faith alone had "justified" him. But what is this faith?

a) To begin with, it is a *hope* surpassing all hope (v. 18). The patriarch's faith maintained him in the conviction that God can suspend all determinism in nature where the future naturally

---

*See the doctrinal theme: *resurrection of the body,* p. 51.

stems from the past, and bring about a new and unexpected future. Thus Abraham did not rely upon himself, shutting himself in his own past. He relied upon God as one who could renew everything. Believing as he did, Abraham did not consider his physical state which seemed to belie his hope. He trusted God to find a way of resolving the seeming contradiction.

We should remember that Paul is taking a theological rather than an historical stance in the whole matter; because in actual fact Abraham will subsequently be capable of giving a son to Agar and six children to Cetura (Gn 25).

b) Abraham's faith concerns the person of God himself rather than the content of God's promise (in this case, changing natural laws). It is eminently *personal*. It presupposes an awareness of man's incapacity to shape by himself his future (v. 19), being thus contrary to the view of atheists and idolators (Rm 1:21). Abraham attaches himself to the *person* rather than the promise; later he will be ready to deprive himself of the object of the promise, his son, without relaxing that attachment.

c) In his predominantly theological analysis of this faith Paul finds yet another component: faith in the *resurrection* (vv. 19 and 24), or, more precisely, faith in Him who raised up Jesus. It is impossible to have faith in a miracle, or in the resurrection, without a prior act of trust in the one who works the miracles.

By giving life to the worn body of Abraham God anticipates Christ's own resurrection, and Isaac, the son sprung from the barren loins of Abraham, can be compared to Jesus issuing from the tomb. True, the two events can only be compared allegorically in their material content; but they both presuppose a similar intensity of faith.

The true "yes" of God's promise is the Risen Christ. In him God gives himself to man, a gift that is not merited. In him man is enabled to join God in complete openness and confidence. The order then both of promise and of faith is the reciprocity in Jesus Christ of two personal fidelities.

V. 2 Corinthians This is Paul's apologia for his ministry to the
4:13 - 5:1   Corinthian audience who questioned his voca-
2nd reading   tion, and were scandalized above all by the
2nd cycle   failures and weaknesses of an envoy of God.

His response to his detractors is substantially the same as the exposé in Romans 5:1-5.

There Paul took his stand on the justification that is accorded to every Christian (Rm 5:1); here he depends on the genuineness of his vocation. But general justification or individual vocation have but a single purpose, the "weight of eternal glory" (v. 17) promised to every man.

So far does this weight of glory transcend human life that it can only be reached by passing through *trial*. The justified Christian encounters this in his life (Rm 5:3), and the apostle is not exempt (vv. 16-17). Hope however itself produces the resistance to trial: constancy, above all the love of the Father and the indwelling of the Spirit. In Romans 5:4-5 Paul had already analyzed in some detail this confluence of different virtues which sustain hope during trial. Here there is not so much precision, but talk of the "interior man." Comparison of the two passages gives us the key to the meaning of the phrase. What Paul has in mind is the interaction of the three divine persons in the theological development of the Christian.

Hope does not mean belief in some distant blessedness, which will appear unexpectedly. On the contrary it is the belief that the blessedness is realized ever since glory was accorded to Jesus of Nazareth, and the earnest of glory deposited with us. This is an especially Pauline notion: the hope of a glory that is awaited but already with us, that is capable of sustaining us now through trials and difficulties that can only touch the flesh, the visible.

The Christian however will naturally want to know how, in the midst of all his other, human, hopes this hope can express itself. For this to come about, his hope must be purged of all alienating elements that belong to another order, that the Christian may have inherited, but have nothing to do with the gospel. It must also be clothed in extreme patience, if it is to tolerate the slowness of the human quest for salvation, the fact that realization of hopes can only come at the end of long endurance. This is the task that is crucial for the Christian, and the apostle too, and it is extremely complex. Without doubt it is the source of the trials Paul is always mentioning when he discusses the hope of glory (Rm 8:18-23).

It is in the Eucharist that theological hope and human hope come to terms. Here man is summoned to build the Kingdom and purify himself of egoism so that he can make the best use of his resources. But he is also invited to muster these resources, thus transformed, and build the sort of human society where he can bear the best witness to daily victory over death and hate.

VI. Galatians 1:11-19
1st reading
3rd cycle

Paul is insisting that he owes his gospel not to the Jerusalem community but to a revelation (vv. 11-12). Many formulas and traditions of course he does owe to the community (cf. 1 Co 15:1-3), but the content of his message is of "apocalyptic" order (revelation).

a) To prove this assertion, he recalls events both prior and subsequent to his "conversion." The essential fact that emerges is that Saul, the one time persecutor, underwent not only a personal conversion, becoming a disciple instead of an enemy. This experience coincided with another, deeper one that made him the apostle of the Gentiles (v. 16). For him, the essential dimensions of the event on the road to Damascus were conversion, admission to *apostolate,* and openness to the Gentiles. It absolved him from the need for any explicit mandate from the Twelve.

His gospel does not differ in content so much from that of the Twelve; it differs because of its diffusion to the Gentiles. For him this aspect of his message is quite essential.

b) When he makes contact with Jerusalem (v. 17 or Ga 2:1-2), this is not to assure himself that his gospel is correct, but to maintain his principle of a gospel for Gentiles (an approach to Christ that is without the law and circumcision) (cf. Ga 2:6). There could not of course have been disavowal on the part of the Twelve of a gospel that came from God himself. Paul's main concern with his Jerusalem contacts is to stress the *unity of mission*. When he secures the agreement of the apostles there, it is not because he has any doubts about the content of his gospel, but because he fears any interference with the unity of mission.

In the Church unity and mission are inseparably associated. Ecumenical problems for instance have never received proper treatment in any context other than that of a World-Church. They will founder in the welter of niggling arguments and institutions. But once there is a stir of missionary enterprise the yearning for unity brooks no delays.

And the converse is also true. Without unity no ecclesial mission can be genuine. We have only to consider the dissipation of energy, and the scandal, which accompany conflicting presentations of the gospel on the African and Asian continents. Yet it is true that uniformity, which is a type of unity, militates against mission. If the Church is based on twelve apostles, with Paul a thirteenth, rather than one, the lesson doubtless should be that mission depends on a concurrence of different mentalities and cultures acting collegially. When Paul went to Jerusalem he did so not to seek some sort of monolithic concurrence. His object was to have the collegiate group of apostles recognize the gospel at work in the very originality of his own procedure.

VII. Matthew   This passage describes the meal that reunited
     9:9-13   Jesus, his disciples, and a few sinners im-
     Gospel   mediately after the call of Matthew (v. 9).
     1st cycle   Luke 5:29 and Mark 2:15 affirm that Matthew
           had organized the banquet himself and Luke
comments that it was sumptuous.

The Pharisees express surprise to the disciples that their master eats with sinners. Christ then asserts that he has come for the sick and sinners, not for the just and those who are well-off (vv. 12-13).

Jesus is no doubt referring to "the just" who are incapable of transcending the idea of distributive justice as a sign of God's mercy. Their attitude resembles that of the workers in the vineyard (Mt 20:1-16) or that of the elder son, jealous of the love of the father for the prodigal younger son (Lk 15:11-32), or again that of the Pharisee who is minutely careful to pay his little tax, but who looks down upon the sinner's plea to God's mercy (Lk 18:9-14). Christ contrasts a religion reduced to human justice with a religion built on divine *mercy*. In citing Hosea 6:6 (v. 13), he recalls that the prophets had already rejected the value of rites, even when perfectly performed, in favor of a religion of love and mercy.

The number of meals taken by Christ with sinners, the fact that the father of the family pardons his prodigal son with a sumptuous banquet (Lk 15:22-24), Christ's attitude toward Judas at the Last Supper (Mt 26:20-25) and his anxiety to offer bread and wine for the forgiveness of sins (Mt 26:28), are clear indications of the awareness of the early Christians who regard the Eucharist as a sacrament of pardon (Mt 18:15-18). A theology that was overly compartmentalized on the tracts of the Eucharist and penance has lost sight of the link that exists between the two sacraments, and the way that penance received its proper value from the Eucharist itself. The content of the two sacraments was minimized when the sacrament of penance was thought of only as a rite of purification set before the sacred action, as if the latter was incapable of a purifying effect. Does not a father of the family, who gives his life in the course of a meal where he brings his loved ones together, pardon by the very fact that he gives his life? It is very important that the eucharistic banquet be again celebrated "for the remission of sins."

VIII. Mark
3:20-35
Gospel
2nd cycle

Here we have the Jewish discussion about the source of Jesus' power of exorcism. It is the version common to all the synoptics (vv. 22-30; cf. Mt 12:24-32 and Luke 11:15-23), though each one places it in a different context. Curiously enough, Mark's context associates this with a tradition about an incident that took place between Jesus and members of his family (vv. 20-21, 31-35). Yet his account seems in many ways very close to the primitive events. The discussion about Beelzebub (vv. 22-26) for instance, and the reference to blasphemy against the Spirit (vv. 28-30) seem part of the primitive tradition. After that he becomes concerned with contrasting the lot of the person who allows himself to be drawn by the evil spirit and that of him who obeys the word (as in Lk 11:27-28), and gives us verses 20-21. Verse 27 is an addition made by the common synoptic tradition (cf. Mt 12:29). Here Mark is more discreet than the others, who added rather more in this vein to the primitive account (cf. Lk 11:15-23).

a) The essential theme of this gospel appears to be the *war between the two spirits*. The Jewish tradition, already much elaborated in the doctrine of Qumran, was that the world had been given over to the spirit of evil by followers of that spirit. The last times would see the advent of the Spirit of good, who would turn men again towards good and give them access to the Kingdom. Christ's expulsion of demons now is evidence that the Spirit of good is in action (Mt 12:28).

The scribes do not deny the fact that Jesus drives out evil spirits. But instead of attributing this to the good Spirit, they come up with an explanation that is at least novel. He is driving out inferior demons in the name of the chief demon (v. 22). For Jesus this amounts to blasphemy against the Spirit: it equates him with Satan. This is the sin against the Spirit, denying his presence in the world, denying his capacity to make the world over new. Such a sin is without remission. People who make such an affirmation can never be members of the Kingdom, because they reject the intervention of the Spirit which is the precise manner of the Kingdom's beginning (vv. 28-30).

The two spirits really exist, and the campaign waged by Jesus is that of the stronger against the strong (v. 27). The faithful share this campaign by opting for one spirit against the other. When one opts for the Spirit of God, one hears his Word and puts it in practice (vv. 34-35), making all the ruptures of previous ties, even family ties, that are necessary.*

b) Having just set up the Twelve (Mk 3:13-20) Jesus now encounters his *family* (Mk 3:20-21 and 31-35). We have frequent indications in the gospels of opposition between these two groups: doubtless they reflect rivalry about succession to the Messiah. But the matter of faith is also included. Jesus' fellow townspeople, above all his family, fail to understand his teaching (Lk 4:25). Not even his miracles, or his victories over Satan, bring about a change in this attitude. Consequently Jesus must set up a new family. Membership here will be based on free choice, not natural ties. Hearing the Word takes precedence over sentiment.

Man was created to respond with fidelity to God's loving initiative. Because he is free, he can turn to infidelity and betray his calling. This is sin. This experience in sin is one of being

---

*See the doctrinal theme: *Satan,* p. 46.

engulfed again by some great mass that is anterior to man, and can engulf creatures other than man, demons and nature itself. The state of sin is a conscious plunging further and further into this quasi-cosmic mass.

But man was created free and should never become the plaything of other creatures, even spirits. That is what Jesus is concerned to reveal. He freed himself from this cosmic mass that as man threatened to envelop him, and he freed his brothers from the grip of demonic powers. The liberation was accomplished not so much by his exorcisms, as by that basic obedience with which he victoriously confronted temptation and death.

As he awaits the clear manifestation of this victory, the Christian finds himself haunted by the two opposing forces. He yields to sin and becomes engulfed in the mass. Or he hears the Word and obeys it, becoming absorbed in the Kingdom.

It is in the liturgy of the Word that we become hearers of the Word, and in the obedience of our spiritual sacrifice in the eucharist that we put it in practice.

IX. Luke 7:11-17   Saint Luke is the only one to give us an ac-
Gospel   count of the resuscitation of the widow's son
3rd cycle   at Haim. Doubtless he does it of set purpose.
            A few verses further on he gives us Jesus'
reply to the Baptist: "The blind see . . . the deaf hear . . . the dead rise again" (v. 22). There had been hitherto no instance of raising to life. To justify fully the assertion of verse 22 he had to provide one.

a) The mention of a woman, an outcast in the Jewish society, in this account of a raising to life is deliberate. He wants to indicate Jesus' anxiety to *reassemble* all humanity, men and women, children and adults, rich and poor, Jews and Gentiles.

But the whole incident is meant to justify the assertion of verse 22. The sort of messianic era that the Jews envisaged was one where all human nature, suffering, sinful, humiliated, would be fully restored. The texts of Isaiah 61:1 and 35:5-6 were their authority: a Messiah would come to heal all human suffering and weakness.

b) In this context too Jewish tradition anticipated, at the end of time and the inauguration of the messianic age, a general *resurrection* of those Israelites who had died before the time. Isaiah 26:19 was cited for this: "Your dead will come to life, their corpses will rise." Probably the prophet, in using these words, thought only of the people's restoration (like Ez 37). But it is certain that at least one Jewish group anticipated a genuine corporal resurrection when the age dawned (2 M 7:9-36; Dn 12:2-3).

c) *Elias* was expected to return to preside over the inauguration. Consequently then it was thought that the Messiah would show those evidences of the "spirit of Elias" that ancient tradition had already discerned in Eliseus (compare 2 K 4:25-38 and 1 K 17:17-24). Certainly the evangelists had this in mind in recounting the resuscitation of a child, that had some resemblance to Elias' miracle (compare 1 K 17:23 and Lk 7:16). But what a difference there was between Elias, Eliseus, and Christ. The Old Testament figures performed their miracles in secret, Christ his in full view of the crowds. They used procedures that still have traces of traditional magic: Christ is content to speak and command.

The Jewish hopes are fulfilled by Christ, but this falls far short of the ultimate possibilities of his message. He reanimates a child, but it is after the manner of a "recovery" (v. 15). Soon another type of resurrection is to be revealed to men. It will be more than the mere "recovery" of a dead body. It will mean entry to a royal way of life that transcends all human categories.*

In Jewish terms then, Elias has already come. Jesus is raising

---

*See the doctrinal theme: *resurrection of the body,* p. 51.

the dead from their biers. It is however an indifferent success
when the one destined to be Lord of the Kingdom is taken for
its precursor. All this will be redressed on the day when he is no
longer content with resuscitating corpses, but when his life as
Risen Lord will be the very life of God himself.

The ambiguity continues perhaps to color attitudes even now.
Is Jesus merely the precursor of a kingdom yet to be realized,
the propounder of an ethic that has yet to be defined? Or is he,
in the very depths of his person, the actual Kingdom itself?

The first Christians avoided the danger of reducing Jesus to
the role of a new Elias; this they saw as the function of the
Baptist. In the same way we in our time should reject any view
which makes Jesus the mere precursor of a renewed humanity.
He *is* that renewed humanity, having received it from his Father.

B. DOCTRINE

1. The Theme of Satan

Many Christians no longer believe in Satan. Their experience of temptation does not seem to them to argue the existence of demonic powers; sin is sufficiently explained by human liberty. Personifying evil was characteristic of an epoch, now past, when man saw himself as the pawn of cosmic forces. The popular mythology of yesterday is today rejected, and what used to be called diabolic possession has become just another malady to be explained in terms of depth psychology. Has not the Church itself undergone a similar change and become remarkably hesitant about the practice of exorcism?

There are others who do not take this view. Satan they say has never been more active. Is not his trump card making people disbelieve in his existence? Without opposition, he can work all the more effectively. If we allege that Satan is not active in the world, how can we explain the many scriptural passages about him? Was Jesus himself the victim of folk beliefs? Surely not.

Questions such as these make us reflect more deeply about what we believe. What validity do these traditional affirmations have, about Satan's role on earth? As we review the various stages of salvation history, we shall find that the affirmations are by no means gratuitous. Without them it does not seem possible to see the work of Christ, or the duty of the Christian, in adequate dimensions.

The adversary of Yahweh's plan

Pagan man saw himself under the dominion of a world of spirits who were superior to himself. Very early he made an attempt to explain good and evil by seeing two principles locked in combat. This sort of dualism has had very many manifestations in the religious history of humanity. The very creation of the world was often seen as a victory of good over evil.

In the climate of the covenant, and of Jewish monotheism, this dualist outlook was profoundly changed. There is but one God, Yahweh; the existence of everything else is entirely due to his benevolent creativity. Thus it is absolutely unthinkable that any creature, of whatever kind, should dispute his exclusive domain with Yahweh or jeopardize in any basic way his plan of love and mercy. Man is created to respond by fidelity to the love initiative of God; but, because he is free, it is possible for him to be unfaithful and to betray his vocation.

In fact, man has rejected God and bears responsibility for that. But man's experience of sin leads him to the conviction that what takes place is capitulation by him to temptation. It is as if there were some evil inherent in the object of temptation, antecedent to his voluntary act. In other words experience seems to teach him that what happens when man sins is an awareness of involvement in some evil that existed independently of his sin, and embraces also spiritual creatures other than man. If God has created everything in love, everything he created is capable of rejecting him.

Such was the Jewish explanation. The result of human sin was expulsion from the terrestrial paradise. Man henceforward belonged in a world that was acquainted with death, and this world was the empire of spiritual powers who had themselves rejected God. These powers used death as their most potent instrument for confronting man with temptation, and when he yields he becomes their slave. The hope was for the advent of a man who would not yield, who would open himself to the action of God's victorious Spirit and Word. Then the power of death would be broken. For it is only by his own connivance that man becomes the slave of the demonic forces; he is not by nature the plaything of other spirits.

Christ's victory over the adversary

To ensure human salvation the dominion of demonic forces had to be destroyed; death had to be vanquished on his own ground. Of all this dread dominion Satan is the prince. He it was who at the very beginning took the form of a serpent in order to deceive the first Adam. He it is whom the Messiah must confront and conquer in a new combat. That is the object of Christ's mission "to take away all the power of the devil, who had power over death" (He 2:14).

We should not then be surprised when the evangelists present his public life as a constant combat with Satan: the encounter in the desert, the liberation of those possessed, the challenge to unbelieving Jews, finally the passion where, even when he seemed to be in control, Satan was overwhelmed. By being obedient even to the death on the cross, Jesus dethroned death and deprived Satan of the primary weapon whereby he built his earthly kingdom.

What is the basic meaning of this victory of Christ's? Affirmations about Satan's defeat really mean affirmation of the cosmic dimensions of what he did. We are dealing with something very fundamental indeed. Previously all creation was encompassed in the solidarity of sin. From now on there is a breach in the barrier. Christ, in a cosmic fashion, has opened up the way for a new cosmic solidarity, that of love. In other words, in Jesus Christ, the real creative plan of God breaks through; man becomes the ally of his creator in bringing to actuality his plan of love. Salvation-history, in the cosmic sense, has its real beginning. The day will come when Satan and death will be thrown "in the burning lake" (Rev 20:14). Then the solidarity of sin will have lost all consistency; there will be no kingdom of sin any more.

"He is the image of the unseen God and the first-born of all creation, for in him were created all things in heaven and on earth, everything visible and everything invisible, thrones, Dominations, Sovereignties, Powers; all things were created through him and for him. Before anything was created, he existed and he holds all things in unity. Now the Church is his body, he is its hold" (Col 1:15-18). It is in such terms that Saint Paul reveals the cosmic dimensions of Christ's intervention in history, and delineates the basic role of the Christian.

The adversary of Christians

The Church's mission here below is constantly to widen the breach opened by Christ, the Head of the Body. Satan's empire has been undermined, but it is not yet destroyed; death in all its forms continues to lure sinful man into temptation. Christ has once for all defeated Satan; but each man is summoned to win the same victory in turn.

Membership of the Church by baptism means accepting the duty of working for the fulfillment of Christ's primacy, so that beginning with him the true creation may be shaped. It means undertaking a responsibility of cosmic dimensions. The baptismal rite itself dwells upon this aspect of Christian vocation. Time and again the Spirit of God is dramatically opposed to Satan. The catechumen is made aware that the sacrament is about to snatch him once and for all from the dominion of demonic forces and incorporate him with true humanity. In other words he is about to pass once and for all from the world of sin to that of grace and fidelity, set up by Christ to give real validity to God's creative plan. He is required to endorse personally the triple renouncement of Satan, and the triple confession of Trinitarian faith.

But the struggle with Satan does not cease with baptism; this is a triumphal beginning of something designed for the advancement of all creation. In any man's life it is the initial act of regeneration which equips him to join Christ's struggle against the sin of the world and against all powers that reject God. Christ made the definitive breach in the solidarity of sin: baptism summons us all to continue his work. Because the Kingdom of the Father must be expanded until it absorbs all creation.

Mission and the struggle with Satan

In mission comes the high moment of the struggle with Satan, the time when the Christian must summon all the resources of his baptismal state. We have mission in the strict sense when the Good News of salvation is preached to a new people, when there is question of planting the mystery of Christ in a hitherto untouched cultural *milieu*. Here one has a more proximate sense of the cosmic weight of sin. Not that God's Spirit is not active in such environments. On the contrary, the religious pilgrimage of any non-Christian people is invariably the result in some part of action by the Spirit. But because the mystery of Christ is not yet rooted here, the pilgrimage is tentative, without the key to fulfillment. Death retains its power; Satan's sway is formidable.

What is the work of the missionary? He leaves one cultural milieu already shaped by the Church to bear witness to the risen Christ in another where the Good News has not yet penetrated. His task is to make his own the religious pilgrimage of this people, to use it and shape it in every possible way towards culmination in Christ. This is a sharing pregnant with paschal meaning. He anticipates somehow in himself the experience the people are destined to have when the mystery of Christ is rooted here; he points the way that they must take in order to accomplish their true destiny.

All this, as we said, indicates a paschal rhythm and it is therefore imperative that the people should realize this truth. Their deepest aspirations will only be accomplished, when death, wherever it appears, above all in relations with others, is challenged in obedience. In this sense the object of mission is the overthrow of Satan's empire in an area where it is still jealously preserved, just because death here has never yet been shorn of its power.

The Eucharist, the meal of victory over Satan

Baptism equips the Christian for the triumphal struggle with

Satan, but only sharing in the Eucharist nourishes him for successful combat day by day.

First of all, reception of the body of Christ gradually nourishes the baptized person as a child of the Kingdom. It absorbs him more and more into the true creation built on Jesus Christ, not only for his own personal salvation, but for entry on his cosmic role. Did not Saint Paul say to the Corinthians that on entry to the Lordship of Christ they would judge the angels?

Then, beyond that, openness to the triumphal Word provides each member of the assembly with the impetus he needs for deeper and deeper integration into salvation history. He becomes aware of the concrete terms on which death must be challenged in obedience, or Satan combatted.

2. The Theme of the Resurrection of the Body

The doctrine of resurrection for the body does not have the place it ought in the general structure of the Christian's belief. Nor did it have in recent generations, though the reasons for that state of affairs were then different.

For centuries, at least in the West, dualistic views about soul and body, a legacy from Greek paganism, led Christians to give the body, and indeed material creation in general, a secondary place. Indeed what was corporal was quite often downgraded, or in some cases even despised, as the seat *par excellence* of culpability. After the Renaissance the opposition between the world of the spirit and that of the body became even more pronounced. It was only in the former domain that there could be question of true religion; to introduce the world of the body would mean degradation in some way. Such were the terms in which Christ's phrase about religion 'in spirit and in truth" was interpreted. In a climate like that it is not surprising that the doctrine of resurrection for the body should cease to be prominent in the structure of Christian belief.

Now, the situation is quite different. There is a new scale of values, in some instance a totally opposite one, about the body and about matter. Man's mastery over the material universe leads him to think in terms of transforming the visible world, of hominization of the earth, rather than of spiritual realities. The corporal world has come back into its own. Yet the doctrine of bodily resurrection remains foreign, more often than not, to the average Christian outlook. It is an eschatological doctrine and has never been properly articulated into the project of reconstructing the world that modern man sees as his particular task.

If we are to answer an important Christian challenge of our time, this articulation must be accomplished. Otherwise the gap between the preview of faith and the actual sphere of human responsibility will continue to widen. It seems likely that theological investigation of the problem will assume greater proportions. We may see interesting doctrinal developments.

Resurrection of the body, a late belief in Israel

The God of Israel has absolute sovereignty over life and death. As the miracles of Elias and Eliseus show, he can even bring back to this life people who have already descended to Sheol.

However the resurrection theme is principally related to salvation history, and expresses the collective hope of Israel. The chosen people will not be always subject to the powers of Hell; one day death will be destroyed. This will be the definitive restoration, when the faithful Remnant will arise from the dead. Crushed by suffering and death, the suffering Servant will see the light and have his share of the spoils of victory (cf. Is 53, 11, 12).

It was not until the 2nd century BC that the question of individual resurrection was clearly posed. It was the time of the Maccabees, when there were martyrs. These were sustained by the hope that when final restoration came God would bring them up from Sheol to share the Kingdom. With the wicked it would not be so (cf. 2 M 7, 9, 14).

This shadowy character of the Jewish resurrection belief is evidence of the limitations as yet of the quest of faith. Here, as in so many other areas, Jewish inadequacy is to be explained by their bafflement before death. The real meaning of death as the gateway to eternal life, rather than just the consequence of sin, would have to await the Jewish man who would be capable of the degree of poverty that would find in death the true focus of obedience and love. It would be seen to be a crucial, but necessary, trial, that opened the gate of real life for all humanity.

Christ risen in the body, an essential element of faith

The coming of the Messiah put an end to all vagueness about the doctrine of resurrection. We can even say that the whole Good News about human salvation hinges on the bodily resurrection of Jesus.

It had been the Jewish belief that the Kingdom would come with acclamation, that it would appear suddenly from on high by a mighty act on the part of God and his Messiah. But nothing of the kind happened. Jesus proclaimed himself Savior, and set up, in unforeseen terms, the Kingdom on earth of the Father's own family. Man is created in the image and likeness of God, and is genuinely called by his living link with the man-God to the state of sonship. But this altogether gratuitous status as God's partner is based on his liberty as a creature. And this liberty gets its fullest expression in obedience unto death to the creatural condition.

Where Jewish belief had made the end of death a prior condition for the coming resurrection, Jesus revealed that, in order to reach life, death is a road that must be undertaken in obedience. When he dies on the cross he does so in obedience to the creaturely condition, displaying to the limit, in his radical annihilation of self, the demands made by the love of God and of all men. So encountered, death is placed in true perspective: it is the great avenue to eternal life. When he arises, he does so in soul and body. All of his humanness had been involved in his long pilgrimage of obedience as Incarnate Word.

So, the bodily resurrection of Jesus shows us the basic dimensions of salvation. In Jesus, man is called to enter the family of the Father, but he does so as a creature. That is to say, he must exercise his liberty fully in entering the paschal path that Jesus himself definitively opened. The body as well as the soul will be engaged in this pilgrimage (as indeed will material creation too). There is no human liberty that is not incarnate.

Risen with Christ in the Church

When he enters the Church by baptism, the Christian is established in living contact with the bodily arisen Christ. This development in ecclesial life of this link will enable him in his turn to undertake the paschal pilgrimage of Jesus, and, by so doing, to contribute his share in the building of the Kingdom.

The Spirit of the Risen Lord renews in us what Saint Paul calls the "interior man," so that, delivered from sin, we embark on the way of obedience unto death. Having died with Christ, we are also arisen with him. Here on earth, every encounter with death that follows the example of Jesus opens the way to the Kingdom. In that sense we are already risen with him.

Such an overwhelming affirmation should be viewed more closely. If we are already arisen, that is because the Spirit of the Risen Lord is actively at work here below throughout the whole human reality, not just in the spiritual domain. Man's body, and the material creation with which it is linked, is involved too. The Kingdom here below is made up of men, not of souls. When we say the Spirit of the Risen Lord is at work on earth, we are affirming that a mysterious dynamism gradually leads our universe across the barrier of death. At the end will come the great fulfillment. But meantime, throughout history, the fulfillment is being shaped in terms of what has already been accomplished in Jesus Christ.

Is there anything further that can be said of resurrection as applied to the body here below? The body is the "material medium" of communication and communion among men. Nor is it divorced from spiritual activity. On the contrary it is the vehicle by which the life of the spirit can be displayed in the interpersonal exchange of truth and love. It is indeed the very instrument of Christian charity. We might even say that the practice of universal brotherly love actually shapes the body itself into its true lineaments. Could not this be the sense in which the body here below shares the resurrection, that it is the most effective means of communion with all men? There is no reason why we shouldn't think so.

Witnesses of the resurrection of the body

The doctrine of the resurrection of the body is of quite paramount importance in the actual conduct of mission. It provides an insight into the extent of Christian concern for human salvation in the fullest sense. In addition, it gives meaning to the actual thrust now of human effort, provided of course that this thrust can be articulated into its true position in the general quest of faith.

The missionary thus will be concerned to show that the Good News of salvation is not exclusively concerned with values of the spirit; it touches men at every level of his being. It is man as he is, here and now in the terrestrial condition, who is called to sonship with God. The best way of making this clear is to show that the Kingdom inaugurated by Jesus Christ begins here at the moment when a man makes his engagement of faith. This entails the mobilization of all his resources, corporal as well as spiritual, for the shaping of his pattern of obedience unto death. From this moment onwards, where there can be no attempt to evade the creatural condition in order to achieve salvation, the body, with all material creation, recovers its true dignity in the salvific plan of God.

Remembering then that the definitive Kingdom begins on earth, that the body retains its basic identity both before and after death, we can go further and say that this doctrine has a direct bearing on modern man's search for meaning in his reconstruction of the world. Such a project has meaning not only as an expression of man's fidelity to the creatural condition: it has a salvific dimension as well. The hominization of the earth, insofar as it is really an expression of man's fidelity to the creatural condition, is actually bringing about cosmic death and the ultimate transfiguration of the universe. The dynamism at work is that of resurrection.

The eucharistic assembly and the resurrection of the body

In the chapter of the first letter to the Corinthians where he speaks of the Lord's supper, Saint Paul mentions "unworthiness" among people who eat the bread and drink the cup. Then he adds what seems at first sight an enigmatic verse: "That is why many of you are weak and ill and some of you have died" (1 Co 11:30). As he sees it, the communion with the Risen Lord offered by the Eucharist has such an effect even on the body, that if *per impossibile* one were to receive it with absolute worthiness one's body would be completely transformed and would know neither sickness nor death.

The eucharistic assembly is in fact the chief focus of activity for the Spirit of the Risen Lord. When our "yes" of living faith makes us part of it, the influence permeates us in body as well as in soul, because the yes of faith engages the whole person. Furthermore it is during the eucharistic celebration, because of its ritual character, that the unifying force of the faith reaches its greatest intensity. The Spirit of the Risen Lord reaches down to the very roots of our being and our awareness. Our bodies can truly be said to be sharing in Christ's resurrection. They are caught up in the great movement of universal love and summoned to pass through the gateway of death to glory and transfiguration.

ELEVENTH SUNDAY

A. THE WORD

I. Exodus 19:2-6
1st reading
1st cycle

This passage, which forms the introduction to the episode of the Sinai covenant, is not from any of the usual Pentateuch sources. Indeed it seems to have been inserted at this point by some author of the 4th or 3rd century BC. It is quite poetic in structure, something exceptional in Exodus. We have the theme of the "house of Jacob" in verse 3 (cf. Ps 113/114:1), the image of Yahweh "carrying" his people (v. 4; cf. Is 40:11, 46:3-4, 63:9, 66:12-13; Dt 1:31, 32:10-12), deuteronomic expressions like "keeping the alliance" (v. 5; cf. Dt 29:8, 33:9) "hearing the voice" (v. 5; cf. Dt *passim*), finally the theme of the consecrated people (v. 6; cf. Dt 7:6, 14:2, 21, 26:19, 28:9).

a) The phrase "a people of priests" (v. 6) relates the passage to the context of third Isaiah (Is 61:6). The author sees the people of Israel fulfilling the same role among the nations as the priestly caste does among the tribes. All the tribes belong to God, yet the priests only approach him. Likewise, all humanity belongs to God, but only the chosen people can approach him in the liturgy of the Word. They represent humanity, and are a sign before the nations of God's will. The deep meaning of the events of Exodus and Sinai lies in the *choice* of the people. This entails a separation which is particularly manifested in a special manner of living that bears witness to God's plan for man (v. 5). It does not however mean isolation. Their "consecration" is on the contrary a sign of humanity before the Lord, and a testimony of the Lord before the nations. The mediating priesthood lies in this function.

b) Yahweh took Israel under the charge (v. 4b; cf. Dt 32:11; Ho 11:3-4; Is 46:3-4, 63:9) and brought her across the desert to

Sinai in order to make an *alliance* with her. This is not a bilateral contract, even though there be reciprocal obligations. God alone has the initiative and undertakes the task of preparation (v. 4). But on the other hand it is not a definitive regulation, forever determining the role of the people. Everything is cast in terms of the future ("I shall have you as a people . . . you will be . . ."). The best description of the covenant could well be: the beginnings of a relationship, with all the suggestion this carries of vicissitudes in history.

The Church is genuinely representative before God of humanity. Her function is not to claim a monopoly of salvation and good. These are present indeed in every man of good will. It is rather to express in her spiritual cult what is still latent in humanity, and to be a sign before humanity of the free choice offered in God's plan.

The eucharistic assembly which meets to change the bread and wine into Christ's Body and Blood is the channel of that change we must bring about in spiritualizing nature. It indicates the means and the end. The gathering of the mystical Body of Christ takes within its ambit the struggles of all men, even non-Christians, to build peace and justice in the world. When the assembly is a celebration of penance, it is acknowledging before God not only the faults of the members, but the sin of the world itself. It is in the name of this world, of which it constitutes the first fruits, that it secures God's pardon. In this sense the priesthood of the people of God is something very real, a mediation between men and God, and God's own message to men.

II. Ezechiel
17:22-24
1st reading
2nd cycle

Judah has just lost her independence: King Joachim has been taken captive: the symbolic tree of the people has lost its royal summit. About 590, Ezechiel had already lamented the topping of the tree's summit by the eagle

Nabuchednezzar (Ez 17:1-21). Now, thirty years later, Assyria's defeat was jeopardizing his conquests. Consequently the prophet hastens to add to his previous poem about the decapitated tree an oracle full of hope (Ez 17:22-24).

He sees God himself take the initiative in planting a tree on Mount Sion, a shoot taken from the old rotten cedar (v. 22). The shoot becomes a tree, spreads and extends her sway over the whole world (Dn 4:1-34; Ez 31:6). The tiny "Remnant" of the people becomes the messianic people of the final times (v. 23). He concludes the oracle by pointing out that God's judgment is inspired by the law of compensation (v. 24).

The tree-theme is important in Scripture. The tree of life (Gn 2:9) has mythical sources, but Jewish tradition had purified these by making the enjoyment of its fruits conditional on obedience to God's Word (Gn 3:22). The schools of wisdom take up the tree of life theme again, but always in a moralizing and desacralized context (Pr 3:18, 11:30, 13:12, 15:4). Prophetic tradition was more historical. Here, the ideal tree is Israel herself, which produces marvelous fruits because of her fidelity to the covenant (Is 5:1-7; Jr 2:21; Ez 15, 19:10-14; Ps 79/80:9-20). The Israel-tree is stricken when it bears no more fruit, but it comes to life once more when God takes the initiative of replanting it. It is a theme connected always with the divine initiative which keeps it in being.

Another prophetic tradition compares the King (and also the Messiah) to a tree (Jg 9:7-21; Dn 4:7-9; Ez 31:8-9). This is a cliche in oriental literature; but it personalizes the theme, and introduces the notion of the people benefiting by the life of a single person.

Finally, as a result of all these applications, comes the comparison of the just man to a tree. He bears fruits full of flavor and goodness, but among the other barren trees he is lost (Ps 1: 91/92:13-14, a responsorial psalm; Dt 2:1-3; Si 24:12-22). The tree however has to be irrigated by God. Ezechiel (47:1-12) foresaw that the fruitfulness had an eschatological meaning. Jesus denounces the tree-Israel which fails to bear fruit (Mt 3:8-10, 21:18-19), and proposes himself as the fruit tree (Jn 15:1-6), to which moreover people must be grafted if they wish to bear fruit. Finally we find the tree of life definitively planted in Paradise, surrounded for all eternity by fruitful trees (Rev 2:7, 22:1-2, 14:19).

Our fruits, when we are grafted on to the tree of life, are the "fruits of the Holy Spirit" (Ga 5:5-26, 6:7-8, 15-16), that is, the things that increase our awareness of the new life, of our share in the new humanity.

III. 2 Samuel 12:7-10, 13
1st reading
3rd cycle

We have just had, in Chapter 11, the account of David's wrongdoing against Uriah. This account is contained in 2 Samuel 12:15-25 when the child of this adultery was in agony. The primitive tradition represented here suggests that the death of the child is a punishment for the father's sin. Gradually however a more valid theological view gained currency. It was expressed in the tradition of Nathan's visit to the king (2 S 12:1-14), and was subsequently, before the 8th century, incorporated in the primitive account.

a) Nathan, following an ancient procedure of the prophets (cf. 2 S 14:4-17), begins his mission by telling a parable (vv. 1-4). David reacts violently to this, and delivers a death sentence (vv. 5-6) without realizing that he is condemning himself. Nathan at once (v. 7) abandons the role of story-teller for that of prophet and addresses David in the second person ("it is you") in the manner of the old oracles of Yahweh (cf. 1 S 2:27-36). It devolves then upon the prophet to pronounce the *sentence of death* on David's child (v. 10). But the sentence is not clear. In verse 10 David is punished by the constant presence of the sword in his family. In fact his sons, Ammon (2 S 13:29), Absalom (2 S

18:14-15) and Adonias (1 K 2:25) are destined to perish by the sword. This represents a very Jewish concept of history. The father's sin becomes "original sin" for the family and leads to steady downfall.

Verses 11-12 give us another version of the chastisement. Perhaps we are dealing with a later addition, which follows another Jewish concept: the law of retribution. The prophecy however is not destined to be fulfilled in the latter. In any case the reading we have does not include it.

Finally, in verse 14, with the announcement of the death of the child of adultery, we have a third version of the punishment, this is the work of the final editor, who wanted to reconcile Nathan's prophecy with what actually ensued.

b) All of these versions of the punishment of David are too numerous and too different to be original. Subsequent authors, who read and reread the history of David's descendants, wanted to find evidence of chastisement in the dynasty, and for that reason drastically manipulated the primitive text. This procedure of course has its price. It means that verse 13 can be directly related to verses 7-9, and that David's *repentance* is made to be the result of Nathan's prophecy, not the threat of punishment. In other words he is led to repent by the discovery of his crime, not by the fear of punishment.

His repentance wins absolute and immediate pardon from God (v. 13b). "God does not will the death of the sinner, but that he be converted and live." Here too, regrettably, the interpolators place the announcement of the child's death (v. 14) after that of God's pardon, tending to give the impression that God is going back on his word and demanding after all an expiatory victim.

These verses which describe David's chastisement illustrate the deplorable tendency to measure culpability by the concrete harm caused by an act. The real interest of the passage lies in the fact that sin and pardon are meaningless terms outside a personal context, the personal relationship between the sinner and God.

From this aspect the Nathan episode is one of the most important in the whole Old Testament. For the first time the rites and legalities, which obscured the relationship as an encounter of two liberties, are stripped away. A sort of desacralization takes place, which indeed must always get repeated.

Faced with sin, God could be vengeful, break his alliance and intervene at once with judgment. Such a God is suggested by the proclamation of chastisement in verses 10-15. But that would be a travesty of the God of love, who shows himself infinitely superior to such rejection. He replaces the sinner's old heart with something altogether new.

IV. Romans 5:6-11 *2nd reading 1st cycle* — In the first verses of Romans 5, Paul had shown how justification is an accomplished fact (vv. 1-2), contrary to the Jewish view which placed it partially in the future. His proof is the work of love now being carried out by the Holy Spirit in our souls (v. 5). This does not however mean a cancelation of hope; on the contrary it gives our hope a dimension undreamed of in the Jewish perspective (vv. 3-5). Now, in verses 6-11, he takes up the same point, from a different angle and with different imagery.

Salvation-history rests upon those facts: a past event, the voluntary death of Jesus for sinners (vv. 6-8), a present event, the reconciliation brought about by this death, of which we have the fruits in this life (vv. 10-11), and finally the pledge of a future event. To men who have been already reconciled with him God will give his life and his glory, because the Son died for them (v. 10b). Thus, here and now, the essential has been accomplished. If we live in this conviction we are confessing our faith and assuring our hope. Where Jewish hope was in the promise, God is present in the actual texture of the Christian's life. This is the basis of our hope.

Jewish religious life was turned towards Yahweh's future judgment, reward for the good and punishment for the wicked. Observance of the law placed one among the good: one's justice would shine forth at the judgment.

Nevertheless religious experience brought some disconcerting discoveries for the chosen people. God is not only the judge, the guarantor of the good; he is above all the Totally-Other before whom man can have no rights. He can save the sinner, as he justifies the just. His justice certainly does not follow the pattern of human distributive justice.

In his person, Jesus manifested both types of justice. He observed the justice of the law, giving it the new dimension of love. And by his pardon he brought justification to all humanity. The Christian's gaze is not, as the Jews was, directed to a last judgment of the distributive kind. God's justice for him is truly that of the Totally-Other, who has shown what he is by reconciling humanity.

It is in the eucharistic celebration that we particularly feel our justification. Sharing the Bread and the Word is the most effective avenue to the grace that was given once for all in Jesus Christ, above all in the event of his death. But the Eucharist also makes us partners with God in the building of the Kingdom. Justified by Christ, we are called here, in this life, to construct the kingdom of God's justice. Our fidelity to this task, day after day, constitutes the sign that ought to shine before all men. So it will come about that they, justified in turn, will build the future Kingdom and there be gathered in the life and glory of the God of love.*

V. 2 Corinthians 5:6-10
2nd reading
2nd cycle

The verses in our reading, where Paul gives us a particularly complicated formulation of his hope, are understandable only by keeping in mind the first verse of the chapter.

*See the doctrinal theme: *hope*, p. 180.

Paul indeed is subscribing to the New Testament doctrine of the spiritualization, in Jesus Christ, of the *temple* (compare v. 1 with Mk 14:58). He is certainly influenced by Stephen's discourse on the subject (Ac 7:48-56). For Christians of Jewish origin, secluded or removed from the temple, it was important to realize that, in the person of the Risen Christ, they had a definitive temple. (Jn 2:9), the channel of mediation, and a new source of blessing. Yet there was a sense in which they, like the Jews of the Diaspora in regard to the material temple (v. 6), felt themselves at a distance from this spiritual, eternal temple. Their exile however is not real, because the Christian's own terrestrial body is in some way a temple ("tent" in v. 4; cf. 1 Co 3:16).

There remains of course the painful passage through death, that sometimes the Christian would wish to escape. But would he really? Is not our hope that of ascending to the temple, of seeing there the face of God (Ex 23:15, 34:23-24; Dt 16:16) in all its splendor (Is 2:2-5), and dwelling with him (vv. 6-9)? What Paul is doing then is transposing the themes of cult and temple, by spiritualizing them, into the context of Christian hope. In the glorified Christ we shall see the face of God, as Isaiah did in the temple of Sion. How then can we hesitate to undergo the trial of exile and death?

VI. Galatians 2:16, 19:21 *2nd reading 3rd cycle* Having considered his ministry to the Gentiles historically, Paul now turns to it again, this time from the doctrinal point of view. He does not confine himself to a catalogue of his peregrinations, but attempts to define the gospel as a religious system in contrast with Judaism.

In so doing he relinquishes his own particular meaning for the word "gospel" (access for the Gentiles to salvation) in favor of the primary meaning (the proclamation of the death and resurrection of Christ).

a) Paul is one of the first to liken the *death and resurrection* of Jesus to the Christian life (vv. 19-21). Above all he is the first to become interested in Christ's death for its own sake. His procedure differs from that of Peter, who likes to gloss over the death by pointing out that Christ "had" to die. As he sees it, it is Jesus' death which is the primary source of the Christian's justice (v. 21). By his resurrection he becomes present for his own in a definitive way, but by his death he liberates and justifies them.

b) *Justification,* in this context, has a quite precise meaning. It denotes that one is now on the plane of God's designs for man, and responds to his hopes for man. The law was powerless to aid us in this response, because it did not change the heart, nor did it prevent death (it actually went the length of condemning to death). What God wants for man is that he be victorious over death and have a new heart in order to obey the covenant.

Christ on the cross is the first justified man. He is the first to show a sufficiently loving heart and to accept from the Father whatever comes after death.

Justification then is a summons to go beyond the limits. Every Christian life that challenges the rigidity of law and the boundaries of egoism is life with Christ on the cross.

VII. Matthew
9:36-10:8
Gospel
1st cycle

The missionary discourse, of which the present passage forms the general introduction, has been handed down in different traditions. We have a very short account in Mk 6:8-11, which is taken up by Luke (9:3-4) and incorporated in his version of the sending of the Twelve. But in Luke 10:2-16 we have a longer version of the same discourse, which he associates with the sending of the seventy-two disciples. Here he is following his customary policy of avoiding a context that was limited to the activities of the Twelve and Judeo-Christian thinking.

Matthew, for his part, chose to combine the long and the short version. And he adds certain points taken, for instance, from the eschatological discourse. This broadens considerably the limits of Christ's original statement. We are dealing not so much with the actual mission of the twelve apostles to Galilee, but rather with a short treatise on general missiology.

a) This discourse opens with the *harvest* theme (cf. Mt 9:37-38; Lk 10:3; Jn 4:35-38). As in the case of fishermen who are invited to become fishers of men. Jesus summons the grain-harvesters to become spiritual harvesters.

The image suggests the figure of God bringing human history to an end, and inaugurating the Kingdom of the final times (v. 7; cf. Am 9:13-15; Ps 125/126:5-6; Jl 4:13; Jr 5:17; Mt 13:28-39; Rev 14:15-16). Hence comes the idea of judgment; of good grain separated from the chaff. As a consequence it is not surprising that the harvesters become the object of persecution: they will be as lambs in the midst of wolves (Mt 10:16).

b) More important is the idea Jesus seems to have of himself as *rabbi* in his own country. Contrary to the other rabbis of his time who gathered some followers round about them in a school or at the gate of a city, he wants to be an itinerant rabbi. He does not wait for disciples to come to him; he goes to meet them and encounters them in their various avocations. He is not going to be like the temple clergy who receive victims and money from the faithful, without concerning themselves with the salvation of souls. Nor will he be like the Pharisees who are only concerned with the souls of the elite. He is going after the "lost sheep" of Israel, the neglected and forgotten (v. 35). When he accepts disciples he does not do so after the manner of contemporary rabbis, to engage in discussion with them. He wants them to join his missionary excursions and give attention to the forsaken sheep (vv. 36 and 10:1).

This is a completely new concept by contemporary Jewish practice. It immediately makes of Jesus' mission a work of "pity"

(v. 36) and mercy towards the poor, the sick and sinners. These are all "sheep without shepherds" (v. 36), because neither priests, nor Pharisees, nor rabbis condescend to deal with them.

c) Matthew differs from the other synoptics in giving us the list of the twelve apostles, not at the moment of their calling (Mk 3:16-19; Lk 6:14-16), but at the time of their sending. He is more sensitive to the importance of mission than of vocation. By listing the apostolic college at the beginning of the mission discourse, he is very probably concerned to establish a link between *apostolic collegiality* and *mission*, something that is also stressed in Acts 2:14; Mark 1:36; and Luke 9:32.

However the mission is to be confined to the sheep of *Israel*. Jesus explicitly excludes Gentiles and Samaritans (vv. 5-6). Doubtless he sees his Messiahship at this stage as something for the chosen people. The belief of his time, which he shared, was that the entry of the Gentiles to the Kingdom would take place only in the eschatological future, by the gratuitous act of God. So carefully does Jesus await this eschatological intervention by the Father for the gathering of the Gentiles, that throughout his public life he does not concern himself with their calling (Lk 13:23-36; Mk 7:24-30). He is observing an economy of salvation that is "first for the Jews" (Rm 1:16). Luke, in the Acts, respects this scrupulously, by describing the dissemination of the Good News from Jerusalem and Judaea.

It is undeniable that the missionary awareness of the Church and the apostles was something that developed gradually. Passages like Matthew 10, where the author is actually concerned to elaborate a theology of mission, are still limited to the horizon of Israel. It would take persecution to drive the apostles out from Jerusalem among the Diaspora.

However, the essence of the Church is mission: her function includes a relationship with the non-Christian world. The eucharistic assembly, to be adequate, should imbue all its members with this universalism.

VIII. Mark
4:26-34
Gospel
2nd cycle

The two parables in this passage, the patient husbandman and the mustard seed, form, with the sower (Mk 4:3-8) and the leaven (Mt 13:33), a separate group designed to indicate the same conclusion: a justification of the Messiah's attitude when he encounters failure in his preaching. It does not seem impossible that they were composed with special reference to Simon the Zealot and Judas Iscariot (the Licarius). These two disciples belonged to an extremist group who wanted to undertake a holy war against Rome in order to reestablish the messianic kingdom.

a) In the story of the patient husbandman (vv. 26-29) the Kingdom of God is compared to the *slow growth* of the seed until the harvest, and simultaneously to the prolonged inactivity of the husbandman before the feverish work of the harvest (something already mentioned in Jl 4:13; cf. also Rev 14:14-16). The harvest, as the Joel reference and the Bible generally indicate, certainly denotes the judgment of God as he inaugurates the definitive Kingdom. In other words God is the husbandman who will one day be active, just as feverishly as the harvester at gathering. True, in actual fact, and especially throughout the ministry of Jesus, God does not seem to act. He leaves Christ isolated, without success, rejected more and more by his own. This inaction though is connected with the judgment to come, just as surely as the inaction of the husbandman who planted the seed is related to his future worth as harvester.

The Jews challenged Jesus, if he claimed Messiahship, to provide the signs that would herald the kingdom. His reply was that there are no spectacular signs. God allows the seed to grow slowly, but there is nothing to be lost by waiting: there is absolute continuity between the growing pains of the kingdom of God and its manifestation in plenitude. Those who wished to collaborate in the inauguration should not lose heart. God had given the beginnings; without doubt, after his silence, he would bring his work to completion. We should wait in patience and not press for developments. Those who refused to accept the Kingdom until the moment of its manifestation should beware. The Kingdom had actually come close to them in the person of Jesus. One had to have the insight to see it at work, even with inadequate means and slow development.

b) The parable of the mustard seed fosters confidence in God by stressing the contrast between the humble beginnings of the Kingdom (v. 31) and the dimensions of its eschatological future (v. 32, where the rest *motif* is borrowed from Jewish eschatologies about the incorporation of the Gentiles in the people of God, cf. Ez 17:22-24). In the story Jesus is doubtless anxious to provide an answer to people who contrasted the *feebleness of his means* with the glory of the expected Kingdom. They ridiculed the poverty and ignorance of his disciples, by contrast with the triumphal cortege that should herald the inauguration of the final times.

But the truth is that in the tiny seed what is destined to grow great is active. In a world that does not know the Kingdom it is already there in germ: in the heart of the most hardened sinner a tiny spark may yet become a devouring fire. In spite of all appearances we must take God seriously.*

IX. Luke
7:36-50
Gospel
3rd cycle

This passage which tells of the anointing of Jesus by a woman who was a sinner and gives us in conjunction the parable of the two debtors, raises a problem on which exegetes are not yet agreed.

The tradition prior to the gospels was of an anointing at Bethany, in the house of Simon the Pharisee (Mt 26:6-13; Mk 14:3-9) by a woman who was not named. The expensive anointing was justified by Jesus by reference to a Jewish tradition

*See the doctrinal theme: *abundance*, p. 73.

which made the anointing of corpses more valuable than alms given to the poor.

John gives us this tradition at a later stage, when there were new elements (Jn 12:1-8). He names the woman: Mary: the sister of Martha and Lazarus. He stresses the fact that the anointing was not of the head, as Matthew and Mark have it, but of the feet, and that Mary dried them with her hair. Finally, though he retains the discussion about the cost of the anointing, he mentions that the oil would normally be used for Christ's burial. However, in that Christ was destined to arise again, this burial rite was pointless. When Mary provided it before Christ's death, she was expressing her conviction, confirmed by the raising of Lazarus, that Jesus could not die (Jn 11:25).

Luke's version too (7:36-50) has some original details. He mentions a host called Simon (Lk 8:40; Mt 26:6). The anointing, contrary to Matthew's version, is of the feet, and the woman dries them with her hair (Lk 7:38; Jn 12:3). He does not however mention an anointing at Bethany, aware, doubtless, that this would be a doublet. Nor does he mention any discussion about the opportuneness of this anointing (Mt 26:10-12; Jn 12:5-8), probably because this was a matter of Jewish classification of "good works," not intelligible to his Greek readers. He chooses to replace this by a parable that is more in accord with his general doctrine about pardon.

Whatever we are to say about the episode recounted, whether it is the same or not, it is at least evident that in Luke's version we must distinguish the episode itself (vv. 36-39, 44-47, 48-50) from the parable he appends (vv. 40-43).

a) The *meal*-scenes in Saint Luke constitute in fact a special literary genre, which follows precise lines (cf. 7:36-50, 5:27-32; Lk 14). He probably saw in these occasions an opportunity for presenting, more or less artificially, some unchronicled parables. He always ties these in adroitly by the mention of some incident or other during the meal (in one case, the placing at table, in another, the omission by Jesus of the ritual ablutions). However, there is no reason for attaching theological importance to the meal in the Pharisee's house. For Luke this is simply an occasion, borrowed perhaps from Mark 14:3-9, and used to fit his "symposium" genre. He uses items from oral tradition (the sinful woman, vv. 37-38; the parable of the two debtors, vv. 40-43), or from written tradition (Mk 14, the anointing: v. 37). But he adds other details appropriate to his genre (vv. 44-46), and comments appropriate to his theology (remission of sins: vv. 41-42 and 47-50).

b) The essential lesson for Luke in the episode is the *pardon of sin* by Christ.* In the context (Lk 7:34, 8:1-4) there is direct allusion to his familiarity with sinners.

The scandal taken by the Pharisee (v. 39) is based on the prohibition, in Deuteronomy 23:19, of accepting the gifts of a prostitute for sacred use. If Christ were a man of God he should have refused the woman's offering. Immersed in legalism, like the hardened Pharisees of Mark 2:23 - 3:5, this man did not seek to understand Christ's reason for disregarding the prohibition. Faced with "hardness" of this calibre, Jesus displays his openness towards the sinner. Their personal contact, their encounter in love and pardon, cancel the prescripts of Deuteronomy about purity and discrimination. So potent is this person to person encounter, where God's gift (the remission of sins) is joined with human love (the woman's gratitude), that it becomes a substitute for the traditional means of justification: ablutions and various rites (v. 48).

c) The parable of the two debtors (vv. 40-43) is extremely nuanced. It opposes to the pharisaic obsession about debts and duties the notion of a creditor who *remits debts*, and of debtors with feelings of love and gratitude, something not altogether usual in ordinary life.

True indeed, the parable is somewhat disconcerting when

*See the doctrinal theme: *pardon*, p. 77.

there is talk about loving more or less, and when the situation between the debtors becomes one of overbidding. Love and gratitude are not measured in figures. We should remember that the quantitative emphasis belongs to the polemical context in which the parable was delivered.

Nor is the context ultimately important. The parable is really designed to lead the audience from a quantitative notion of religion to one where divine pardon meets the loving fidelity of man.

Our gospel indeed will not be comprehensible unless we discern behind it the very person of the man-God, the ideal point of encounter between man and God. It is because Christ has made a success of this encounter that he can take the most desperate human situations and make sinners themselves aware of what they must do. They must be open to God's gift (or his pardon), and respond with a loving "yes" to his initiative.

When these conditions are verified in the Eucharist, we can dispense with the contrived reconciliations brought about by ablutions and exterior rites. We are emancipated from the excommunications and ostracisms of over-abstract legalism.

B. DOCTRINE

1. The Theme of Abundance

Dreams of abundance have invariably colored notions of happiness. Only perpetual plenty it seems can fully satisfy man's aspirations. All the golden ages of mythology are depicted as terrestrial paradises of endless richness.

However, where man in the past naturally evoked towards the gods for this plenty, modern man means to attain it himself. The golden age has come within the bounds of concrete possibility.

When we view the matter from the point of view of faith, we shall find that the sign of abundance is just as essential a note. It is important however to realize what kind of abundance we have in mind, and what we must do to attain it.

The abundance promised to Israel

Like other peoples, Israel dreamed of abundance. It is the subject of patriarchal blessings and ancient divine promises. For a considerable time the salvation designed for his people by Yahweh is seen in terms of fruitfulness and material riches. "I shall multiply the fruit of your womb and the fruit of your soil." It was natural for people to regard fruitfulness of the moment, or goods already possessed, as signs of the abundance to be.

Very soon however, harsh reality put an end to such foolish dreams. Israel continued to be a tiny people exposed to the rivalry of the great powers in that epoch; her survival as a political entity was always in jeopardy. The deepening of faith which came about as a result of this forced her to take a second look at the ancient promise of abundance. Yahweh, true, will keep his promise, provided only that the people remain faithful to the Law. In time of trial they must not take refuge in the illusory security of idolatry. To guard against this, it is better that Israel remain in the insecurity of small numbers and sometimes absolute inadequacy of material resources. Where richness brings injustice, poverty is preferable. Political weakness is a surer reminder than political power of the gratuitousness of divine choice. On the day when God actually does shower abundance on his chosen folk, they will realize that he acts from love and that they owe everything to him.

Thus, as interiorization grew, Israel began to realize that true riches are not material riches. Little by little new horizons opened up concerning the nature of the abundance God had in store for his elect.

The abundance of the Kingdom inaugurated in Jesus Christ

It was Jesus who revealed to men the true nature of the abundance that was destined to bring satisfaction. It is the abundance of the Father's family. Those divine blessings which alone are capable of satisfying man lie beyond man's power: they are not in the category of possessions. God, in absolutely gratuitous love, has these in store for man to give full richness to his being. So priceless is this abundance that all other riches must be sacrificed for it.

The gift of the Spirit which is the epitome of this divine abundance shone forth in the resurrection of Christ. Plenitude of this order however was only achieved at the cost of complete rejection of any form of human power. In his death and resurrection Jesus showed that true abundance does not consist in having possessions. It is of the category of being, not having, of openness and self-giving, not controlling or owning.

Because this gift of the Spirit met in Jesus the perfect measure of human fidelity, he became the center of universal reassembly. In the Risen Lord a project of catholicity is inaugurated that extends to all men everywhere, at any time. All humanity is invited to share the blessings of the Father's family.

In all this the linked themes of abundance and multitude again are prominent, but it is a far cry from the primitive view. We are not dealing with a chosen people, multitudinous and powerful, who extend their sway over the nations of the earth. The terms define a Kingdom that is not of this world, but is yet the only one capable of satisfying mankind.

The Church of abundance

Saint Paul marvels when he describes the riches enjoyed by Christians, the power of the Spirit at work among the primitive communities, and the evangelistic enterprise. These first Christians realized that they were the recipients of every sort of blessing.

It is important to understand the real character of this messianic abundance. The sense of fulfillment that these people had was altogether different from that of people whose contractual demands have been met. It was a source of responsibility. Their blessings were something conferred on free people, who were asked to respond by dependence on Jesus Christ. The abundance of the Kingdom is an absolutely gratuitous gift of God, but it cannot be received passively. It imposes a task, and presumes on our part a sort of growth. When we affirm that abundance is ours, we are saying that in Christ, after the resurrection, all has been accomplished, but that yet, somehow, all remains to be accomplished. The eschatological Kingdom is a task still to be undertaken, an edifice to be built, a project of catholicity that will be realized only gradually.

Furthermore, and paradoxically, the principle in all this growth is one of poverty. Saint Paul is the first to stress the contrast between the riches he possesses and the poverty attributed to him. The Body of Christ continues to grow across the hazards of our insufficiency, and, sometimes indeed, in a context of apparent failure. In any case it is essential to remember that developments are not visible to the material eye. Catholicity goes forward on the principle of the "seed" or the "leaven." Growth escapes notice. Thus if we take a superficial view of the Church now it could well seem a failure. True failure however would only arise if the Church were to behave like secular powers, if the ecclesial impact about which Christians dream were to be construed in terms of secular procedures.

Finally, the abundance of the Kingdom, and the growth it fosters, are in fact the basis for those human values which correspond to the gospel. Here and now, in the world we inhabit, there is an "abundance" which all men should be seeking. Brotherhood, that is, between all men. Every other material benefit that men pursue should be subordinated to the achievement of brotherhood and peace.

The sign par excellence of true abundance

Mission is this sign. It is so first of all because it is an invitation to all men to join in brotherhood, around the first-born, in the family of the Father. Secondly, because for every man, every people, every cultural climate it elicits the gift of the Spirit who is there at work, and makes the riches of the Father's family flower in the Church.

But it is the sign under certain conditions only. If it is to be really a channel of universal salvation in Jesus Christ, it is essential that mission respect the priority of the poor. Once the poor are properly evangelized, the others follow freely. This supposes of course that the Church relinquish all power tactics, all propaganda. Furthermore, if missionaries are to penetrate to the Spirit that is at work in the heart of every man, they must be open for this task. They must be ready to renounce self and share the other's experience. There are many roads that lead to recognition of Christ. When a new one manifests itself, we must realize that this is the very abundance of the Kingdom finding a new form of expression.

Saint Paul, in many instances, emphasizes the evangelic force of example. The Good News is best proclaimed when the non-Christian begins to discern in the Christian's life the answer to the spiritual thrust he feels in himself.

The spirit of abundance at work in the Eucharist

It is in the eucharistic celebration above all that the Spirit is at work. Here we partake of the body of Christ, and his risen body is the one point of creation where the plentitude of the Spirit rests. Here are concentrated all those familial blessings that God has set aside for humanity.

When we share the Eucharist, we have here below the eschatological fullness of the Kingdom. We are already living the life of the Risen Lord, sharing his victory over death, and over those walls of separation that divide human beings. We are here and now accepting all men as brothers in Jesus Christ. These are the things that ought to be made evident in the actual eucharistic celebration as organized by the Church.

Wherever the Eucharist is celebrated its whole thrust is towards catholicity. The call to salvation in Jesus Christ is always a universal call. No matter what barriers divide them, all men who hear this call are asked to come together in the fraternal unity that comes from sharing the same bread. Complete response in these terms may be beyond possibility, but we should always aim at it. When men share the body of Christ, men of whatever origin should realize that there is a fraternal bond between them, that it can be experienced here and now, that the hope which is theirs is capable of surmounting any obstacles. When they go out again into secular life, the walls of separation will be there, but they know that these have been broken down in the death and resurrection of Jesus.

2. The Theme of Pardon

Insofar as modern man has lost the sense of God, he tends to query Christian ideas about sin and divine pardon. However to the extent that the God he rejects is a mere substitute for the God of Jesus Christ, it is possible that his notions of sin and pardon are a deformation of the true Christian notions. For that matter the judgments that Christians, increasingly, tend to pass on their non-Christian brethren are based, not on valid concepts of sin and pardon, but on the erroneous concepts that have gained currency.

What in fact did happen? The relationship between supernatural and natural, which has been analyzed theologically since the 13th century, has been very slow in influencing the everyday routine of Christian life. Sin, which doctrinally speaking is essentially a personal rejection of the God of love, tends in fact to be understood in natural terms, in terms of the disorder which it creates. By emphasizing the material act in the objective order, one runs the risk of obscuring the encounter of two liberties, and the notion of guilt becomes encumbered with material elements that do not properly belong to it.

And as for the notion of pardon, the images frequently used to illustrate it do not go to the heart of the matter. Quite certainly, the distaste evinced by modern man suggests that our notions in both domains need to be purified.

Yahweh the God of pardon up to the day of judgment

Man has been created in God's image and likeness, and he is called by his Creator to a supernatural destiny that he can only accomplish by responding to the divine initiative. Man is a creature and only God can divinize him. Yet, in fact, man has tried to divinize himself, to satisfy by his own resources his thirst for the absolute, to touch somehow the sacral world that keeps eluding him. In other words, he is a sinner. At the very beginning of human history we have original sin, at the very beginning of the history of the chosen people the sin of the desert. The Bible, which recounts all this, sees human history and Jewish history as a constant recrudescence of these two great sins. Instead of following God's way, man turns away and follows his own.

Thus, in the perspective of faith, sin is essentially a rejection of love: Jewish man sees the relationship of the people to Yahweh as a personal one. If man blocks this channel of love which links him with God, he destroys himself.

What is Yahweh's reaction to sin? Unquestionably he could exercise vengeance, break his covenant and intervene at once with his eschatological judgment, letting man condemn himself. But to take that view simply would be a misunderstanding of the God of love. Yahweh is a God of mercy and pardon. His love shows itself altogether larger than the rejection which challenges it: even in his state of sin he reaches out to man. When he pardons, Yahweh shows himself superior to hate.

Man however, to be pardoned, must turn away from sin and be converted. Little by little sinful man becomes aware that even this conversion depends on divine love, that man in every single detail depends on this gratuitous divine initiative. When Yahweh pardons he replaces the sinful heart with a new heart.

A final insight was the believer's realization that his own pardon depended on his pardoning in turn. The just man should model himself after the mercy of God. The extent to which he pardoned would be limited by the frontiers of Jewish universalism, but there was a deep realization of the link between this and divine pardon.

The messianic pardon of the Son of Man

When John the Baptist proclaims the imminence of the Kingdom he summons people to conversion in view of the judgment that is to be. But when the Messiah comes, he affirms that he has come among men not to judge but to heal and pardon.

The unexpected revelation showed the true character of divine pardon. God pardons by becoming incarnate; he so loved men that he gave what he most loved, his own Son. It was the infinite generosity of this gift that made possible a total response by man. Jesus of Nazareth made that total response. God's pardon became fully effective when he in his humanity set in motion the same pardon, a human pardon of divine dimension. He manifested this pardon, this total gift of himself, by a love for men that vanquished all hate, that reached out to man in his rejection. Concretely it took shape in his pilgrimage of absolute

obedience unto the death of the cross "for the remission of sins."
On the cross sins were remitted, because the love displayed on
the cross was stronger than hate. Divine pardon had found in
man its perfect response.

So that it is with Jesus of Nazareth that the history of pardon
begins. His victory over hate was destined to be extended bit by
bit. When others, in dependence on him, followed in their turn
the path of obedience, God's partners were multiplied. The
pardon of the cross began to flow through history. The history of
pardon in other words is the history of true love, the history of
salvation. Because he is the only mediator, the man-God is the
only one among man to have the power of pardon. But by our
link with him we all in turn become capable of limitless giving
and limitless pardon.

The history of pardon then links indissolubly divine pardon
with our pardon for one another. It could not be otherwise; it
is the lesson of the whole life of Jesus. His supreme moment on
the cross was a manifestation of God's pardon for men, and of the
man-God's pardon for all his brothers.

The Church of mercy

Because the Church is Christ's Body, it is the establishment in
history of the task of mediation. By virtue of this the Church
can forgive sins. If it were otherwise she could not be the Church
of Christ, nor would he be present in her. She would not be the
sacrament of human salvation. And when we affirm that she has
the power to forgive, we are saying that in her the history of
pardon is being continued. The exercise of God's pardon requires
an agent on earth. She is that agent.

To his apostles Jesus communicated the power of pardon, to
those people, that is, whose responsibility it is, throughout the
time of the Church, to ensure ecclesial presence in the world.
And when the apostles or their successors pardon in the name of
Christ, it is in fact the whole people of God who find themselves
involved in the mystery of the cross, and in the act of pardon

which is at once divine and human. The existence of the whole Church indeed is an act of mercy for the benefit of all humanity.

However true it is that the whole Church is engaged in the act of pardon, it also remains true that all members without exception are obliged to subject themselves to the ecclesial channel of pardon. All are sinners and must have recourse to what we call the power of the keys. By baptism we are all marked with the inviolable sign of divine pardon. Yet the baptized person is still a sinner and knows his need of the power of the keys.

All sacramental activity on the part of the Church is an exercise of mercy, but this is particularly true of the sacrament of penance. Here God encounters the confessed sinner as the father did the prodigal son. His whole concern is the preparation of the family feast. At this moment the whole Church should join with God in restoring the penitent to ecclesial communion.

Mission, an application of ecclesial pardon

Pardon being the ultimate expression of total giving, of brotherly love without limits, is one of the great signs of salvation in Jesus Christ. We should not however misunderstand the objective nature of this pardon, or the aspect it should present in the conduct of mission.

In the first place the missionary can never afford to forget that the pardon which is a sign of salvation is always an ecclesial pardon. Otherwise it would not be related to the unparalleled mystery of the pardon of Jesus Christ. In the case of non-Christians pardon will always be concerned with the realities of daily living, and we should be mindful always that the Church is present even in those members who are not yet assembled. She must be present in the texture of life as the leaven is in the bread. Today indeed more than ever the Christian must realize that he is not likely to communicate the pardon of Christ, unless he can be a true member of the Church in diaspora among men. That is to say that he must maintain contact, in his non-Christian environment, with the other members of Christ's Body, clerical and lay, who are embarked on the same adventure as himself.

He must also take care that the pardon which he offers is really an expression of absolute brotherly love. It can never be merely a warm human impulse; it must be related to the precise tensions of the moment. Today, anyhow, the collective aspect of pardon is, from the missionary point of view, more important than the individual. A Christian of our day, in order to dispense pardon, is called upon to bring about peace among peoples, to work for true social and international justice. To the extent that non-Christians believe the Church to be in alliance with the rich and powerful of this world, they are unlikely to listen to the gospel message. The price they will have to pay for Christian pardon will seem intolerable.

The penitential dimension of the eucharistic assembly

Over-narrow ideas about sacramentality have tended to make people restrict the ecclesial power of pardon unduly to the sacrament of penance. The eucharistic celebration has been losing its penitential dimension. This is a serious matter, because it is in relationship to the Eucharist that the real character of the sacrament of penance can best be discerned.

It is only necessary to survey the actual Mass formularies to realize what a prominent penitential dimension the Eucharist does have. There is constant exercise of ecclesial pardon. It could scarcely be otherwise indeed, when we remember that the eucharistic assembly is the best symbol of the assembly of the Father's family, which is altogether based on mercy. The great moment of ecclesial pardon comes when the celebrant invites people to approach the holy table. Very evidently the Church cannot summon members to share the Bread unless she is also offering pardon. The universal brotherhood into which the communicant is ushered was set up by Jesus on the cross in that great act of divine pardon "for the remission of all sins."

TWELFTH SUNDAY

A. THE WORD

**I. Jeremiah
20:10-13**
1st reading
1st cycle

It seems that the prophet Jeremiah was of profoundly depressive temperament. At the beginning of Joachim's reign, a violent indictment by him against a temple cult had resulted in a prosecution for sacrilege. He was exonerated (Jr 26:24) but was deeply wounded. Realizing his fate he then turned to composition of his "confessions," a literary genre new to Israel. They reflect the tension set up in his sensitive soul by the call of God (Jr 16:1-13, etc.). Our reading today is but a brief extract from that section, where he laments the day he was born and likens God's call to a seductive enterprise.

It would be wrong however to regard these confessions altogether as the outpourings of depression. The fact that they are (like many psalms indeed) in the first person singular is not sufficient reason for singularity in interpretation. In fact the "I" is normal in collective community prayers, above all when the liturgical assembly is aware of its mediating role between God and the people. Jeremiah is assuming a liturgical role. Having proclaimed God's will to the people, he moves from his personal situation to formulate a prayer to God of general intercession, and he describes, in lamentation form, the plight of Israel.

a) There were in fact several persecutions of the prophet (v. 18; cf. 12:3-6, etc.). In the view of contemporary sages one prophet's death would not be calamitous. Always, because of the presence of priests and sages, there would be sufficient "Words of God" without having recourse to those of Jeremiah.

b) This reflection leads Jeremiah to formulate a prayer. Its dominant note is the desire for *vengeance* (v. 19; cf. Jr 20:12), a normal sentiment in Jewish prayers of the period (Ps 5:11;

10:15; 30/31:18; 53/54: 7, etc.). In a religion based on temporal retribution this is understandable (cf. Ws 2:10-3:12). Only in the New Testament was such an idea transcended (Mt 5:43-48).

c) Preoccupation with his fate leads him likewise to certain imagery, which is destined to characterize the portrait of the *suffering Servant*. Here we have the theme of conspiracy (vv. 18-19; cf. Is 53:8-10; Ac 4:25-28; Jn 11:47-54) and that of the lamb led to the slaughter (Jr 11:18-19; cf. Is 53:7; Ac 8:32-35).

d) However, the most original theme in his thinking is that of his *seduction* by God. Most narratives of a calling indeed emphasize the manner in which those called are received. For Moses we have the urge to give up (Ex 32); for Elias discouragement (1 K 19); for Jonah deception (Jon 4); for Jeremiah depression (Jr 20) etc. It is particularly painful to feel excluded from a community because one has pointed out certain needs or borne witness to the spiritual. And the prophet's quailing before his mission (Jr 20:10-11) and its demands becomes that of the people too (Jr 20:9). All this is valid insofar as it underlines the gulf between personal wishes and the will of God. It is valid also, even to the point of psychological disturbance or crisis of faith, insofar as it points up the immense distance separating man from the true God.

All in all, then, the tension endured by the prophet is simply the natural disturbance inevitable wherever the mystery of God strikes the life of a man. Doubtless the man to whom God is but an idea or a definition will never experience the drama of such encounter, or have to be emptied of self in order to be aligned with the will of God. How was it that Jesus, that supreme example of total encounter between God and man, managed to evade the law, not to lose himself totally?

Human liberty I suppose, even in this blinding moment of mystery, is not crushed by God. Man lets himself be "seduced": he gives himself only to the person who has a right to take.

Here we have the *raison d'être* of Christ's obedience on the cross, and the Eucharist summons us to follow that.

II. Job 38:1, 8-11   When overwhelmed with suffering Job had
    1st reading   protested his innocence, and rejected the
    2nd cycle   sophistries of friends who were anxious to
    discover in his life a justification of God's chastisement. He went so far as to demand from God a reason for his misfortunes.

At this point God speaks. He does not do so in order to answer Job's questions, or to join the friends' discussion. He wishes to bring their thoughts up to the level of divine mystery. How could Job, merely to satisfy his curiosity or alleviate his anguish, violate this mystery?

He asks Job to consider creation, above all the *creation of the seas*. Here we are dealing with echoes of ancient cosmogonic myths, and the superiority of the creator over recalcitrant elements is stressed.

Judaism had inherited from older mythologies the notion that creation was a combat between God and the waters. God's creative power triumphed over these waters and the evil monsters they contained (Pss 103/104:5-9, 105/106:9, 73/74:13-14, 88/89:9-11; Ha 3:8-15; Is 51:9-10). Very often such descriptions will see God's victory as a "threat" (Pss 105/106:9, 103/104:6-9; Gn 1:9; Jb 26:5-12; Ps 18-19). Salvation history even may be seen in terms of Yahweh's victory over the waters. That is the point of the accounts of the Red Sea (Ps 105/106:9) and Revelation 20:9-13, where the victory is that of God's Kingdom over the elements of this world.

For contemporary man of course the mythical chronicle of Yahweh's battle with primordial waters has lost the validity it had for the ancient pagan or the Jew. Today man has acquired over natural forces a mastery that is constantly growing. He no longer fears nature: in any case he sees no reason whatever to suppose divine intervention in her changes. If there are still upheavals of an unforeseeable character, he does not turn to heaven for an explanation. He will concern himself with finding the scientific reason, so that one day he can control it.

There is good reason then for asking what relevance God's discourse to Job could have now. The Christian concept of God is no longer concentrated on omnipotence, which carried so much weight with primitive man. But the Christian concept is for that reason the more authentic, as we shall see from the moral of our gospel (Mk 4:35-41).

III. Zechariah   In the final five chapters of Zechariah we have
    12:10-11   a series of fairly disparate oracles, which were
    1st reading   gathered into a collection certainly by the be-
    3rd cycle   ginning of the 4th century BC.

a) The first of the oracles probably refers to Ezechiel 36:16-28. Verse 10 for instance should be compared with verses 24-26 of Ezechiel. In both cases it is God himself who gives the people the interior disposition that leads them to *conversion*. This is more than what we have in Jeremiah 31:18-20, a preliminary condition for God's gift. It is itself a grace and an initiative by God. There are many other resemblances between the two passages. The spirit of grace in Zechariah is equivalent to the new heart of Ezechiel; his mourning to the repentance in Ezechiel 36:21; his spring (13:1) to the sprinkling of water, Ezechiel 36:25.

b) The Greek version, in alluding to "pierced" (v. 10) is modifying somewhat the probable sense of the original word. The translator doubtless had in mind the suffering Servant of Isaiah 53. In any case they create the impression that conversion is not just a gift of God. It is related to the mysterious mediation of a victim who must be contemplated with faith, as the serpent of bronze was in the desert (Nb 21:8-9). Our oracle then, as handled in the Septuagint, represents a very advanced theology. It regards repentance as a gift of God implanted in man's heart, and makes the gift depend on the faith of the sacrificed servant.

Conversion always means that we pass beyond ourselves and seek resources other than our own. It means that we come to realize that the source of life is something given from above, and that we refresh ourselves constantly at that source.

This avenue to the very depths of one's being was opened up by Jesus, and it was only when he had delivered absolutely everything of himself to death that he reached this point.

IV. Romans 5:12-15
2nd reading
1st cycle

We recall that in Romans passages of kerygmatic proclamation (like Rm 3:21-31) alternate with scriptural analyses or pieces of dialectic (like Rm 4).

In chapter 5 Paul is broaching a new kerygmatic section. He has, since chapter 3, been talking about justification, and he presents it now in the very first verses of chapter 5 as a reconciliation (vv. 10-11). He wants to show that not alone does man not have any right to justification; but, because he is basically sinful, he is incapable of any valid work whatsoever ("feeble," "sinners," "enemies," vv. 6, 8 and 10).

The justification-reconciliation is brought about by Jesus Christ (vv. 2, 6b, 8, 10). Paul shows how, even anterior to any movement of faith on the part of Christians, in the event of Jesus the divine initiative to justify and the adequate human response come together.

a) The understanding of verse 12 raises a problem, in particular concerning the nature of the *original sin,* to which Paul seems to allude. Paul's style (he was accustomed to dictate his letters) is not quite precise. Verse 12 opens with a conjunction (*dia touto:* that is why) and a comparison (*ôs ei:* as if), both of which remain suspended. Then it is not clear whether death, personified in a manner that is almost mythical, be death in a physical or a spiritual sense (similarly in vv. 13-14). Nor is it clear whether the relative *eph'ô* should be translated "*in whom* all have sinned (the Augustinian notion of original sin), or "*because* all have sinned" (in reference to personal sins only), or again "*from* the moment at which all have sinned." (There is a sense in which each person, by personal sin, ratifies and adds to the corporate weight of guilt. From generation to generation man's fundamental revolt against God is passed on in such fashion that the coming generation is always placed in a state of weakness and quasi-impotence.)

Furthermore, when Paul says that all have sinned (*anastein*), it is not clear whether he is using this term in the classical sense (*the act* of sinning), or in the passive sense that we sometimes find in the Septuagint (*the state* of guilt: Is 24:5-6). The research of exegetes on these delicate questions is still too inconclusive to allow a doctrine of original sin to be based solely on this verse. Finally, we must always keep in mind that, as in the preceding chapter in regard to Abraham, Paul is dealing with Adam as theologian not as historian (cf. further Rm 7). In considering human existence at its basic roots, he makes corporate responsibility and the dominion of "death" extend to all humanity.

b) Verses 13-14 imply that after Adam's conscious sin, God's will was not again made known to humanity until the Sinai revelation (a situation that, outside the confines of Judaism, among Gentiles who do not know the law, is still the case). Of course personal sin is not imputed to that element of humanity which is without the law and without knowledge of God (v. 13b); but death falls upon this element, unaware as they are of their sin (v. 14).

To understand Paul's thought behind these verses, we must keep in mind the biblical distinction between conscious and unconscious faults. The texts in Numbers 15:22 - 16:35 are very revealing. The sinner who acts deliberately (Nb 15:30) with knowledge of the cause should be exterminated without any possibility of remission. But the many who share his fault, through ignorance of inadvertence, can escape death by offering a sacrifice for sin (cf. Lv 4). The legislation is very clear in the case of Korah. He and his family are exterminated (Nb 16:31-34), whereas the "community" which shared his sin is spared (Nb 16:22).

Turning then to the case of men without knowledge of the law: they sin unwittingly because they are involved in the human totality. They die (a death either natural or spiritual) . . . until such time as the "sacrifice for sin" is offered by Christ on the cross (Rm 5, 6, 8, 11). In Israel the feast of *expiation* had been set up for precisely this reason: to secure remission for personal sin unwittingly committed, or for guilt falling upon the community through the sin of an individual (Lv 4:1-3). The suffering Servant had taken upon himself personally this ritual (Is 53:10). Christ brought it to accomplishment on the cross, offering the true "sacrifice for sin" of people who shared more or less unwittingly in the fault of an individual.

Thus in the hinterland of Paul's thinking lies this ritual of expiation, which is so often used in the New Testament to describe the sacrifice of the cross. It enables us to distinguish two types of sin: the formal personal sin of an individual (here Adam) which leads to death without reprieve, and the sin through ignorance or involvement which can be remitted by the expiation ritual or the suffering Servant.

We should not expect from Paul an explanation for this solidarity between Adam and the people. For him, in the context of the expiation ritual, it went without saying. The originality of his doctrine lies in the proclamation of remission for collective sin by the sacrifice of the cross.

The rest of the passage is constructed as a series of antitheses between *Adam* and Christ.

Verse 15:

— how much more —

by the fault	by the grace
of one	of one man, Jesus
the many	on the many
died	poured out in profusion

Verse 16:

The judgment	grace
of one sin	
brought condemnation	led to the justification of
(that is, the multiplicity of	a multitude of sins
personal faults, on the part of	
a humanity, more and more	
given over to its passions	
(cf. Rm 1:18-32)	

Verse 17:

— how much more —

by the fault	by the ... gift of justice
of one	
death	in life
has reigned	those who receive it shall
by this one man	reign through the one
	Jesus Christ

We should note that in this verse Paul passes from the idea of Christ's expiatory sacrifice to consider eschatological life with Christ. This is a gift still to come, but it is related to the gift of justification which has been already given.

Verse 19 (conclusion):

by the disobedience	by the obedience
of one man	of one man
the many	the many
were made sinful	shall be justified

This parallelism of course between Adam and Christ does not mean that both are given equal importance. We should beware of seeing in Christ merely the person who was capable of restoring a humanity that had faltered in Adam. His obedience and sacrifice did more than cancel the disobedience of Adam and the guilt of the many. He became the Lord of eschatological life (cf. the "how much more" of v. 17). More than a mere restoration or expiation, his sacrifice opened the gateway of a new economy.

This final affirmation is indeed crucial for Christian *anthropology*. If Christ were simply someone who retrieved the disaster brought about by Adam, Adam would be the primary figure and Christ would only be understandable in terms of him. But, given that the gift Christ brings ("life") is radically different from anything Adam himself could have brought, then Adam is only understandable in terms of Christ: "Adam is no more than a figure of him who was to come" (v. 14b). They are not simply obverse and reverse of a single coin, the justice of one counterbalancing the sin of the other. Christian anthropology is constructed altogether in terms of man in Jesus Christ, destined for "life." Adam represents no more than a backward glance, what used to be: he has no claim to represent humanity in Christian terms. Christ only, and not just Christ on the cross but Christ become Lord, has the key to the human mystery. The basis for the whole comparison is Christ, not Adam. The analysis of the religious situation prior to Christ is a theological exercise in the contemporary idiom.

The passage we have been discussing is the most difficult one in the letter to the Romans; but it is also one of the most important in Pauline theology. There is of course a parallel between Christ and Adam: their relationship to the many was unique. But there is not really an old and a new, a first and a second. There is only Jesus Christ and the other figures, whose only meaning is the announcement of his coming. So unequal are the two terms of the antithesis that it makes no difference to Christian faith whether one day polygenism is proved, or it is proved that Paul was dealing in terms of myth when he talked of Adam. The only important thing is that humanity can only find meaning in the lordship of Christ. It does not matter where humanity springs from; what does matter is that humanity realizes whither it is bound.

V. 2 Corinthians This passage is certainly the most important
5:14-17 portion of Paul's long apology for the apostolic
2nd reading ministry, to which the first chapters of the
2nd cycle second letter to the Corinthians are devoted.

The basic reason for Paul's ministry is to be found in the constraining love of Christ (v. 14). This means love in the objective sense, Christ's love for him, and in the subjective sense, his love for Christ. As he sees it there is nothing sentimental in this love; it springs from deep reflection ("thought": v. 14). At the outset he could not comprehend Christ's love in dying for everyone on the cross (v. 15); but once he did understand that he could no longer resist the love that impelled him to devote his life to Christ (v. 15b).

Liberty is not destroyed by this constraint of love, because the apostle has taken time to reflect. It is a new faculty in man (vv. 16-17) which enables him to act as a "new creature," no longer with the hesitancies and calculations of the "flesh." It is grace and dynamism which the flesh cannot contain (Col 3:14). It yearns for sacrifice after the pattern of the cross (v. 15). It is the unifying and balancing principle of all one's life (*suneho* is found in this sense in contemporary philosophical writing).

Jeremiah had complained of being "seduced" by God, and now Paul speaks of being "constrained" by his love. It is not any exterior constraint such as might for instance keep a priest from leaving his ministry. On the contrary it is an inner logic which makes one analyze and interpret everything in terms of Jesus

Christ, a logic which cannot be denied without disturbing one's whole balance. It is a knowledge which lays bare the inner meaning of oneself and everything, a fidelity to what one is. Truly, one cannot rid oneself of God once the traces of his intervention are recognized.

VI. Galatians
3:26-29
2nd reading
3rd cycle

This letter is an answer to the attacks made by Judaizers. These had infiltrated into Galatia, and were questioning Paul's teaching about the unique role of Christ among humanity. Furthermore they challenged his claim to apostleship. The early chapters are a defense of his ministry and of his personal behavior. Now, in the third chapter, he takes up the doctrinal point which is the basis of his polemic against the Judaizers. Once we are placed in dependence on Christ, do we have any further need of the law?

This principal argument is based on his concept of salvation history. To begin with there was God's appearance to Abraham, the promises, the patriarch's faith, and the blessing in him of all nations. Then there was the Law, but it was God's angels only who transmitted this to Moses, and it was only Israel that benefited by its blessings (Ga 3:1-18).

a) The conclusion is self-evident. The function of the Law was relative and transitory, a pedagogic function (v. 24). With the appearance of Christ, the decisive event in salvation history, the Law must disappear and yield to the earlier and more fundamental stage: the promises made to Abraham, which are fulfilled through faith in Christ (v. 25).

There remains the demonstration that Jesus is the *decisive event* which justifies the change of economies. He has already in fact demonstrated this, in rabbinic fashion, in Galatians 3:15-18, by showing how Christ is *the* seed of Abraham. But now he does so more precisely (vv. 26-29). The promise is perfectly fulfilled in Jesus because he is the man-God. As Son of God (v. 26) he is the greatest gift God could promise or give to humanity. As man he can provide the most adequate response to this gift of the Father. He is the heir (v. 29) best fitted to enter into the promised blessings and realize God's plan for humanity.

b) So it is because the whole meaning of human history rests upon fidelity to the Father that the Christ event is the great event of that history. Each one is summoned to "put on Christ" (v. 27),* that is, personally, in his turn, to respond to God's design for humanity.

Christ having thus rendered null the economy of the Law, the question arises how the individual must be linked with Christ in order to be freed from the Law. For Saint Paul the means are two: *faith* (v. 26) and *baptism* (v. 27). They are not exclusive in ambit, but are open to every man on a basis of complete equality with his brothers (v. 28).

Verses 26 and 27 indicate the connection between faith and baptism. They are not disjunctive, but together ensure a man's communion with Christ (cf. further Ep 2:8; 1 Co 6:11). They are the human response to God's initiative. Thus, *mutatis mutandis* we can compare the faith-baptism conjunction with the man-God conjunction in Jesus himself. The gift of God elicits a human response first in Christ and then in the baptized. Every baptism truly incorporates us with Christ, enables us to "put on" (v. 27) Christ, and offers us a state of divine filiation in God's image which Jesus possesses by nature (*ibid.*). These new relations with God that we achieve by baptism also transform our relations with our brothers. Barriers fall down, all men become equal, and finally the blessing of all nations in Abraham becomes a reality (vv. 27-28).

So, the old economy is supplanted by the new Christian order. No longer is salvation determined by incorporation through

---

*See the doctrinal theme: *clothing*, p. 107.

circumcision or ablutions into a particular people, nor indeed by observance of a law. Everything is now changed because God by sending his Son has intervened in history. The Son in his person brings together God's gift and the response of a human partner, thus saving humanity. Every man shares this salvation insofar as the meaning of his life too is focused at the meeting point of divine initiative and human response. It is these two realities that are sanctioned in the faith-baptism process.

VII. Matthew
10:26-33
Gospel
1st cycle

This is an extract from the mission-discourse where Matthew attempts to analyze precisely the thought of Jesus on this matter. Verses 24 and 25 were a commentary on verse 17: similarly verses 26 and 27 are a commentary on verse 19. He uses *logia* of Jesus, the original meaning of which he doesn't quite grasp. Previously, Luke 8:17 had applied them to the dynamism of the gospel, which could not remain hidden, and Luke 12:2-3 to the adversaries of the gospel, whose wrong proclamations would be eventually exposed.

Matthew gives us a new interpretation. Christ, according to him, wished to say that he could not deliver his message with all the clarity required (Mk 4:22; Jn 16:29-30), and that now this further task devolved upon missionaries. He is transposing into a missionary context sayings by Jesus that had been originally delivered, doubtless, in a moral context.

Verses 28-31 are a commentary on verse 19. They describe the attitude Jesus prescribes for his followers during persecution. There are two motives for reassurance. First: there is only one enemy to be feared, Satan, and God has control here. Second: God looks after each of his own (v. 30).

Verses 32-33 describe the mutual fidelity between Christ and the Christian at the time of judgment.

a) Thus, the unity of the whole passage is somewhat impaired.

The author has brought together *logia* of Jesus from a different context. They are linked together by connecting phrases, and whatever unity we have comes from his purpose of elaborating a theology about the difficulties and obstacles of the *missionary life*. He does not treat the matter as extensively as Paul (Rm 5:1-5; 2 Co 4:16-18). But he does stress some important topics: the solidarity that unites a disciple under challenge to his master; the obligation of the disciple to go deeper than the master in the revelation of the message; the trust the missionary must have in God's protection; and finally the missionary's assured reward at the judgment.

For Matthew, as for Paul, mission is destined to encounter persecution. The Kingdom of glory and transcendence cannot really be built without a laceration of the human heart, without challenge from a world which purports to find in itself the means of salvation. Between the wisdom of the world and the wisdom of Christ the opposition is really irreconcilable. It was necessary that Vatican II should enter again into dialogue with the world because this was really of the essence of the Church. We should not however be misled into believing that as a result of this reconciliation all men are going to march hand in hand, always we are going to have people who put the gospel beatitudes into practice and in consequence encounter challenge.

The Christian, whenever he celebrates in the Eucharist Christ's victory over hate, realizes how far his sin and that of others stands in the way of the Kingdom. He offers sacrifice to be delivered from this obstacle.

b) Our gospel passage delivers perhaps its most consistent message in the summons to be free from all *fear* (vv. 26, 28, 31). The reasons for confidence are multiple. First we have the assurance that the work of Christ, hitherto confidential, is destined to become public in a spectacular fashion (v. 27): its slight success thus far should not cause discouragement. Secondly, "life" (the soul of v. 28, in the Hebrew sense) cannot be affected by persecution: it comes from God only, and men have no power over it. Thirdly, we have the assurance that Providence watches over all creatures, even the weakest (v. 31). How much more so over those who confess the name of God (vv. 32-33).*

VIII. Mark 4:35-41 The account of the stilling of the tempest as
Gospel   we have it in the synoptics has some sig-
2nd cycle   nificant variants. Our discussion then will
                include examination of the *synoptic texts
generally, among which Mark's seems to be the primitive one, and a closer study of the Marcan text itself.**

a) All the synoptics give us the account immediately before the exorcism of the Gerasene (Mk 5:1-20). Tradition had juxtaposed the two episodes for doctrinal reasons: to show in Jesus the *power* that dominates evil forces in nature as well as in hearts. Elsewhere (1:23-27) Mark had given an account of exorcism that is constructed exactly after the pattern of his version of the stilling of the tempest (compare Mk 1:25 with Mk 4:39: threats; Mk 1:24 with Mk 4:38: the reproach to Christ of coming to destroy; Mk 1:27b with Mk 4:41: obedience to Jesus by elements and spirits; Mk 1:27a with Mk 4:41: fear). Apparently then the stilling of the tempest is a manifestation by the one who is undertaking again the creative work that has been compromised by evil powers (cf. Jb 38:1-11). It is a christological affirmation. God is in Christ bringing the cosmogonic myth to accomplishment by a decisive victory over evil. Men are rendering to Jesus the admiration and fear reserved for the Creator-God (v. 41; cf. Pss 64/65:8-9, 88/89:10, 106/107:28-30).

b) Mark however, throughout the gospel, is concerned to show that, before the resurrection, the apostles could not have true faith. Thus he inserts verse 40, which should be rendered in a particular way: "have you no faith yet?" Before the Pasch the

---

*See further the doctrinal theme: *persecution,* p. 102.

**See the doctrinal theme: *resurrection,* Eastertime volume, p. 84.

apostles could not have faith: the only true faith was in the Risen Christ. As Mark sees it then, the real meaning of the stilling of the tempest is that it already includes the *resurrection*. For this reason he likens the tempest to that which Jonah encountered (compare especially v. 38, a detail exclusive to Mark, with Jon 1:56; v. 41a with Jon 1:16, etc.). It seems possible indeed that Mark's thoughts in his account were of the famous sign of Jonah (Mt 12:38-40). Like Jonah, by his power over the tempest, Christ is triumphing over the "inferior waters."

c) All through his gospel Mark stresses the theme of messianic secret, and in this episode he is particularly conscious of Christ's *silence*. God remains silent, does not allow himself to be discerned, appears to sleep, even in the case of people who do not believe him dead. . . . But he is in fact living and taking sides.

It is too easy to rely upon the omnipotence and transcendence of God. That is not the kind of faith to which we are summoned by today's gospel. Faith means reliance on a conquering God to be sure, but a God who is absent and silent. It may mean realization that God is "dead" and "powerless," but yet living in communion with him. It may mean wandering without knowing where one is going, being ready to perish on the way, without ever personally accomplishing one's enterprises, and yet being convinced that God is by one's side all the time. Faith means struggling with adversity because we are convinced that Christ arose from adversity.

IX. Luke 9:18-24 Peter's confession (vv. 18-21), the prophecy of
  Gospel   the passion (v. 22) and the teaching about the
  3rd cycle   conditions for becoming a disciple of Jesus
                      (vv. 23-26) were not originally recounted to-
gether. Peter's confession, of which we have the primitive version in Matthew (16:13-20), was originally the introduction to the discourse called "ecclesiastical" (Mt 18; cf. in both passages

Peter's predominant role and the identical phrases, etc.). The prophecy of the passion on the other hand, and the list of conditions for discipleship, must have belonged originally to the passion narrative, of which they would have formed the prologue. The first portion then is of apocalyptic genre, and ecclesiological in purpose. The second is prophetic, and concerned with the passion.

Before the final redaction of the synoptics, these two differing traditions had been conjoined, for literary and theological reasons, to the point that Mark (8:27-31) makes them the central axis of his gospel. His first part which is centered on the Messiah, ends with the first; and his second part, centered on the suffering Servant, begins with the second.

The Lucan version of the traditions is the least satisfactory, unfortunately. Luke is at this stage eager to broach the most important part of his gospel, the journey to Jerusalem (9:51 - 18:14). Consequently he makes chapter 9 a sort of hasty appendix, dividing his first part from the account of the great journey. It contains some important elements which he could not avoid mentioning, but his treatment of them is sometimes cursory. Thus he says nothing about Peter's vocation (Mt 16:17-19), or about Jesus' response to Peter's lack of faith (Mt 16:22-23). He omits all geographical precisions. These would tend to distract attention at the point where he is about to give us the journey to Jerusalem and concentrate upon messianic suffering.

a) Jesus wishes to have from the Twelve an affirmation of his *Messiahship*. They do so affirm it through the mouth of Peter, having first discarded other possible hypotheses. However according to current notions, their idea of Messiahship remains ambiguous, with some suggestion of a restoration of the Kingdom by violence and a judgment of the nations. Accordingly Jesus imposes silence on them, suggesting that there can be no true Messiahship without death and resurrection.

At a particular point in his ministry Jesus became aware of

what Messiahship would really mean for him, and he conveyed this knowledge to his followers. It is noteworthy that the insight came to him during prayer (v. 18). In his anxiety to respond as perfectly as possible to God's will he did not wish his Messiahship to have any political or vengeful overtones (cf. Mt 8:4-10). It would be all gentleness and pardon. The choice was not an easy one to make, or to sustain. It engendered opposition of every kind, and soon he became aware that it would lead him to his death (v. 22).

The agony of the decision can be imagined. The messianic call must be answered: it must be pursued with inadequate means in an atmosphere of gentleness, and there was always the realization that death must intervene before it could be realized. Surely the meaning must be that God's design was accomplishment on the other side of death. God would not abandon him to death. So Jesus begins to think of his resurrection, and to proclaim it (v. 22).

b) Doubtless it is this point about mediation on the other side of death which explains the original placing of the passage as an introduction to the ecclesiastical discourse (Mt 18). By announcing his death, Jesus is in fact beginning to set up the *community* which will continue his work.

So it is that he is concerned about the faith and loyalty of his disciples. At this point, Luke condenses, vv. 23-26, some sentiments drawn from the apostolic discourse (Mt 10:33, 38, 39). If the disciples remain fundamentally loyal to their messianic role in the world, if their mission exhibits the essential roles of suffering and poverty, they can expect no better lot than the master.

c) Each time that he is about to make an important decision, or embark on a new stage of his ministry, Luke shows us Christ in *prayer* (c. Lk 3:21, 6:12, 9:29, 11:1, 22:31-39). Indeed he is the only one to tell us (v. 18) of Christ's prayer before he secures a profession of faith from his followers and tells them of his passion. As in the other Lucan instances, the suggestion is that Jesus is praying about a mission, the dimensions of which he can see only in vague outline. To say that his prayer is simply meant to give example to the apostles is an insufficient explanation. The purpose is not just one of edification. When he prays it is because the object of the prayer does not seem certain to him, and theologians who maintain that Jesus had an exact knowledge of the future fail to provide adequate basis for his prayer. One cannot pray for the law of gravity to have effect. As in the case of any man, the future was dark to Jesus, and he was troubled by uncertainty about what would happen. His human will was incapable by itself of accomplishing the mission; consequently he turned to God for light and help.

His prayer is very real. It shows us that he is facing the death that had appeared on the horizon with an uncertainty that is altogether human.

B. DOCTRINE

1. The Theme of Persecution

The teaching about persecution that we find in the formulary of today's Mass (1st cycle: 1st reading and gospel) is an invitation to penetrate the very least of the paschal mystery. It is here that we find the ultimate secret of love's victory.

The general theology of suffering does not deal adequately with the theme of persecution, because persecution differs from all other sorts of suffering. Suffering could be described as something essential to the human condition which should be patiently accepted. But the only explanation for persecution is human sin. It is because of his justice that the "just man" encounters it. Sinful man is attempting to wreck God's plan of love by destroying the witness to it.

Throughout the centuries the Church has encountered much persecution, and she encounters it still today. However, we should beware of making the assumption that any grave conflict in which she happens to be engaged is automatically a persecution. The word ought to be used with extreme caution. The following reflection, we hope, will prove helpful.

The Israelite prophets persecuted by their people

Throughout her history Israel encountered violent opposition from other peoples. Her unusual geographical position tended to involve her in the power struggles between Egypt and Mesopotamia. Each time this occurred the chosen people would see their cause as that of Yahweh, and too easily raise the cry of persecution. It led to a good deal of misunderstanding.

There was however another sort of tension, something altogether more religious, that paved the way for the revelation of the New Testament. This was the opposition, sometimes dramatic, encountered by the leaders of the people, kings, and above all prophets, in carrying out their mission. Love for

Yahweh and fidelity to his word would bring persecution on their heads. Moses was rejected by his own, David was harshly opposed, and what are we to say of Elias, Amos, Jeremiah? Jeremiah indeed occupies a special place in the roster of the persecuted. He, rather than anyone else, described the close link between persecution and the prophetic mission. Quite probably the notion of the suffering Servant, someone who fulfills the divine plan by accepting the punishments inflicted on him by his people, emanates from a prolonged mediation on his exceptional career.

The deep meaning of this agony of the prophets is clarified by the Book of Wisdom. For the wicked the just man is a "living reproach" (Wi 2:14), a "spoilsport" (Wi 2:12), a witness of the living God one would like to ignore.

Jesus of Nazareth, the persecuted just man

When the Jews condemned Jesus to the death of the cross, they followed the example of predecessors who persecuted the prophets. But there was an added dimension. He had put himself forward as the Messiah, the witness *par excellence* of God. And, for the Jewish people, his witness was particularly embarrassing. One had to divest oneself of everything, one's goods, one's self, the privileges of the covenant. . . . God's plan was represented as one of universal love, with no acceptance of persons. The new commandment is that we love all men, our enemies too. All are called, in him, to sonship with the Father. If one accepts him it means the way of total renunciation, of absolute poverty. He puts himself forward as the expected Messiah, the one who will save man by bringing him to the Father. Belief in him implies something altogether extraordinary: accepting his divinity, accepting the Incarnation as God's way of saving man, accepting the fact that the perfect human response to God is itself a divine gift. This is too much. It were better that such an idea be suppressed; death will be at least a solution.

Yet the event was to prove wrong the conjectures of sinful

man. When they crucified the "Lord of Glory," the "princes of this world" were in fact the instruments of divine wisdom (1 Co 2:8). Jesus' doctrine of universal love meant that death would be forever challenged. When encountered in obedience it has a different meaning. It delivers up its secret; it is the moment of supreme truth in the giving of self. There is no greater love than laying down one's life for those one loves. In this perspective the defiance of death takes on the fullest significance, because death is rooted in hate, it is the direct consequence of sin. The reason the Jews condemned Jesus to death on the cross was because they rejected the new commandment. But by accepting that death Jesus showed that love was stronger than hate. Even a death so charged with the sinfulness of men could be made to change its meaning.

Blessed are those persecuted for justice' sake

One of the beatitudes is about persecution: "Happy are you when people abuse you and speak all kinds of calumny against you on my account. Rejoice and be glad for your reward will be great in heaven; this is how they persecuted the prophets before you" (Mt 5:11-12). Or again: "The servant is not greater than his master. If they have persecuted me they will persecute you also" (Jn 15:20). And Saint Paul adds: "Anybody who tries to live in devotion to Christ is certain to be persecuted" (2 Tm 3:12).

These affirmations are uncompromisingly clear. Persecution is regarded as something that touches faith at the quick: it touches the deepest roots of human sinfulness, but also the unfathomable depths of the love which conquers that. It is inevitable, because sinfulness is so deep-rooted that the most marvelous initiatives of divine love are rejected. Man is created in the image and likeness of God, but he will not show fidelity to the creatural condition. He tries to divinize himself, and by refusing the divine offer allies himself with everything creatural that opposes God. Sin makes him an actor in a cosmic drama. Persecution is also in some way necessary. Through it the Church, and the individual Christian, are set in a light that manifests the victory of love over hate. When a martyr is put to death we have a resplendent sign of love at its most intense: in that very moment he pardons his executioners.

The eschatological significance of such incidents is very obvious: they bear witness to the definitive victory of Christ and his followers. The more evident the presence here below of the Risen Christ, the more intense the resistance to sin. The behavior of the martyr demonstrates that the Kingdom has really come upon the earth.

Persecution an important stake in mission

Mission is the greatest work of universal love; consequently it must expect to encounter persecution. But the missionary who accepts that fate with constancy will experience joy. When Saint Paul reviews the vicissitudes of his career, it is the tribulations which strike him always, and he shares this insight frequently with his correspondents. "In all my trouble my joy is overflowing" he goes so far as to say (2 Co 7:4). There is not the slightest trace of masochism here. He is just convinced that the Kingdom grows by challenge and opposition. His joy is the joy of hope. He tells the Romans: "We can boast about our sufferings. These sufferings bring patience, as we know, and patience brings perseverance, and perseverance brings hope, and this hope is not deceptive, because the love of God has been poured into our hearts by the Holy Spirit which has been given us" (Rm 5:4-5).

Any genuine mission will encounter persecution, but not all difficulties encountered deserve the name of persecution. For that, the people concerned must in fact be genuine witnesses of universal love, with a witness that is capable of being discerned by others. The two conditions of course become in practice one. Genuine love will display itself very unmistakably in the concrete domain of human relations.

In our day witness to universal love will necessarily be concerned, first and foremost, with the great tasks that confront all humanity. The fact that John XXIII's two most important encyclicals concern, first peace, and second, problems of international and social justice, is not without significance. The whole conciliar experience brought the Church again in contact with the world. Let us not however for a moment think that this reconciliation means men are going to march hand in hand. Some people will continue to encounter persecution because they will continue to practice the evangelical counsels in the conviction that here lies the true road to human advancement. There will always be an irreconcilable opposition between the wisdom of Christ and the wisdom of the world.

The eucharistic celebration and the triumph of love over hate

When we celebrate the Eucharist we proclaim the death of the Lord until he comes. The sacrifice of the cross, the victory of love over hate, is actualized. Each one of us, as he shares the Bread and the Word, forges that link with Christ which renders him capable of the Just One's obedience, the obedience of limitless love. Yet we all realize how much sin, our sin and that of others, stands in the way of this obedience. So we pray for deliverance from sin.

Sharing the Eucharist too makes us victorious over evil, not alone because of the interior grace we receive, but by reason also of the bonds of brotherhood that are developed. The catholicity which is so essential a note of the Eucharist should always be expressed somehow in the assembly. On those occasions when brothers of every race and of every class are united in the same celebration, and fraternally share the same bread, it is as if, by anticipation, they have already achieved the definitive victory of love over hate. Strengthened by their experience, they go forth among men with a lucid awareness that they are engaged in combat against sin.

2. The Theme of Clothing

The simplest components of daily living have in fact served as models for the revelation of the mystery of salvation. The dawning and development of faith has tended to center around these things. The believer would meditate upon the basic meaning in physical life, and gradually pass to the deepest religious insight.

Clothing is a case in point. This simple matter has a profound importance in living. Israel was very conscious of the image: we have in fact in the Bible all the elements of a philosophy of clothing. Little by little reflection about it would tend to suggest ideas about the terrestrial state of man in its relationship with God. Clothing or the lack of clothing would be referred to man's spiritual state. In the New Testament the theme is taken up again, to depict the essential dimensions of the mystery of Christ, and to describe the Christian's relationship to Christ.

The theme of clothing in Israel

Clothing humanizes the body. It determines the plane of a person's interpersonal relations with his fellow man. It indicates sex and social function. By diversifying it, people mark seasons of festival, or of work. In general it establishes one in a fixed order of values. Furthermore, bestowing one's garments is a sign of brotherhood. Clothing the other when he is naked helps him to emerge from anonymity, to be reborn into society.

Thus, the symbol was ready made as an indication of what the Covenant between Yahweh and Israel meant. Yahweh was establishing personal relations with his people, sharing with them something of his glory. A royal bridegroom would spread the shelter of his mantle over his spouse. If she were unfaithful and showed herself to every passer-by, this clothing that ought not to wear out would disintegrate in rags and tatters.

Clothing also is a reminder of the sinful state of man. The body has to be concealed from the regard of lust, which objectifies it, and jeopardizes the interpersonal relation. Nudity in paradise was an expression of man's harmony with the divine. Sin destroyed that harmony. Again, clothing may be employed by its wearer as a badge of wealth, something that is attention-getting, that provides a security that is illusory. From this point of view nakedness has more value in the eyes of God than clothing: it denotes that poverty of spirit that is pleasing to God. The Servant of Yahweh, whose destiny it is to save and heal Israel, is presented as "one without comeliness or luster."

Christ denuded and clothed in glory

All the evangelists point out that when Jesus arrived at the place of crucifixion he was, according to the Scriptures stripped of his garments. This is the ultimate stage of his pilgrimage of obedience to the Father. He goes to the very limits of love in renouncing absolutely everything. Nothing lies before him except death in utter desolation on the cross; his disciples have abandoned him. It is clear from the agony in the garden that he encounters this fate with full lucidity. The only immediate reality is death; all human security has been withdrawn. Humanly speaking, his person has become blurred and indistinct.

Yet, paradoxically, the truth lies beyond all this: not for a moment does the man-God cease to be clothed in glory. During the brief moment of the transfiguration the veil was lifted; his vestments then were shining like light. This is the light in which he was invested at the resurrection, and in which, with all its brilliance, he appeared to Paul on the road to Damascus. It is only the eye of faith that can discern the garment of glory.

Putting on Christ through faith and baptism

The clothing image is used by Saint Paul to depict the Christian's new state of being as a result of faith and baptism, and to stress the moral consequences of this phenomenon.

It is because Christ is at the very heart of creation as willed by God that he turns naturally to this figure of "putting on

Christ" (Ga 3:27). The whole order of salvation depends upon
his paschal mystery: consequently sharing in salvation means
putting on Christ. Saint Paul will speak likewise of "putting on
the new man" (Ep 4:24; Col 3:10). In two separate instances
what this image will conjure up for Paul is the whole creative
design of universal recapitulation in the unique Family of the
Father. "All baptized in Christ, you have all clothed yourselves in
Christ, and there are no more distinctions between Jew and
Greek, slave and free, male and female, but all of you are one
in Christ Jesus" (Ga 3:27-28). And again: "You have put on a
new self which will progress towards true knowledge the more
it is renewed in the image of its creator; and in that image
there is no room for distinction between Greek and Jew, between
the circumcised or the uncircumcised, or between barbarian and
Scythian, slave and free man. There is only Christ, he is everything and he is in everything" (Col 3:10-11). But putting on
Christ or the new man means stripping off the old man, all his
lusts and all his doings (Ep 4:22; Col 3:9).

The very same insights are stressed in Matthew's parable of
the nuptial feast. The feast is open to everyone, particularly to
the poor and to sinners, but to share it one must wear the
wedding garment. We must manifest our determination to con-
form our lives to the state of sonship that we have acquired
in Christ.

There is too of course the eschatological dimension of the
wedding garment. To the extent to which her members are clad
in this garment and ready to put on, on the other side, the
garment of incorruptibility, the Church is preparing herself for
her encounter, attired as a bride, with her Spouse (Rev 21:2).

The wedding garment of the eucharistic banquet

In the eucharistic celebration all these aspects of the clothing
theme take on particular significance. It is here above all, in this
prelude to the unending nuptials of the Kingdom, that Christians
are initiated to their new state of being in Jesus Christ. Here, as

nowhere else, they are clothed with Christ, renewed in the image of the Creator, introduced to the universal family of the Father, which is open to all men, irrespective of race, sex or social condition.

For participation in it the wedding garment is a prerequisite. The moral requirements, in other words, are there; if it is to have meaning each member must have determined to respect them, and undergo the conversion they imply. Indeed the very close bond between rite and life that distinguishes Christian worship is underlined by the clothing theme. So far from being a fringe activity, added to our actual life, the eucharistic celebration is the heart of that life. We should never assist at Mass without having our determination renewed to practice the gospel precepts.

THIRTEENTH SUNDAY

A. THE WORD

I. 2 Kings
4:8-11, 14-16
1st reading
1st cycle

Here we have one of those narratives that are so frequent about a miraculous birth from a seemingly barren womb.

a) The particular interest of this account is that the *prophet* is regarded as the bearer of God's authentic word of power. What the angels did for Sarah and other women when they were made fecund, the word can do for a gentile woman. The prophet is accordingly the recipient of God's creative and vivifying word.

b) That a childless woman will very easily extend maternal affection to a stranger is a well-known fact. Here Eliseus, who has left his family for the service of God, is the recipient. Thus what is basically a psychological attitude becomes one of welcome and *hospitality*.

To receive the little one is to receive God himself (Mt 10:40), as the woman now discovers. Because she gives herself altogether to the task of hospitality, she discovers in God the secret of goodness.*

II. Wisdom
1:13-15;
2:23-24
1st reading
2nd cycle

The author of this passage has received a training in Greek circles that enables him to pose the problem of human destiny more clearly than his predecessors. Today's reading is concerned with the question of death.

The author's basic idea is that life of itself is corruptible. If we live it according to God's purpose, it has some interior dynamism which is constantly ongoing and renewing. Yet, in concrete fact,

*See the doctrinal theme: *hospitality*, p. 210.

111

life comes to an end; it fails to secure its destiny. As the author sees it this *death* is accidental. It is not part of the law of life; it comes from outside, the result of man's sin.

The link between sin and death, spiritual death that is and physical, is of course classic in Jewish thought. Nor is it all that difficult to translate the notion into contemporary idiom. If the author of our passage were alive now, he would certainly challenge the biologist's right to say the last word about life. Biology touches only some aspects. Life cannot be reduced to what is clinically observable; on the contrary it has reserves of power and dynamism that open up limitless possibilities. But man of course is afraid of life, of the risks and horizons it implies. He bottles it up in egoism, in a sterile comfort. Life perishes in this confinement; it is strangled by sin.

The person who releases life from such bondage, who fulfills the aspirations for the absolute and for sharing, is incorruptible. He is no less than God, and his name is Jesus Christ.

III. 1 Kings 19:16, 19-21
1st reading
3rd cycle

This narrative of Eliseus' call belongs to the extremely old (8th or 9th century) "Eliseus cycle." This prophet-to-be is a rich fellow who owns many cattle. Elias chooses him as disciple by casting his mantle over him, an ancient rite indicating proprietorship (Rt 3:9; Dt 23:1, 27:20; Ez 16:8). In this instance we have the additional point about magical powers in the mantle (2 K 2:14).

A summons of this nature could not really be rejected; it bound the disciple very firmly to his master. We still have traces of it in Jesus' relationship with his apostles (Lk 9:59-62). The disciple must not look back towards all that is his (v. 20); he must reject his profession, his way of life (v. 21), in order to follow the master. Henceforth the master would regard him as a servant; his business would be one of ministering to the needs of the master, surrounding him with every possible care (cf. Lk 8:3; Jn 4:8). Jesus however will regard his disciples no longer as servants, but as friends (Jn 15:15).

a) This sort of bond between *master and disciples* is one that shuts out all sentimentality. Jesus too, in choosing his followers, seemed quite intransigent. Subsequently however he overwhelmed them with his attention, initiating them to the mystery of his relationship with the Father, sharing with them his friendship. The disciples, for their part, do not come just because of his enchanting doctrine, or his powers as miracle worker, but to share his mission in God's name, a mission based on love (Jn 15:15).*

b) The story of Elias' search for a successor has much in common (compare 1 K 19:9 and 13 with Ex 3:6 and 33:22; 1 K 19:11-12 with Ex 19:16) with Moses' choice of Joshua (compare v. 21 with Ex 24:13, 33:12; and 2 K 2:9 with Nb 27:15). Such parallel vocation narratives show that in the line of the prophets the influence and style of the great legislator is carried on.

Eliseus' call, so unconditional, is an indication of the absolute requirements imposed by the discovery of a summons from God. We have the conversion itself and the unreserved abandonment of a previous state of life. The literary genre used, which resembles in many ways the *fioretti* of Saint Francis, has embellishments which tend to soften the peremptory nature of the call. Yet two other essential characteristics of vocation are prominent: the fact that it takes shape in the midst of workaday occupations, and the fact that the response of the person called, however unreserved, is nevertheless a voluntary acceptance of the will of God.

---

*See the doctrinal theme: *discipleship*, p. 134.

IV. Romans   Throughout this whole letter Paul is always
  6:3-4, 8-11   contrasting the justice that men, whether
  2nd reading   Jewish or Gentile, seek to procure by their
  1st cycle   own resources and that which God grants to
  the person who seeks in faith.
The instrument of this justification is baptism, which is the
point of encounter between God's justice and man's faith.

a) The essential theme of our reading is *death with Christ*. In
biblical idiom God is life and his plan is a plan of life. Physical
death is an accident which the Jewish mind attributed to sin
(Gn 3:3, 19; Ez 18:23, 32, 33:11; Si 25:24; Wi 1:13, 2:23-24).
Saint Paul is thinking in this context when he relates physical
death to the spiritual death of sin. The thought can be quite
precisely analyzed. Physical death is not an external punishment
appointed for man's sin by God. Man shutting himself in sin,
that is, by depending on himself alone for his destiny, shuts
himself also in death. He can only be released again by an initiative on the part of God, and a reaching out to God by man.
Jesus was the first to encounter death sinlessly; he displayed
complete fidelity and attachment to his Father, confident that the
Father would save him. Thus his death destroyed the previous
association between death and sin. It was really the instrument
of liberation from sin, because it showed that there was someone
capable of defeating death and rising again, simply because he
had gone back to the Father. No longer is physical death an
accident in the divine plan of life; it is the very point at which
God communicates his life to man.
b) *Baptism,* for Saint Paul, is something that joins us to the
death of Christ, in the sense that it binds us not now to ourselves
but to the Father. It is also the rite by which we signify our
desire to achieve our destiny in communion with God (vv. 3-6).
It resembles Christ's death (v. 11) because it establishes us in
his very own dispositions under the same decree of the Father's
salvific will. The Christian of course is destined for physical

death, like every other man, but, because of this baptism which is like the death of Jesus, he can encounter death as Jesus encountered it, altogether submissive to the other. He can, too, overcome the spiritual death of sin, which is a refusal to accept divine intervention in human destiny. Death in other words is the experience which brings us closest to God, in the self-despoliation it implies. The one great lesson we have learned about God, in Jesus Christ, is that he only lives for giving, even if this means dying. If we can die with the same readiness to surrender self to the other, we are living the very life of God, and that is what baptism provides for us.

c) More than that, because baptism enables the Christian to die to sin, it introduces him also to God's plan of life. Though he be destined now for physical death, he is living a *new life,* the gift of God (v. 4). In these terms he can look upon death as something already in the past; he who is dead is freed from sin (v. 7; cf. Col 3:3; Rm 6:10-11). The baptized Christian has already undergone the essentials of death, the death that is that sin means. Thanks to God's own intervention, he has emerged.

In the Old Testament the idea of a future restoration of the people had shaped itself, including a previous resurrection for the just who were worthy to share the restoration. The corollary of this was a belief that the living could pray and expiate for the sins of the dead and thus enable them to share it (2 M).

Apostolic preaching followed this tradition, but added the proclamation that in Jesus Christ the resurrection of the body had begun, that, since the Lord was established as judge of the living and the dead, the restoration of the holy people was under way. Yet the letters to the Thessalonians and the Corinthians are altogether concerned with the future resurrection, when we shall be "with" the Lord, sharing his glory and incorruptibility.

In the letter to the Romans Saint Paul develops this insight by insisting that Christ's resurrection is not an isolated fact, the pledge of future resurrection, but that here and now it involves us with him. We are already dead "with him" (v. 3), already buried "with him" (v. 4), already living "with him" a new life (v. 5). Five times the word "with" recurs in verses 3-6, to make the Christian fully aware that baptism has launched him on the road to resurrection, and the restoration of the chosen people. No physical death can ever interfere with the spread throughout our being of divine life. It is a process that is measured by the extent to which we imitate the service, the self-employing, the love that are characteristic of the death endured by the man-God.

V. 2 Corinthians This passage was probably the conclusion of
8:7-9, 13-15 the letter sent to the Corinthians after the
2nd reading difficulties were settled. Chapter 9 seems in
2nd cycle fact to be an independent note, and Chapters
10-13 reproduce very probably the material covered in a previous letter sent at the very height of the crisis.

As usual, the apostle concludes his letter with practical details, among them, in this case, the collection he is making throughout the Gentile churches for the Christians of Jerusalem.

Apparently the *collection* was a gesture decided upon by the Corinthians themselves (v. 10; but see Ac 11:29), and accepted by the Jerusalem community (Ga 2:10) as a gesture of solidarity between Gentile and Jewish Christians. The arguments put forward by Saint Paul to induce his listeners to take part in it are the most interesting feature of our reading.

First, the imitation of Jesus Christ (v. 9). For Paul, indeed, Christian ethic consists in reproducing the action of Christ. We should receive one another because Christ has received us (Rm 15:5-7). Husbands and wives, masters and slaves must love one another as Christ loves the Church (Ep 5, etc.). Nor is it merely a matter of following some ideal that has become the sign of salvation. By his concrete performance the Christian can prolong the Lord's incarnation and spread its benefits throughout all humanity. The value of the collection will lie in the theological and salvific insight of those who make it.

The second argument reflects Paul's desire for equality among Greeks and Jews (vv. 13-14). He is not thinking of economic equality to be brought about by social assimilation, but of exchange on the basis of faith. The Jerusalem Christians have not retained for themselves the privileges of the faith. They have extended them to the Gentiles, letting their abundance and "superfluity" supply this great dearth for the nations. It is only fitting that the Gentiles in turn should share their economic superfluity with the deprived Christians of Jerusalem. So between the two groups a solidarity and unity will develop that was hitherto unknown.

Thus the Christian's participation in contemporary movements for human solidarity takes on a new significance. He seeks solidarity with his brethren on the same basis as other men, but, in doing so, he is following the pattern set by the Savior himself, and what he shares with his brothers becomes the authentic sign of God's salvation for men. During these years when secular institutions can do more, better, on an international scale than Church organizations, so that the latter are tending to lose their traditional monopoly, it is important to have a deep understanding of the real Christian meaning of almsgiving. It is the activity wherein the Christian carries on the redemptive work of his Lord. Confronted by it, a redeemed humanity does not cease to offer thanks to God for the gifts received.

It sometimes happens that ecclesiastics whose duty it is to collect money among Christian communities resort to such down-to-earth arguments and procedures (raffles, etc.) that all theological perspective is lost. Donors tend to give with some notion of eventual profit. A collection carried out at a level like this can scarcely be regarded as a sign of salvation. Merely giving money is not enough: the gesture must be consciously placed in a salvific and ecclesial context.*

VI. Galatians   Chapter 5 really gives us the true conclusion
     5:1, 13-18   to Galatians. Subsequently Paul gives no new
     2nd reading   insights about Christian liberty, but merely
     3rd cycle   recapitulates with great intensity the essentials
               of what he has said. His main anxiety is to
lead his listeners towards a way of life that will bear witness to
their freedom in Jesus Christ.

a) Today's reading recalls at once the general theme of the whole letter: the *liberty* we acquire in Jesus. It shows that this liberty really comes when we live in obedience to the truth and to the gospel.

The very first verse affirms our liberation, but it does not describe what we have been liberated from, or how. For this we must turn to the first chapters of the letter. Basically, it is the cross that liberates a man (Ga 1:4; 4:5): on the day that he hears apostolic preaching and accepts it (Ga 3:1-5) he becomes free. The teaching that we have here then concerning liberty follows the pattern that Paul had already developed, in Romans 5:6-11 and in 2 Corinthians 5:14-21, concerning justification or reconciliation. Liberty is something that has been already achieved for humanity by God's initiative and the death of Christ. But the task of integrating the individual man into this mystery of liberty becomes the business of the apostle.

From what are we liberated? In Galatians Paul thinks above all of the practices of the law (circumcision, days of observance, etc.: Ga 3:10-22; 4:9-10). These he characterizes as a yoke (cf. Sl 51:31-37 and Mt 11:28-30). The liberty of the gospel however is opposed not only to the slavery of the law, but to all religious slavery (Rm 8:21) to everything that is alienating in this way.

*See the doctrinal theme: *ecclesial communion*, p. 127.

b) The expression of this Christian liberty is *love*. It is so in the first place because love fulfills the law (v. 14). One's whole religious and moral life, once freed from the innumerable requirements of legalism, can be concentrated on this single great precept. In the second place love and the service of others (v. 13) release us from the slavery of the flesh: from selfishness, in concrete terms.

c) Verses 16-17 go on to develop this opposition between *flesh and spirit*. Flesh stands for the way man will tend to take when he wants to be self-sufficient, ignoring God's aid which is his Spirit. When Paul exhorts the believer to choose between flesh and the Spirit, it becomes clear that there is no automatic entry to salvation. The believer is no less carnal than the unbeliever; the Spirit of liberty is offered him as a means to victory over himself.

When we speak of liberty, the question arises concerning an objective norm of morality. For modern man indeed the question has become very actual. He tends to query the very basis of his ethic, its overly juridical bias, its alleged respect for the human being.

If a moral doctrine is unduly spiritual and supernatural, it cannot easily develop as it ought side by side with the development of psychology. Sometimes too it becomes so identified with a particular culture that it grows rigid and unadaptable. Often indeed moral doctrine is presented in such theocentric terms that there seems to be a genuine fear of the human being. This is altogether too rigid for a world that wants to develop. It is furthermore rather ineffective. The Christian is in fact no different from other human beings, but such presentation seems always to be canonizing the past and failing to look forward.

The Pauline insight about love in liberty can provide an answer to these difficulties that moralists have to face. The only way to be moral is to have one's conscience involved. The only function of an exterior law is to confront the conscience with its surrounding environment, to draw it towards a relational ethic that abjures all enervating individualism. In an atmosphere of love liberty finds a congenial field, while it is opposed to the selfishness of the flesh.

However, it is only when moral doctrine is frankly "theological" rather than "theocentric" that we have true freedom. If God is just the God of law, punishing and rewarding, we can have no true conformity between moral doctrine and the mystery of liberty. If however he is the "God with us," if he gives his Spirit to assist our liberty, there can. If our morality were no more than external imitation of Christ, it would be theocratic. But if it is a sharing with Christ through his Spirit, it is theological. It is a morality of presence and relation, thus of love and liberty, and it is the Spirit who guarantees these two realities. When human conscience and the Spirit are blended together, morality becomes creative. Charity begins to inform all interpersonal relations.

VII. Matthew
10:37-42
Gospel
1st cycle

This conclusion to the mission discourse is almost altogether made up of different materials, drawn by Matthew rather arbitrarily from varying contexts. We find verses 34-36 in Luke 12:51-53; verse 27 in Luke 14:26; verses 36-39 duplicated in Matthew 16:24-25. Verses 40-41 have more or less close parallels in Mark 9:37-41 and Luke 10:16.

Thus the whole piece is composite.

a) It seems possible that the verses about carrying the *cross* after the example of Jesus (38-39) were spoken just as he was about to embark on his final journey to Jerusalem. He was convinced that the opposition which had hardened against him would lead to his death. At this moment he turns to his apostles to see who among them would share his journey towards the cross (cf. Mt 16:21-25).

b) Those who are sent forth by the Lord, who are content to accept all the deprivations and crosses that following him entails, are promised an extraordinary reward. Whatever is done to them will in fact be done to Christ himself (vv. 40-42). This is as it should be. If the envoy resembles his Lord in deprivation and the cross, so, when he is welcomed by Christians and offered *hospitality* and nourishment, his lot resembles the Lord's too. This will free him from worry about ordinary needs, and he can devote himself completely to the good of the Church.

In that hospitality constitutes the major theme of both the first reading and the gospel of this cycle, it is worth while to consider the relevance of this for the modern Christian. Living as we do in a dehumanized and urbanized world, the witness of hospitality, where houses are regularly opened to the outsider, can be quite prophetic. Monastic orders which have a long tradition of hospitality in this sense, should revitalize this aspect of their work as witness. Other groups should follow suit. Then it will be possible for the individual person to recover identity, in a world where he tends to be a cipher. Regard for the other person must be the distinguishing characteristic of our hospitality, if we are to assist uprooted and alienated people to rediscover themselves by discovering the meaning of spontaneous relationship and exchange.

| VIII. Mark 5:21-43 Gospel 2nd cycle | In the three synoptics the account of the raising of the daughter of Jairus (vv. 21-24, 35-43) is complicated by the inclusion of the cure of the woman with an issue of blood |

(vv. 25-34). Consequently the association must be primitive, but we do not know the reason. Possibly the coincidence of "twelve" years (vv. 25 and 42) may explain the conjunction, or this may be due indeed to what actually happened at the time.

Mark's account seems to be the most primitive. Indeed his version of the woman with the issue of blood conveys a quite magical impression of Jesus' thaumaturgic powers, whereas Matthew and Luke make this an instance of faith. Again, Mark does not trouble to determine whether the child was really dead or in a coma (v. 39).The others already interpret the incident in the light of the paschal mystery.

a) In Mark, the woman approaches Jesus with a magical outlook. She thinks he is the possessor of mysterious forces which can be used by those who need them, to the discomfiture of physicians who fail to heal (v. 26), and priests who excommunicate for uncleanness (Lv 15:25). Mark sees the incident as another instance of misconception on the part of the crowd concerning Jesus and his real nature. Luke on the other hand, at the price of some manipulation of the tradition, makes it an example of the conditions of faith required for a miracle. He has the woman make a public profession of faith (Lk 8:47), whereas in Mark (v. 28) her touching Jesus' garment takes place in absolute secrecy.

This dynamism radiating from the garment in a manner which Jesus cannot control (Mark is the only one to give us this detail) accords well with the general purpose of the second evangelist. He wants to demonstrate the epiphany of the Son of God as something quite inevitable, taking place even when Jesus does everything in his power to preserve the secret, even when the crowd fails to recognize it.

b) In the daughter of Jairus incident too, we get this same version of Jesus' situation, unrecognized in spite of his *miracles*. He does not seem as yet to be in control of his power. He is awkward and withdrawn with the crowd whom he quickly disperses (v. 40b). He brings no one with him except the three disciples (precisely the number required for authentic witness), and he pays no attention to the parents (v. 37; contrary to Lk 8:51). His tone even is one of reproach (Why . . . v. 39). It will require a good deal of manipulation on Luke's part to give this episode an atmosphere of gentleness.

Lastly his attitude towards the child is that of healer (v. 41; a warmer attitude in Lk 8:54). The formula he uses is ambiguous: it could be interpreted in a magical sense by Mark's Greek readers (v. 41; curiously similar to Ac 9:40 *Tabitha knoum*). It is indeed clear that Jesus is somewhat embarrassed by his healing power. He has not yet managed to control it (cf. vv. 30-32): he has not yet determined the conditions of faith necessary for its exercise. Meanwhile he continues to impose silence on the beneficiaries and the witness (v. 43).

This passage of course must be taken in its context. Herod is plotting against Jesus; John the Baptist has just been executed; the passion is already looming on the horizon. Confronted now by an apparently senseless malady and a senseless death, Jesus must sharpen his own weapons against death.

Just three disciples are admitted to the secret, though their understanding is minimal. Jesus finds himself involved with a humanity whose situation seems beyond hope. He revolts against these hopeless situations — that is often the meaning of his miracles — but he undertakes them all the same. The revulsion he feels will only be extinguished by his own death. This will lead to the foundation of a new humanity, where evil and death will be overshadowed by grace.

IX. Luke 9:51-62 This passage begins a long section, exclusively
    Gospel   Lucan, that concludes only with Luke 18:14.
    3rd cycle   It contains of course a number of items that
                      we find in other synoptics, but Luke modifies
them much more arbitrarily than he does in other chapters. He adds special comments and in general manipulates everything to illustrate the particular theme that is so characteristic of him: the journey of Christ and his followers towards Jerusalem. Indeed, when we consider style, the rarity of geographical and chrono-

logical data, the Aramaic vocabulary, and the repetition of certain times that have already appeared in the earlier section, this section seems almost like an independent gospel within a gospel.

a) The first verse is a very solemn introduction to the great theme of Jesus' journeys to Jerusalem. There is emphasis on the Johannine themes: the fulfillment of time (cf. Jn 13:1), the "taking up" from the world (John will speak of "glorification" Jn 7:39, 12:16, 22, 13:31-32; cf. Jn 12:32), and Jesus' determination to follow his destiny to the end ("resolutely"; cf. Jn 18:4, 19:11). Thus, in this verse which foreshadows clearly the mystery of Christ's death, we have the key to the whole passage. The evangelist immediately goes on to consider the conditions necessary in order to be Christ's disciple, not only just now, in the journey to Jerusalem, but also, in a very definitive way, in the conduct of daily life.

b) The first condition is *patience* under trial. James and John thought they should have fire from heaven to deal with the hostile Samaritans (cf. 2 K 1:10-12). Jesus however, consistent with his teaching in the parables of the darnel and the dragnet (cf. Mt 13:24-35 and 47-48), recommends his disciples to allow the necessary time for conversion and development (vv. 54-56).

c) The second condition is *common life* with the master. As in all the rabbinic schools, this is manifested by the material services which the disciples perform for the rabbi (vv. 52-53; cf. Mt 26:17-19). Christ being an itinerant master above all, common life with him will entail discomfort and poverty (vv. 57-58). The disciple may have to live in the open air, or content himself with whatever hospitality is offered, something that will train him to share the tragic destiny of the suffering Servant (Lk 14:27; 17:33).

d) A third characteristic of the disciple must be his *missionary involvement*, to which everything else is subordinated (vv. 59-60). The passage immediately following in Luke (10:1-11) will stress this heavily, but it is already clear in verse 60.

Christ demands from his disciple the severance of ties necessary for "proclaiming the Kingdom," and he brooks no delay.

e) Finally the disciple must *renounce all human ties* (vv. 61-62). This follows the severity of Elias with his disciple (1 K 19:19-21). Several rabbis followed this tradition, and it was inherited by ancient monasticism (cf. again Lk 14:26). "Following" Christ then becomes really a state of life, of common life, which parallels a family life (vv. 59-62).

These recommendations of Christ to his disciples seem harsh, but they must be properly understood. He is not imposing a "law of poverty" or a "law of celibacy." He does not intend to determine the guide lines of subsequent ecclesiastical law for certain states of life. He is speaking to concrete persons about a concrete situation.

After Christ's death, the recommendations tended to be interpreted rather more in the context of personal salvation than in that of service to the kingdom of God (cf. Mk 10:17-26). The concept of disciple, which was originally confined to those persons who followed Jesus in his journeys through Palestine, was extended to the actual Christian state (Mt 10:42; 7:21-23).

There can be no doubt that Luke's text was influenced by the idea the Christian community formed of itself. It is quite significant that the persons addressed by Jesus remain anonymous. Where Matthew and Mark give us particularized accounts of apostles' callings, Luke by contrast uses anonymity in order to address the message to each reader.

This means that even within the synoptic tradition the concept of following Christ has different meanings. In the gospel of John, and in Paul's letters, the meaning will be completely different again. But there is always a common ground, and that is imitation of Jesus by communion in his life. Such imitation has three principal components: detachment from material things so that one will remain open and ready; freedom from the fear of death (the more necessary because the disciple, with Christ, is required to communicate life); finally a rejection of any fetters with the past (Ph 3:12-14), so that one will be open to the event, to newness, to initiative and the unforeseen.*

*See the doctrinal theme: *discipleship,* p. 134.

B. DOCTRINE

1. The Theme of Ecclesial Communion

Saint Paul's action in organizing a collection among the Churches he founded for the mother-Church of Jerusalem, which was threatened by famine, deserves our notice in these days. It is clear that he wanted this collection to be a great sign of ecclesial communion to counteract the tensions that troubled the primitive Church. In many ways these tensions resemble those of the Church today (see 2nd reading, 2nd cycle).

Let us for a moment go back to these Christian origins, which were so profoundly marked by the entry of the Gentiles to the Church. Like Christ's first disciples, all convert Jews thought wrongly that practice of the law of Moses was necessary for following the Messiah. Consequently the Gentile entry at once encountered an objection in principle, that was fairly rapidly solved by reference to the universalism of faith. Many Gentiles became Christian, and naturally introduced new cultural elements into the Church. Very soon their churches began to present an aspect markedly different from those of the Judaeo-Christian communities. The same Christ was confessed in both of course, the same baptism was conferred, the same Eucharist celebrated. All the brethren were assembled in the same communion of the Spirit. Yet the communion was far from being automatic; considerable differences of mentality and religious sensibility went on dividing people. Always there was the danger of trouble, if means were not adopted of developing and consolidating communion.

What of the Church today? Not only are there differences in Christendom; there are actual ruptures, the most profound ones not necessarily corresponding to confessional differences. The future looks like it will bring greater differences still. Asian, African and Latin American Christians will tend to vary from the traditional model of Western Christianity. And, everywhere,

Christians who look towards the modern world will find themselves at variance more and more with those who are traditional. Notwithstanding, the people of God have a great yearning for unity. If ecclesial communion is to develop a proper witness in our time, what is the most urgent measure that should be taken? Perhaps this Pauline collection can point the way for us in the future.

Communion and particularism in Israel

There is a sort of communion towards which all men naturally aspire because of the security it provides. That is family, social and cultural communion. In such a group the individual is likely to find in the other a kindred soul, both in style of life and in value system. These are the common denominators which provide security, and the security is more pronounced when the individual conforms to the role determined for him by the group. Conversely, when the group feels its security threatened, it reacts by excommunicating the rebel or the nonconformist. Confronted by other groups, it will aim at assimilation, coexistence, or destruction according to circumstances.

In Israel, the regime of faith tended gradually to upset these standards. Little by little believers became conscious of genuine spiritual liberty, and began to see the true meaning of human relationships. Instead of being taken as the expression of some divine ordinance, established once for all, they were restored to their real human signifiance. The believer's awareness of personal sin led him to think that fidelity to the alliance necessarily entailed a transformation in human relationships. They must be aligned more and more with the "justice" of Yahweh. Then the awareness of God's absolute transcendence naturally led people to widen their horizons where human communion was concerned. Yahweh is creator of the universe. He is Lord of all nations, and consequently concerned with their destiny. The prophets' pictures of the Kingdom of the future see Israel side by side with other peoples.

All this notwithstanding, it must be admitted that, before the advent of Christ, the tendencies in this direction left much to be desired. Interdicts against certain categories of the chosen people continued to be the rule. Inequality was general. People excommunicated one another. The better Israelites avoided all contact with publicans and sinners. As for outside nations, there was always talk about divine vengeance. Where contacts were inevitable, among the Diaspora for instance, there was never any concept of communion that was not centripetal. Israel is and always will be the chosen people. The nations, to find their destiny, must turn to the people of the Covenant. If they wish to be saved, that can only be by passing under the "Caudine forks" of Israel. The true God can only be adored on Sion.

The evangelic sign of communion

The coming of Jesus of Nazareth meant a profound challenge to these attitudes. Their inadequacy was vigorously assailed. By his attitude and his preaching he made it clear that faith required the recognition of every man as a brother. Man to his fellow-man is always someone other, and it is in recognition of this otherness that we really see him as brother. Whoever they are, all men have a fundamental equality before God, and the God of faith is above all a universal Father. When Jesus put forward the new commandment of brotherly love without limits he was fulfilling the Law and the Prophets. Love which embraces enemies means love that is prepared to find an enemy in the other. Herein lies the originality of the gospel, an originality that is disconcerting, but that discloses the true nature of God and the true nature of man.

We have the true gospel concept of communion when a man deliberately undertakes to love the other to the very limit of differences that cannot be dissolved. Jesus does not say: "Make friends of your enemies." He simply says: "Love your enemies." Love like this means absolute renunciation of self, which only the state of sonship and liberation from sin make possible. It is an amazingly vulnerable love. It does bring about genuine communion; but its efficacity is rarely recognized and it encounters much rejection. Sinful man does not easily embark upon a path that obliges him to "lose his life."

The sign *par excellence* of universal communion is the sign of the cross. It is a paradoxical sign, because under the appearance of failure it bears witness to victory. At the beginning of his ministry Jesus had hoped that the chosen people would follow the new commandment, and be a witness before the nations of genuine love. But he had to accept the fact that Israel did not want such a Messiah. In the end he had to go alone to the cross. Having loved his own, he loved them to the end. The failure seemed absolute. Yet it was from the root of the cross that the Church took shape, that it became possible for all men to be reassembled in love.

The scope and structure of communion

It is the task of each individual Christian to follow the example of Jesus under the influence of the Spirit, and contribute his share to the building of genuine communion among all men. To undertake this responsibility a man must be a member of the Church, must be himself in other words already bound by that communion which Jesus set up. Communion must be a reality among Christians themselves before they can presume to build it amongst men. They cannot be "gatherers" without being themselves "gathered." That is why ecclesial communion is basic in the missionary responsibility of the people of God. Throughout the centuries, however, ecclesial communion has undergone frequent mutations, and today, when we consider the major Christian confessions, the aspect it presents is very different from what it used to be.

During the apostolic age, and throughout the first three centuries, Christians were deeply aware of the connection between ecclesial communion and the Spirit of the Risen Lord. They realized that the cross of Christ had in fact broken down the walls of separation between the Jews and the nations, but that only the action of the Spirit could build communion between local assemblies of believers who differed so much in mentality and religious tradition. There was no attempt whatsover to organize this communion juridically, but very naturally attempts were made to manifest it by demonstrations of one kind or another. Saint Paul had arranged a collection in order to reinforce the rather uneasy communion between Jewish and Gentile Christians.

At a later stage the spectacular spread of Christendom, and the diminution of spiritual fervor consequent upon the huge influx of Gentiles, led to attempts at concrete organization of ecclesial communion. Structures became more important than demonstrations. In the Latin Church Rome came to be more and more a centralizing influence. The underlying principle of communion began to be uniformity of laws and observances. Unquestionably there were immediate advantages that flowed from this development, but in the long run, so far from providing against deep cleavages, it actually tended to produce them.

Vatican II marked the end of an epoch, at least for the Catholic Church. Diversity of every kind begins to be evident within her fold, and the law of uniformity is yielding place to a greater concern for the new commandment. Undoubtedly we need demonstrations of various kinds to reinforce communion. Only the future can tell what kind of ecclesial structure is destined to preserve both communion and diversity.

Ecclesial communion in the service of mission

Ideas about the duty of mission to non-Christians have always been colored by the manner in which the people of God have actually practiced ecclesial communion. Thus, throughout the Christian centuries, within the framework of the Catholic Church, communion tended to be achieved by the law of uniformity. People found a close link between the content of the faith and its institutional expression (structures, formulation, style of worship, etc.). The extent to which Christianity was influenced by Western culture itself was inadequately understood. Nor was it understood how far the divisions that actually developed in European Christianity were produced by cultural diversity within Europe. Mission has as its object the presentation of the faith to all men. Inevitably, in the conduct of mission, there was a tendency to transfer the Western institutional expression of this faith to other peoples, because it was considered immutable. In Christian centers established in Asia and Africa, it was thought natural by the greater number of missionaries that everything should follow the Western pattern.

Since the beginning of the 20th century a profound change has come about. It is being finally realized how very different men are, individually and collectively. Man must always be other to his fellow man. Believers realize that within the actual confines of the Church we have this diversity, and that it can be a source of richness if handled properly. Gradually the law of uniformity falls more and more into disrepute, and people are rejecting the idea of a close link between the content of the faith and its institutional expression. The "language" of faith, as it has developed in the Catholic Church, however authentic, is recognized to be just *one* of many possible languages. In such a climate, mission to the modern world, or to other cultural environments, cannot obviously be a mere matter of transference. It must be a genuinely creative process, entailing much more than mere "adaptation." The one essential requirement is that ecclesial communion be actually practiced. If, as a result of mission, the Church is to flourish creatively, with diversity, in new soil, it will be absolutely necessary that between local churches, bishops and the faithful there be interchange of life and energy. In the Church solo performance is not really possible. The interchange will be that of fraternal charity, which depends on the action of the Spirit. And it is in this sense that the lived experience of ecclesial communion can be beneficial to mission. It was John XXIII's great achievement that he clearly perceived this.

Initiation to ecclesial communion

Ecclesial communion is of course above all the work of the Spirit. Being as it is a gift, it is always antecedent to any initiative on the part of the believer. But there is a sense too in which it is the work of the believer, the fruit of fidelity to the new commandment. Under this aspect it is always something fragile and precarious. The Church should be ever watchful about these two aspects when it assembles the faithful to initiate them into ecclesial communion.

The truth is that the people of God have lived for centuries as if this gift were solely a grace. The Institution of the Church has seemed the unique instrument of divine intervention. In order to be correctly established in ecclesial communion one had merely to respond to her summons. True, the faithful were required to show fidelity to the new commandment, but their fidelity was not a constitutive element of communion. The Institution was everything. Ecclesial communion was organized before it was lived.

Nowadays however it is evident that personal initiative on the part of the faithful is becoming more and more a constitutive element. There is realization that this is more than a gift; it must always be getting shaped. Thus, when Christians are assembled in the eucharistic celebration, it is of the first importance that they feel themselves in communion with their brethren throughout the world. They must, in all lucidity, declare themselves ready to assume the responsibilities of the charity to which the celebration summons them. Can we say that the current liturgical reform takes sufficient account of this second aspect of ecclesial communion? One cannot be sure. In any case the issue at stake is very grave. Unless personal initiative on the part of the faithful be part and parcel in this domain, there will always be the risk of organization on the part of the Institution. Except for a few minor details we shall be back again with the law of uniformity.

2. The Theme of Discipleship

"It was at Antioch that the disciples, for the first time, received the name of Christians" (Ac 11:26). To be a Christian then is to be a disciple of Christ, and to become that more and more. From the very beginning the term was understood in its evangelic sense. A man's salvation depended on Christ's own person. One could not be his disciple without following him, without attaching oneself personally to him. The lives of saints bear eloquent witness to this. One day they all heard the call of the Risen Lord and answered it, each according to his fashion. They gave all their energies to the service of Christ, and never ceased to strengthen their link with his person through prayer.

Yet how many people profess themselves Christian, without having any idea, or scarcely any idea, of all that it means. The Christian is merely an exponent of Christianity in the sense that the Moslem is of Islam, or the Buddhist of Buddhism. He is bound of course by a series of obligations, certain duties of worship and a way of life that conforms to gospel wisdom. The person of Christ however enters very little into the whole pattern. For a great many such Christians the phrase dear to Saint Paul "For me, to live is Christ" has no great meaning.

In our day, the situation is even more serious still. Many of our more involved Christians, that is to say those who are most concerned to put the gospel into practice in every aspect of individual and social life, do not necessarily see themselves as disciples of Christ in the traditional sense of the word. True, they have discovered the gospel. They consider that the new commandment of Jesus is of capital importance for human destiny. They sincerely try to follow it. Yet, the person of the Risen Lord is not the central thing in their lives. Indeed ordinary religious practice, just like traditional spiritual concepts, tends to leave them cold.

Such considerations are sufficient to indicate the prime importance of reflection about discipleship. The New Testament understanding of this concept touches the very fundamentals of faith. We should carefully examine it. It could be that the crisis we describe is more one of language and imagery than of the underlying reality. Today, as always, being a Christian must mean being a disciple. But what does discipleship really mean?

The disciples of Yahweh

In all the great religious traditions the great masters have had disciples. These were meticulous about the master's teaching and anxious to preserve his sayings as a heritage. A few Old Testament allusions indicate a similar situation in Israel. We have an Eliseus attaching himself to Elias (see today's first reading, third cycle), or a group of disciples surrounding Isaiah (8:16). The word disciple is hardly known in the Old Testament, but we do have the institution. Followers gathered round the prophets and the sages, frequented their schools and shared their views.

The comparative imprecision of the Old Testament in this area may perhaps arise from a difference of outlook under the regime of faith. The Covenant is not based on traditions handed down from master to disciple, but on itself. Once the people began to see the event, whether in individual or community life, as the focus of encounter with Yahweh, each person was led to estimate his fidelity to the Covenant in this context. He must accept the will of God as it manifests itself in history. From day to day the God of the Covenant intervenes in the life of the chosen people, and his living Word has to be discerned in these interventions. Guides of course were needed by Israel in the spiritual pilgrimage. But such guidance was no more than provisional. The prophets themselves nourished the hope of a future where hearts would be directed by Yahweh himself, without mediation by any human master (Jr 31:31-34), when all men would be "disciples of Yahweh" (Is 54:13). As faith deepened then, interiorization grew. The ideal of the believer was to be a listener before God, to attach himself, not to a human master, but to God's Word.

During the later Jewish era however there was a change. The disconcerting reality of the Word was there, but the voice of prophecy was silenced. The Law had become rigid, a preserve for the teachings of the doctors. Traditions had become established and were handed down from generation to generation. The word disciple came into common usage. Masters of the Law opened schools which attracted pupils. The viewpoint of faith was less sharply defined than it had been formerly.

Jesus of Nazareth and his disciples

Throughout his public ministry Jesus gathered disciples about himself. Some, the Twelve, received a special sort of summons, but, in a wider sense, the term was applied to those who chose to follow the Master. They shared his life, were modeled by his teaching, and would eventually assume a particular charge, as Saint Luke tells us of the seventy disciples. Doubtless the followers were numerous, but because the demands of the Master were so stringent, many would have abandoned him along the way.

While following this procedure, Jesus nevertheless lost no opportunity of distinguishing himself from the doctors of the law. He placed himself, by contrast, in the tradition of the great prophets. When he referred to the Law it was not to comment on it, but to restore it to its proper place. It was integral to the regime of faith, and should not be degraded to a catalogue of observances. He made it his function to assist believers to see in events the interventions of God. For any believer the event *par excellence* was encounter with the other, and consequently the

Law could be reduced to the single commandment of love. But this was a very exigent commandment, with undreamed-of demands. True, more than any other prophet Jesus summoned men to become disciples of the living God. Yet, at the same time, his precept was "follow me." He delivered his teaching with an authority that has nothing in common with the prophets who preceded him.

One had to do more than follow his teaching. One had to follow him, answering a call that originated with him. Following him meant being attached, for always, to his person. It meant going where he went, conforming one's life to his, carrying the cross in his wake, sharing his destiny and being granted by him the Kingdom. So that his disciples have nothing really in common with those of doctors of the law, or indeed prophets. Discipleship here defines the state of the believer under the new covenant.

His coming then gives the theme of discipleship an altogether new meaning. In the Old Testament the ideal for the believer had been discipleship of the living God, without intermediary. In the New Testament we learn that discipleship of the living God is rendered possible only by discipleship of Jesus. Jesus is not an intermediary; he is the unique Mediator. Only through him can the believer discern the living God at work in history.

Disciples of the Risen Lord in the Church

A final dimension is given to the theme of discipleship by Christ's Pasch. The people of the New Covenant have been definitively established. The constant activity of the Risen Lord among his own means that they enjoy a new being and a new mode of action. The members of the new people are disciples of the Risen Lord and members of his Body which is the Church. They are disciples because the Master is always present in their lives, because they can do nothing apart from their attachment to his person. They look for him in every moment of their daily existence. But they realize too that they are disciples who count; they are called to make up in their flesh that which is wanting in his Passion. They are his partners in the accomplishment of the Father's plan.

It has been true, thus far at least, that liturgical celebration has been the area where Christians could best experience the presence among them of the Risen Lord. Their awareness of discipleship has been most intense in sharing his body and blood. The Eucharist was regarded as a major event in salvation history, because it was here, and only here, that Christ became present to his Church in person. For true disciples, religious practice in these terms became a matter of course. We can easily understand why daily Mass became the norm for them, and why it was prolonged by visits to the Blessed Sacrament and other such marks of respect.

As long as liturgy, or, in a wider sense, religious expression, was central in people's lives this mode of procedure had very much point. But today, when liturgy is being gradually displaced as a center of gravity by secular life and secular language, can we say the situation is the same? For Christians in our actual world now is it sufficient, is it indeed possible, to have the sense of discipleship of the Risen Lord that comes during the eucharistic celebration? Must they not begin to realize that Christ intervenes personally in every sphere of their lives? Must they not make the judgment that the human endeavor, towards which they bend all their energies, will only succeed when it is thoroughly permeated by the action of the Risen Lord? In the actual context of living the encounter with the Risen Lord cannot be dissociated from the encounter with other men, above all with the poor (see the last judgment scene in Mt 25:31-46). In other words it is by fidelity to the new commandment of love without limits that we encounter the Risen Lord, because, without Christ, such love is impossible. Christians in our day, if they want to be true disciples of Christ, must find their Master in the other. And so the gospel is always new.

Make disciples of all nations

The theme of discipleship is equally important for an understanding of mission. Early Christians clearly realized this, because they recalled that this was the theme of the Risen Lord when he addressed the Eleven. "All authority in heaven and on earth has been given to me. Go therefore, make disciples of all the nations; baptize them in the name of the Father and of the Son and of the Holy Spirit, and teach them to observe all the commands I gave you. And know that I am with you always; yes to the end of time" (Mt 28:18-20). This affirms that the salvation of all the nations depends upon the actual intervention at all times of the Risen Lord among his own. The proper end of mission is the winning of disciples in all the nations. The Risen Lord has all power in heaven and on earth; only he can lead to fulfillment the spiritual pilgrimage of any and every nation. In each case his way of doing so is by finding disciples.

This is a very strict ideal, which missionaries at all times must keep before their eyes. It is easier to make converts than to make disciples. In the conduct of mission there is always the possibility that people will become converts for inadequate reasons. In the past men have requested baptism because of the material or cultural advantages to be gained. But, in order to make disciples of the Risen Lord, the presentation of the faith will be of paramount importance. The missioner must accept men as they are, join them in their spiritual pilgrimage. He must demonstrate to them the newness of the gospel, and lead them gradually to realize how Christ is the only answer to their groping search. All this is arduous. Inevitably the wisdom of the gospel gives scandal, and sometimes missionaries will be tempted to resort to other, less committing, messages.

Because of their increasing mastery over nature, men nowadays take the view that they can make the earth a more livable place by the use of their own resources. The great immediate objectives are those of world peace. This is precisely the area where missionaries must put forward faith in the living Christ.

By their own lives and conduct they must somehow show that, as long as men stop short of a radical conversion of heart, such ideals will continue to be ambiguous. The true road to development lies through mutual recognition of differences and mutual acceptance. All men must work towards a genuine universal brotherhood. They will never achieve this unless they have recourse to the one and only Liberator, and become his disciples.

The fraternal banquet of the Lord's disciples

We have said earlier that it is in their relationship to the other that Christians of today will come to discover the true nature of their discipleship. Evidently however, in the ordinary pattern of existence, this can be more than an intuition. To deepen our awareness, we must regularly express this discipleship in the eucharistic celebration.

In actual practice, this aspect of the celebration is too often overlooked. The reason is simply that in the past this aspect was not understood. People had become so accustomed to the virtual isolation of Christ in the sacramental species, that they had become blind to the essential connection between encounter with Christ and our encounter with the other which the gospel underlines. It is absolutely imperative that this be recognized. Indeed the disinterest shown in religious practice today may be to some extent explained by this very inadequacy in our Masses.

In our celebration two things must be emphasized. First, that the object of the celebration is the actual lived experience of the people of God, with Christ at its center, what we are celebrating is the "today" of salvation. Second, the celebration must be manifestly a sharing between brothers of the Word and the Bread. It must be the sort of banquet in which believers, whoever they be, can discern as they encounter one another the very face of the Risen Lord who is present among them.

FOURTEENTH SUNDAY

A. THE WORD

I. Zechariah
9:9-10
1st reading
1st cycle

Though it is very brief, the book of Zechariah was put together by two different authors, and "Second-Zechariah" (Ze 9-14) was probably written in the third century BC. The author is for the most part an anthologist, borrowing images and themes from his predecessors, and modifying them according to the requirements of the contemporary situation.

a) Second Zechariah revives the theme of *davidic messiahship*, which had suffered eclipse during the Persian period. Thus verse 9 alludes to David, who did not mount a horse (cf. Gn 49:11), and verse 20 inveighs against Solomon and his successors, who introduced horses and chariots to Israel (1 K 10:26-29). Prophetic tradition invariably opposed this tendency to "cavalry" (Dt 17: 16; Is 31:1-3; Ho 1:7, 14:4; Mi 5:9). It made men rely on their own resources rather than God; Solomon's horses were regarded as one reason for the people's failure. Being mounted on an ass was at once a return to the humble style of David, and a sign of fidelity to Palestinian tradition.

b) Yet the opposition between David and Solomon is not absolute. The author compares the Messiah to Solomon as well. The reference to Psalm 71/72:8 and to the book of Kings is unmistakable: the themes of peace (etymology of "Solomon") and of the extension of the kingdom from sea to sea (1 K 4:9-14). The future Messiah is destined to have from David his simplicity and from Solomon his brilliance.

This double association for the future Messiah on the prophet's part is not without interest. When he makes him a descendant both of David and of Solomon, he is perhaps anxious to exclude

141

other descendants of David. In any case his image of the
Messiah combines the poverty of David and the majesty of
Solomon. We have both extremes of the human experience.

II. Ezechiel
2:2-5
1st reading
2nd cycle

These verses are taken from the "vision of the
book," which was doubtless once, before the
vision of the chariot (the introduction to another book), the introduction to Ezechiel's
oracles.

We have no trace here of the solemnity which traditionally
characterizes *vocation* narratives. Ezechiel is called forthwith to
challenge a people who have been rebellious for centuries (v. 4).
He is no superman, but a simple "son of man," no one remarkable, that is (v. 3). That is to say, his call is represented under
the most dramatic and tense aspect. Against a powerful adver-
sary, the only means of sustaining the ideal he undertakes are
exceedingly frail.

III. Isaiah
66:10-14
1st reading
3rd cycle

This reading comes from the apocalyptic poem
(Is 65-66) that concludes a series of oracles
published under the name of Isaiah. The piece
is certainly postexilic, and is probably meant
to rekindle the hope in Jerusalem's restoration, which was slow in coming.

Its author is completely an anthologist. Not a single phrase is
original: the summons to joy for Jerusalem (v. 10; cf. Ze 9:9; Is
3:14; Is 60:1), the proclamation of a river of grace for the city
which will replace the little brook of Cedron (v. 12; cf. Ps 45/
46:5; Ez 47), the reference to the theme of consolation (v. 13;
cf. Is 40:1; 52:9). One insight is somewhat original: Jerusalem's
maternity with regard to her children (vv. 11:12). Frequently

enough there had been allusions to the imminent fertility of the reconciled spouse, and promises of abundant progeny (Is 62:4, 12; 60:15), but this is the first time that Jerusalem's tenderness for her children as a mother has been stressed. It is a gift for her from God; the consolation she spreads is God's very own.

So she becomes the sacrament of God's loving presence among his own.*

The image of the people of God is of course the most expressive one for describing the Church, but it can be interpreted too horizontally. The people are not set up merely by the association of its members, or a federation of local assemblies. It depends on a founding act that is outside itself. The image of motherhood then is valuable in stressing the antecedent act: children, or men, only exist because a mother preceded them. The Church is logically prior to the elect. She calls them into life, and the life whereby they live is hers. The Church is a convocation before she becomes an assembly.

IV. Romans
8:9, 11-13
2nd reading
1st cycle

Here we have an extract from Paul's long catechesis about Christian life in the Spirit. The main interest lies in the contrast he makes between the flesh and the spirit (vv. 12-13; cf. Ga 5:16-24), and in the way he associates life in the spirit with Christ's resurrection (v. 11).

a) Flesh stands for the way man takes when he depends on himself, without reference to the *Spirit*, who is the special aid God sends. The Law itself, though it is a gift of God, can pertain to the flesh, when its observances are so perverted by man that he confronts God with a ledger of titles and merits. "To live in the flesh" is to seek after the autarchy Adam sought when he disobeyed, and that legal observers seek in their formalism. Both

*See the doctrinal theme: *Jerusalem*, Eastertime volume, p. 176.

attitudes lead to death; they isolate one from God and from the eschatological era. "To live in the Spirit" by contrast is to accept the fact that he is "dwelling" in us, that our being is open to God's initiative so that he may lead us to life and to peace. When he dwells in us it is as master (theme of authority in vv. 7-9), even though he is lodged in a body that is dead (v. 10), as he was when Jesus was buried.*

b) This life in the "spirit" is closely associated with the *resurrection* of Christ. In either case it is the same power of God, and the gift of his Spirit (cf. Rm 1:4) that is at work (v. 11). So it is that the Christian life in the Spirit is the best witness to Christ's resurrection.

V. 2 Corinthians 12:7-10
2nd reading
2nd cycle

Paul's enemies, in order to discredit him with the Corinthians, made much of their own superiority in charisms. It is not then sufficient for him to stress the action of God in his ministry by contrast with his own weakness (2 Co 11:14-33). He has to show that even in the domain of charisms he has no reason to feel inferior to his adversaries. If, even here, he still stresses his weakness, it is because he is not defending himself personally but the very nature of apostolic ministry.

Our reading is taken up with the theme of *weakness*. It is always thus when Paul describes his ministry (1 Co 4:9-13; 2 Co 4:7-15, 6:4-10, 11:23-33, 12:9-10). His weakness is very prominent, but it yields place to the power and dynamism of Christ.

If apostolic ministry happens to be accompanied by charismatic phenomena, that, for Paul, is no proof of mandate. As he sees it, his very weakness is the only thing that reveals the profundity

---

*See the doctrinal theme: *flesh and spirit,* p. 154.

of his mission. It is also guaranteed by the buffets of Satan and by the sting in the flesh (vv. 7-9), symbolizing probably the hostility of false brethren (this is the meaning of the phrase in Ng 33:55; Jos 23:13; Ez 28:24), rather than by any charisms.

It becomes very evident then that the true criterion of apostolic ministry is the acceptance, with patience and joy, of everything that resembles the Lord's humiliation. If it is applied to the false apostles at Corinth, their hypocrisy becomes evident.

Of course Paul does no more really than apply the essential criteria of Christian life to Christ's minister. One must imitate the wisdom of Christ. He humiliated himself to the point of weakness in order to glorify God. He reveals divine life to all believers (2 Co 13:4; 1 Co 1:18-19; 2:2; Ph 2:6-11) and offers them a share in the power of the resurrection.*

VI. Galatians   This is the conclusion of the letter to the
    6:14-18   Galatians, where Paul recapitulates the most
    2nd reading   important of the themes he has treated.
    3rd cycle

                 In the theology of the *cross*, the death-resurrection antithesis is applied to the life of the Christian, and more particularly to the life of the apostle (2 Co 4:10-12, 14:4; Col 1:24). When one follows the way of the cross, it becomes a matter of glory as Calvary was for Jesus, because it leads to the resurrection. The cross sets up the Christian in a new existence. He is more than someone destined to resurrection. The certitude of his resurrection is provided by the fact that he is crucified by trial and opposition.

All previous means that people have used in the past in order to reach the glory of God have been abolished, among them circumcision.

---

*See the doctrinal theme: *growth in weakness*, p. 160.

The letter to the Galatians is the first to attribute such large importance to the cross in the work of salvation. This enables Paul to find a meaning for trial and demonstrate its efficacy. He can develop reflections about its redemptive and prophetic value, because of the associated notions of glory and resurrection, and the natural corollary of all this, the idea of freedom from any brand of alienation.

He does not see trial simply as an ascesis destined to purify people of false values, and shield them from the alienation that leads to wrong use of happiness. Nor does he see it as a basis for moral life. He is not a teacher of ethics, but a prophet of the new age. Nor, again, is it a simple imitation of Christ's cross. It is not just because Christ suffered that the Christian should suffer. All of these considerations have value, but in Paul's thinking are trivial beside the fact that trial is first and foremost the basis of hope, an earnest of the Kingdom that is coming.

The trial of the cross is a challenge to the world and the Church. Trial is resurrection not alone for the individual, but on collective, economic, social and political levels as well. It is only men who have endured trial that are capable of building the revolutionary community that will change the world. It is only such tried and persecuted people that can give us a Church that will be purer and more faithful, because trial has a prophetic value.

The challenge is a grave one for the Church. How can she sincerely preach the hope of the cross at times when she finds herself ranged on the side of the comfortable, those who succeed in evading all trial and misfortune? Throughout the centuries she has often strangled prophetic movements of the poor that would have given her a nobler visage had they succeeded. Trial becomes the cross of glory whenever Christians who have undergone it reassert their membership of a prophetic community dedicated to a better world, and a kingdom of God that is evident.

VII. Matthew   Numerous exegetical problems arise concern-
11:25-30   ing this passage with regard to authenticity,
Gospel   unity and doctrine. The first portion (vv. 25-
1st cycle   27) rather resembles Luke's account (Lk 10:
21-22), but the latter portion (vv. 28-29) is
notably different (Lk 10:23-24). Matthew's version however
appears to be primitive, if one is to judge by the frequency of
Aramaic expressions.

To begin with, we have a thanksgiving by Jesus to his Father
(vv. 25-27) for all that they mean to one another, and for the
mission he has received of revealing the Father to the little ones.
Then he turns to those little ones (vv. 28-30) and invites them
to communicate with him.

a) The biblical background of this hymn is extremely revealing. Jesus is actually using for his own purposes the hymn of the
three boys in Daniel 2:23. The three "children" (cf. Lk 10-21)
are contrasted with the "sages" of Babylon. Thanks to their
prayers (Dn 2:18) they have been granted "revelation" of the
mystery of the kingdom (a phrase characteristic of the book of
Daniel, which we also find in Lk 10:21), something that has
escaped the wise men and the sages.

He is then comparing the contrast between his disciples and
the Jewish sages with the gulf that separated *children and sages*
in the time of Nabuchadnezzar. He is opening his kingdom and
offering "revelation" to the very precise category of "poor," those
poor in intelligence. Here he is marking himself off from certain
Jewish teachers who frequently showed no understanding for
the ignorant people (cf. Is 29:14; 1 Co 1:19, 26).

b) There is another passage in Daniel (7:14) where "everything is handed over" to the Son of man by the Ancient of days
. . . and this is the subject of the revelation made to Daniel. In
this context, Christ, who claims the title Son of man (Mt 24:36),
blesses the Ancient of days, under his new name of Father, for
having "handed over everything" to him, that is to say for having

given him, as in Daniel 7:14, "power over all things" (Mt 28:18; Jn 5:22, 13:3, 17:2), and also a fuller *knowledge* of the Father to be revealed to men (v. 27). Christ is then both King and Revealer of the kingdom of the little ones. When they gather round him, they will be able to know God and set up a community apart from those "who do not know God," the Gentiles, that is, in the first place (Jr 10:25), and in the second place the Jewish sages (v. 21; cf. Jn 12:39-50).

c) Those who "labor and weep" under the burden (v. 28) are the same as the little ones and the ignorant of the preceding verses. In concrete terms, the burden or the *yoke* often means the observances of the law in the Jewish context (Si 51:26; Jr 2:20, 5:5; Ga 5:1). These were so surcharged by the scribes with multiple precepts that the simple and ignorant, unable to distinguish the essential from the trivial (Mt 23:4), were overloaded. Christ's followers then are not so much the afflicted generally speaking, as the simple and ignorant, who were victimized by Jewish legalism. He is affirming his opposition not alone to over-intellectualism but to over-legalism as well.

d) Yet he presents himself after the manner of the rabbis and sages who sought disciples for their schools (v. 29; cf. Si 51:31; Is 55:1; Pr 9:5; Si 24:19). He imposes a yoke too, but it is easy to carry (1 Jn 5:3-4; Jr 6:6). He is himself part of the community of poor announced by Sophonias 3:12-13, and he gathers round him the meek and humble of heart. The new master of wisdom is himself a *poor man*. He is that from the bottom of his heart, because he has freely accepted this state.

The point of the whole passage is this poverty of Christ. By contrast with the intellectualism of the sages who thought they knew everything, he turns to the ignorant, as one of their own number. He affirms that all that he knows comes not from his own resources, but is the gift of the Father (vv. 21-22). By contrast with the legalism of the rabbis, he turns to those who groan under the yoke of the law, who are made guilty because of this law, and he makes himself one of them. He is someone who has been accused of faults and sins (the context in Mt 12:1-11 makes this evident), but he has liberated himself from this sort of guilt, and recommends that other victims do so in their turn.

The originality of his attitude will be clarified by a comparison with Ben Sira. Both enjoyed a special relationship with God. But for one it was of the intellectual and sapiental order, for the other filial. God shared his secrets with one; he share his life with the other.

Both had problems with the law. Ben Sira saw it as the emanation of God's wisdom and an instrument for encounter with him. Jesus found the yoke of the law, or at least of legalism, a block to encounter with God. It led the ignorant astray, and made their relationship with God a false one.

Both were particularly concerned with the poor and the humble. Jesus however enlarged that circle to include the ignorant, and those who were victimized by a false wisdom and narrow legalism. Both were masters of wisdom. One thought his skill could cure the poor; the other joined the ranks of the poor, and presented even his relations with the Father as the acme of poverty, because of himself he was nothing and had received all.

The conclusion is that, with Jesus, poverty becomes essentially different. It used to denote a material condition, a state of ignorance, sometimes a spiritual or moral attitude. Now it is an ontological state. His poverty is that condition of exclusive relationship with the Father. It is a salvific poverty, because it does not depend on human resources.

His disciples must be people who accept renewal at the very depths of their being. This makes them open to the divine initiative. They will live in the ecclesial community of the poor. They will bear witness to the world of God's adoptive sonship and actually live this mystery in the eucharist.*

* See the doctrinal theme: *poverty*, p. 263.

VIII. Mark   During the course of a missionary journey,
6:1-6   Jesus finds himself at Nazareth, the village of
Gospel   his own family. On the Sabbath day he speaks
2nd cycle   in the synagogue, taking advantage of the
               usual regulations concerning the homily on
the second reading (Lk 4:16-30). He meets with misgiving and
rejection.

a) Mark is confronting his readers with another instance of the
people's *misgiving* where Jesus is concerned. He speaks of
"authority" (cf. Mk 1:22), not only because his presentation
differs from the traditional dialectic of the scribes, but principally
because his message will not meet acceptance unless there is attachment to his person. Not only is he a "rabbi" confronting his
disciples and pupils, he is someone anxious to establish relations
of mutual confidence (cf. "follow me" in Mk 2:14) before he
gives any teaching.

In this he is giving the role of rabbi a deeper dimension than
it had traditionally. When he requires the sort of openness and
confidence that constitute a true movement of "faith" (v. 6), he
is placing his doctrine on an unusual level.

b) What is his title for addressing his peers and compatriots?
His training could not have been furnished by his family circle
(v. 3; cf. Jn 6:42). The family itself was much too modest to
presume to any part in the accomplishment of God's plan. Indeed
it refused Jesus the sort of confidence he demanded (v. 4; cf. Jn
6:44, the reference to parentage is peculiar to Mark).

The Jews here refer to Jesus as "son of Mary" (v. 3), a phrase
which suggests illegitimacy. Matthew, particularly concerned
with demonstrating the "davidic" ancestry of Joseph, retouched
the text of Mark in order to soften the offensive suggestion (Mt
13:55). Even a premature birth, suggesting too early intercourse
between the betrothed, would be matter for comment in Nazareth. Mary must have suffered from the like (the meaning perhaps to be given Lk 2:35), and often absented herself from

Nazareth, during her pregnancy above all (Lk 1:56; Mt 2:21-22). Being the mother of the Messiah was a privilege, but it had other consequences. As Jesus had to bear the cross, Mary had to bear opprobrium.

c) To the proverb cited by Jesus in order to explain the lack of comprehension he encountered (v. 4), Mark adds a precise reference to the lack of faith among "his relations" (cf. Jn 4:44). Faith cannot be acquired by ancestry or heredity. A covert hostility on the part of the evangelists, particularly Mark, to the family of Jesus (Mk 3:20-35; Lk 11:27-28) is to be explained by the conflict in the primitive community between protagonists of *dynastic succession* from Jesus ("succession according to the flesh": James, the brother of the Lord) and those of *charismatic succession* (succession "according to the Spirit": the apostles). Whenever he makes a criticism of Jesus' family, Mark will refer immediately afterwards to the mission of the Twelve (here, Mk 6:7-13 and again Mk 3:13-19). He is contrasting two different concepts of the Kingdom.

The poverty and obscurity of Jesus' parents was a stumbling block for people who expected a resplendent Messiah (Jn 7:2-5). Jesus, on the other hand, wants to show the salvific import of this poverty. Happiness is not achieved by extraordinary phenomena that demonstrate the divine power. It is something provided by a God who takes on humanity, and the poverty which that entails.

For men, this is the only path that is not alienating. Abandoning him to his poverty would be so, or rescuing him from it in a miraculous or paternalist gesture. Poverty, with Christ, becomes a means of salvation and achieves its proper dignity.

IX. Luke 10:1-12, 17-20
Gospel
3rd cycle

Two different versions of the mission discourse have been preserved. We have the brief version in Mark 6:8-11 and Luke 9:3-5 which concerns the mission of the Twelve. The longer version, Luke 10:2-16, concerns the seventy (or seventy-two) disciples. Frequently Luke stresses the particular traditions he inherited from the disciples' circle, where Matthew and Mark keep strictly to those traditions that emanated from the Twelve. Matthew 10:5-16 takes account of the two versions and fuses them into a single one, which is further embellished by outside material. Indeed the originality of Luke's account can be best appreciated by simply comparing it with Matthew 10. Today's reading adds to verses 1-12 verses 17-20 as if to show that Christ's teaching about poverty is contradicted by the apostles' worry about prestige.

a) It was perhaps the sight of a *harvest* field that provided the occasion for the discourse (v. 2; Mt 9:37-38; Jn 4:35-38). Jesus will change harvesters of wheat into harvesters of men just as he has already done with fishermen. However the harvest theme had in Scripture an important eschatological dimension (Am 9:13-15; Ps 125/126:5-6; Jl 4:13; Jr 5:17; Mt 13:28-29; Rev 14:15-16). It also contributes a particular dimension to the disciples' mission. This becomes the involvement here and now of humanity in the Kingdom that is coming. The mission is a prelude of the judgment of God, because every divine Word has its function in judgment, in discernment of hearts. Consequently it is not surprising that the mission is destined sometimes to encounter persecution (v. 3).

Where Matthew's version gives a distinct apocalyptic flavor to this note of persecution (Mt 10:16-20), Luke prefers to confine himself to the practical counsels which Jesus gives the disciples. Buoyed up by messianic hope the object of which is close at hand, the disciple must no longer attach value to the means employed by the present world. Because the Kingdom is at hand he is dispensed from any preoccupation with terrestrial security. His poverty has a prophetic meaning (v. 4; cf. Lk 6:20).

Verse 7b however ("the laborer is worthy of his hire") gives a more sociological and institutional emphasis to the missionary's poverty, in contradistinction to the eschatological. It is because this poverty announces the advent of the Kingdom, and because Christians realize this fact, that they will give God's minister the material assistance necessary to maintain him in his calling.*

The second counsel given concerns relationship with hosts (vv. 5-9). The disciples must always be careful to preserve their role as *pilgrims,* nomads who never rest, but continually journey towards the Kingdom (1 P 2:11; He 11:8-14). They must be grateful for hospitality but unconcerned about the length of their stay or the fare proffered. Their true function lies at a deeper level, and this should be evident.

*See the doctrinal theme: *poverty,* p. 263.

B. DOCTRINE

1. The Theme of the Flesh and the Spirit

The contrast between 'flesh" and "spirit" is essential in biblical anthropology; it expresses the believer's view about the existential relationship between man and the living God. Man is a creature. He must choose between accepting his link with God or rejecting it. When he freely accepts this dependence he is "spirit" and shares in some sense the divine blessings. When he rejects it he becomes no more than "flesh," weakness and sin. Such an anthropology accepts man precisely where God has placed him, in a supernatural state. The most important item in it is the free human decision, for or against God.

The context of such a view is of course religious. The grace-sin dialectic plays a preponderant, not to say an exclusive, role. The whole ideal of human happiness, on the spiritual level as well as on the temporal, is an expression of divine benevolence. But if man dissociates himself from the will of God, he empties himself as it were, he becomes nothing, he becomes the plaything of evil forces.

Modern anthropology is altogether different. Men nowadays tend to have an independent feeling of identity, sense themselves "in existence," quite apart from any ultimate relation to the living God. It is an outlook that has profoundly influenced Christian circles too. For the most part the grace-sin dialectic will only be considered after due allowance is made for man in his own right, and for his capacity to build a human order and humanize the earth. Whether we like it or not, this is the anthropology we live with, and we must remember that, if we wish to bring the Good News to the men of our time.

Is it possible to reestablish the biblical anthropology in our cultural context? This question, a vital one for mission, deserves our attention just now. The formula for the Mass of this Sunday provides the opportunity.

The spiritual man and the carnal man in Israel

In all the ancient religious traditions it was natural for men to feel dependent where the gods were concerned. The sacral world, for which they felt themselves to be destined, eluded them. This feeling of dependence was ubiquitous. To achieve salvation it was necessary to be reconciled with the gods. This is attested by the custom, universally observed, of sacrifice. Yet, on the other hand, even though men believed that the gods meant everything, they still felt they had a role to play in achieving salvation. Without waiting for divine intervention, they would try themselves to manipulate divine energies. In this way we must explain the more or less magical procedures that we find among all peoples.

Under the regime of faith Israel recognized that his God, Yahweh, is the Totally-other. His name is "I am." He is the fount and source of everything existing, the creator of all things. Man's own existence is the result of a free decision by God to produce him from nothing. Between God and creation there stretches an unbridgeable gulf. No creature can presume to remount the ladder of being towards the Creator, not even man, for all that be he created in the image and likeness of God. Jewish man's feelings of dependence towards Yahweh tended to grow more and more intense. There could never be any question of touching God. Man's state is one of radical dependence, in his being and in his possessions. He owes everything to Yahweh, his life, his breath, his goods, his successes, his happiness, his salvation. Yahweh is the living God, always at work in his creation, active through his Spirit, his Wisdom, his Word.

However, this insight about a totally-other God did not mean that Jewish man despised or rejected himself to the point of nihilism. Yahweh saves man in purely gratuitous fashion, but he does not do so without cooperation. What he seeks is not the conformity of slaves but the response of free beings. In Yahweh's eyes man has value. He has the power to accept the divine gift or to reject it. If his reaction is positive, he fulfills his vocation and becomes a "spiritual" man rich in grace and life. But if it is negative, he is now no more than a "carnal" man, cut off from the life-giving source. He is no more than a shadow of himself, a being already dead. Perhaps it took the experience of sin to make Israel fully aware of man's grandeur. He came to realize that man becomes "spiritual" through fidelity to the divine initiative of grace.

Jesus of Nazareth and biblical anthropology
The coming of Jesus revealed the remarkable originality of biblical anthropology, and the new insights provided opened up new horizons. The full grandeur of God had never been so clearly revealed; the obedience that man owed to him was without limits. Man's grandeur too reached heights undreamed of. He did not cease to be a creature, but he was called to become a child of God, God's partner in the building of the Kingdom and of salvation-history.

Jesus did not eradicate the gulf that divided the creature from a transcendent God. On the contrary he made it more evident, and he took every opportunity of unmasking the illusions to which man, through sin, became liable. His message was based on universal love, and summoned men to absolute renunciation; the creatural condition demands obedience at all times to the will of God, and openness without reserve to his interventions. This obedience is highest when it is exercised in face of death, which is an integral part of the human condition. When death is recognized wherever it presents itself, but confronted in obedience, we have true human realism. It is when man refuses to see the pall of death which invests the whole texture of his life that he becomes the victim of illusion. If he sees only the result of sin his view of death is that of sinful man. Jesus became obedient even to the death of the Cross.

But the truth was that by this very obedience to the very end Jesus threw into blinding relief the high dignity of man and the part he was destined to play in the Father's eternal plan. His obedience was more than an expression of man's basic dependence on God. It was a gesture that marshaled every energy of which man is capable for the task of universal brotherly love. By realizing his basic dependence man would come to realize his inherent creatural dignity. And, in the case of Jesus, this creatural obedience was of course also the obedience of the Only-Begotten Son. As such it had an eternal dimension, fulfilling beyond all hopes man's highest aspiration. Once he becomes in Jesus Christ a child of the Father, the spiritual man is henceforward the Temple of the Spirit.

**The Church and
Christian anthropology**

From Pentecost onwards the primitive Church was keenly aware of being the community of the New Covenant that had been sealed in the blood of Christ. It is the Covenant of the Holy Spirit, embracing all flesh. As the prophets had foretold, the gift of the Spirit renews all hearts, filling them with filial love for the Father and brotherly love for men. Even the law takes on a new aspect. It is no longer a heavy yoke, because the man who has received the Spirit of the final times is freed from sin. He can now embark on a victorious combat against the works of the "flesh." The coming of the Spirit is connected with the resurrection. One man, because he was Son of God, has given the perfect response to the Father's antecedent initiative. This mutual encounter in love pours out the Spirit upon all who believe in the Risen Lord and become members of his Body. Such is the high vocation of man; God's adoptive sonship. If he maintains the living link with Christ that membership of the Church offers, man can become a child of God and share the blessings of the Father's family.

The indwelling, in the Christian, of the Holy Trinity, and the relationship it sets up, does not annihilate the creaturely condition. No one realizes more than the Christian the unbridgeable gulf between him and his God. Yet, paradoxically, it is this very insight which gives him a fuller realization of the dignity of human nature. The "yes" to the Father delivered by the child of God is, true, the work of the Holy Spirit. But it is also the "yes" of human freedom. Grace does not destroy nature; on the contrary it presupposes that man is using all his creaturely resources. The filial response is an active response which makes us God's partners in building the Kingdom. But it is erected upon the fidelity man shows to the mission that lies within the compass of his natural capabilities. The Spirit's action does not cancel the man in us; it raises him to the full height of creatural dignity. Any child of God knows that he must use his human resources in order to build the Kingdom. But he knows too that, when he bends all his energies to the task of creating a human order, he is in fact bringing his living stone to the building that is the Kingdom. The contribution of God's Son and that of the creature differ intrinsically, but they are indissolubly linked.

The Church's mission and modern anthropology

It is incontrovertible that the development of Western Christianity has contributed to the birth of the modern world we know. Christian belief always insisted that God's transcendent love was not a cancelation of the human, but an invitation to free human dignity. To that extent it enabled man to realize more fully what his natural resources were, and what his terrestrial destiny was. Its concept of the supernatural order enabled the highest estimates of human nature itself to flourish. The spiritual man who is a child of the Kingdom has the most positive of all attitudes toward "existence." He knows that he is called upon to build a better world. He is responsible. His fidelity to the evangelic law of love is constantly driving him to use every creatural energy in hominizing the universe. If the mutual relations between men are restored to a true balance, it will be in that context that nature can best open itself to supernature.

These developments in Christian thought however had some

serious consequences. Once man becomes aware of the extraordinary power he possesses, the temptation arises to exclude the supernatural, to appropriate to himself this universe of which he realizes he is master. Sin puts on a new visage. Far from seeking solace in divine energy, man will want to accomplish his salvation here below, by reliance on his own resources. In such a context man, modern man, will see the realization of human destiny as a task that does not transcend his capabilities. The temptation will be the temptation to atheism.

What then of evangelization? The atheist will have no difficulty in rejecting the witness of the sort of Christian who confuses the supernatural with the natural. The Christian of course must make it clear that his faith does not withdraw him from the duty of building a better world. He too must work towards the peace of tomorrow. Too often Christians have lost sight of the fact that the idea of man implied in the work of civilization is in fact closely linked with the total vision of man implied in the salvation wrought by Jesus Christ. They have tended to oppose one notion to the other instead of distinguishing them accurately. They have substituted a degraded anthropology for a deepened one.

One of the most urgent tasks confronting the Church now is the presentation of a valid anthropology. It must allow full importance to the consequences of Christ's intervention, and stress at the same time the association between the construction of the Kingdom and the construction of the terrestrial city. Such an anthropology has its roots in the New Testament, and is moreover the only one which sets the history of the Church herself in the proper light. Christians who manifest it are a sign of the salvation of Jesus Christ. It is a constant reminder that there can be no true basis for human dignity except in the evangelic wisdom of the sons of God. Face to face with atheistic humanism, such Christians will be able to discover its weakness while recognizing its nobility. The human condition does indeed carry with it heavy responsibility, but one must do more than accept this fact if a proper humanism is to prevail.

**The anthropology implied in liturgical formularies
of the Eucharist**

The Eucharist being the great focus of activity as sons of the
Father, it follows that the anthropological climate of our celebrations must be one that fits us to manifest our faith in the modern
world. Anything in language or gesture that carries the stamp of
yesterday's sacral regime should sooner or later be reshaped according to the needs of faith now. The use of vernaculars is one
step in this direction. But in the area of preaching we do need
at the moment a considerable effort. Biblical texts of course will
always remain the same. There is no question of forcing them
artificially into some new anthropological context. But that is all
the more reason for requiring those in charge of eucharistic celebrations to be exceedingly careful about commentary and homily.
It is by means of these latter that the constant actuality of the
biblical Word must be made manifest.

2. Theme of Growth in Weakness

We have no shortage of ideologies in the world nowadays. The
various power-blocs who between them control humanity take
particular views of history, and have unusual means of publicity
and propaganda at their disposal for giving "the others" their
"good news" of salvation. The measure of their power to influence
is very often the measure of their technological power. The salvation they offer the masses is the salvation of man by man. Universal peace in the future will depend upon the quality of human
effort now.

The Church, whenever she presents herself under the mantle
of power, is rejected by modern man. More seriously, her religious message meets with little sympathy nowadays, because any
reliance upon God for salvation seems merely alienating. The
Church is simply viewed as some sort of moral influence in the
struggle to achieve justice and peace for humanity.

Such a state of affairs seems to leave the Christian rather help-less. He is well aware of that. The Good News of salvation in Jesus Christ can never be reduced to a mere moral ideal of universal brotherhood. What then are we to do? Remain silent about the true gospel message and wait for better days? That we can never do. In what terms then are we to present the Word now-adays, when and how?

"With strong arm and outstretched hand"

When Yahweh intervenes to save his people, he acts with power, a blinding power so far as Israel is concerned. It is by means of this very power, exercised on behalf of his people, that the nations will come to realize who the God of Israel is.

Thus Jewish man would inevitably tend to see the gifts of God in terms of abundance, overwhelming power and numbers. The great liturgical feasts celebrated not sowing but harvest. The association of weakness with any action of Yahweh, the mighty, the valiant, the victorious, was quite unthinkable.

So strong was this mentality, the exclusion of any possibility of weakness, that it demands explanation. And that we must seek in the very nature of the Jewish regime of faith. The Jews differed from the pagans in being willing to contemplate the heavy bur-den of death and meaninglessness that weighed down human existence. Their interpretation of events made them regard Yahweh as the Totally-Other, the Master of human destiny. Death cannot be the culmination of human history. One day the savior Yahweh will lead men to a blessed land where death will be no more. In the interval what he demands from men in this land of trial is fidelity.

Thus the awaited salvation must above all include the aboli-tion of death. With very rare exceptions (as, for instance, the theme of the Suffering Servant) Jewish thinking excluded all weakness from God's salvific action. This would be giving death a victory. As yet there was no realization that man's great contribution to salvation would be the confrontation in obedience of death.

Jesus Christ victorious on the cross

The whole originality, by contrast, of the Christian view lay in the attitude towards death displayed by Jesus. The result was an altogether new concept of God's intervention in history.

The Good News of salvation now is this. At the moment when death was to all appearances victorious, Jesus actually achieved a victory, that was decisive, if paradoxical. He did not flinch from death. In order to conquer it, he encountered the death of the cross in absolute poverty and obedience, a death seemingly without point. The enemy seemed to have denuded him utterly and ravaged him.

Where then was the victory? What of human salvation? Death was not indeed abolished, because it could not be; it is part and parcel of the human predicament here below. The victory was a victory over the power of death. When confronted in obedience and self-emptying, it can no longer kindle in man pride of the spirit and passion of the flesh. Christ's victory in other words demonstrates that true life is not touched by death. This is incorruptible life, harbinger of eternity for both soul and body, something that begins here and now.

God's salvific power is seen in the humanity of Jesus, especially when in his obedience to the death of the cross he bears witness that he is doing the will of the Father. What seems to be human weakness in the encounter with divine salvation is in reality the weakness of the conqueror, not the conquered. It is at the very moment of salvation that man makes his active contribution.

The growth of the Church in weakness

This principle of weakness governs the growth of Christ's body too, the Church. She must be always dying in order to be reborn and to bear fruit.

Like any human community, she will always be open to the

temptation to rely on her own power. Whenever, in the conduct of mission, she yields to this, she becomes a community like other communities. Her missionaries are mere propagandists who reduce the true message of faith to the level of ordinary publicity. The Good News is perverted.

Fidelity to her true mission will always lead the Church to give priority to the methods of weakness; and she will do this by the actual practice of universal love. Love of this calibre is by its nature vulnerable; it will always be confronted by situations where death seems victorious. If we love our enemies, give priority to the very poorest, are ready to accept the "otherness" of people, we shall be constantly meeting death everywhere. We shall not be using subterfuges in order to turn away our eyes.

In doing all this though we must be prepared for challenge. The non-Christian world, saturated as it is with pagan thinking, is quite liable one day to reject the witness of universal love. The mass of Christian people indeed runs the risk of doing so too, to the extent that it fears the stigma of particularism or search for security. All this simply emphasizes the weakness with which we must live. Let us remember that our weakness, under faith, is something positive. It is the seed of life.

Weakness in mission

The missionary, just because he takes the work of the Lord very seriously, will be worried about the fruits of his action. It will be natural for him to rely on human knowledge; he will want to know what tendencies stand in his way, collectively and individually, and what tendencies aid his enterprise. Here, he must remember the experience of Saint Paul. Paul had the keenest awareness of urgency in his mission, but had to accept the fact that God's salvific power was most evident when his apostolic endeavor seemed weakest, above all when he had to endure the opposition of his brethren.

There is a paradox here that we should ponder carefully. The meaning is not that God will intervene with power when man is utterly helpless. The notion of weakness is positive; it is when we cooperate in absolute fidelity to our creatural condition that divine cooperation is strongest. A missionary will proclaim the good news of salvation in spirit and in truth when he eschews all the ambiguous implications of power and chooses the way of weakness. If he practices universal love he will inevitably do this.

This post-Christian era in which we live challenges all Christians collectively to choose the way of poverty. Our Western world manifests no need for the Church or its services. Under such conditions Christian witness might very well reach great heights of purity and catholicity. But not necessarily. When the Church attempts to reconcile herself with this sort of world a new danger can arise. Missionaries now will talk a good deal about "sharing" and "being invloved," and rightly so. Yet this tendency can never be allowed to develop into a mere anxiety for acceptance by the world. The moments of weakness, where universal love is best displayed, must never be avoided. True, for the most part these will be discountenanced by the world; but we must never forget that it is here God's salvific power is most active.

The proclamation of God's power in weakness

We celebrate the victory of Christ over the power of death when we share the Word and the Bread. All Christians know that the quality of their faith and the value of their witness will be measured by the intensity of their relation to Jesus Christ. If we are to be victorious as he was, in the very moment when death seemed to be victorious, we must live with his life.

There is more still. When the Church assembles the faithful for the eucharistic celebration, the principle of assembly is important. This is a principle of catholicity. The gathering should be a sign of the victory Christ has already won. Everyone present should receive full recognition for his individuality while sensing himself a member of a genuine brotherhood. In other words the ideal atmosphere in such assemblies is really one of weakness, where all realize how heavy a weight of death divides men from one another. During the celebration it will be for each one to experience again Christ's victory, when all the walls of separation were broken down. Each one will emerge conscious of the path he must follow if he is to continue that tradition.

FIFTEENTH SUNDAY

A. THE WORD

I. Isaiah
55:10-11
1st reading
1st cycle

Our reading is the short poem which serves as conclusion to the Book of Consolation of Second-Isaiah (4th century BC). Consequently we naturally expect to find some of the dominant themes of that collection.

a) Throughout all his work Second-Isaiah is the herald of Yahweh's omnipotence and his transcendence (cf. Is 40:27-31; 49:14-16). The two themes are central in this reading. God's thoughts (here, his desire to pardon) are altogether different from the thoughts of men (vv. 8-9; cf. Is 40:21-24; 50:1-3). His power is more efficacious than that of false gods and idols (vv. 10-11; cf. Is 40:12-26).

b) Second Isaiah's vigorous defense of *monotheism* (Is 41:8-14; 17-20 etc.) entailed an affirmation of the unity of world history. God, being unique, has no rival to fear in his manipulation of history. It has been willed by him in all its stages, and all stages lead to the eschatological future. Nothing can interfere with his design (here symbolized by the "Word," vv. 10-11).

Our hope then for the realization of God's plan has no greater support than faith in his unicity and transcendence.

In the preceding chapters the author had been above all concerned to show how all events, good and bad, far from being capricious acts of false gods or dualist forces, are in fact placed by God himself to advance his people. Throughout all vicissitudes, all seeming chaos and unrest, Yahweh is imperturbably carrying out his plan. Even when events seem to hinder his plan, or hinder human progress (vv. 8-9), he is at work. Thus when human sin appears too great to be pardoned, it is found that God's thought transcends the boundaries of human justice.

166

II. Amos
7:12-15
1st reading
2nd cycle

It was about 750, during the long successful reign of Jeroboam II, that Amos made his appearance in the northern kingdom. He was a Judean, a native of Tegoa south of Jerusalem. He tells us himself that he was of lowly birth (v. 14), but that does not mean he was ignorant or countrified. He prophesied at Bethel, the principal sanctuary of the north, which was somewhat opposed to the more artificial cultic centers at Samaria. The message of his oracles is invariably the same. The northern kingdom should not rest on its laurels; the glorious reign of Jeroboam was approaching its end, and then would come the disaster (Am 7:9).

a) These oracles are badly put together. Amos seems to be classed with the antiroyalists, those more or less anarchist schools of prophets who wanted the breakdown of power. It is probably to avoid embarrassment that the priest of Bethel requests Amos to leave. Bethel is a royal sanctuary. It cannot support people who criticize the royal establishment (v. 13). Amos protests. He is no part of any conspiracy, belongs to no school of prophets (v. 14). His *vocation* comes directly from God, a vocation for which he was altogether unprepared. We might be listening to Paul defending himself against the official Judaism of the Twelve. He is not a prophet by profession: on the contrary everything predisposed him for life in the fields. Some impulse more powerful than professional considerations drives him to speak.

b) The priest then takes Amos as one of those prophets who exercise a ministry for pay. The normal sanction against such a one would be deprivation of subsistance. Amos however is unconcerned about the question of *recompense*. His ministry is independent of that. He does not want pay, and the principal advantage arising from this is greater freedom in his speech.

When we consider the history of ministry of the Word, we might well wonder how far the message may have been contaminated by "pay" of one kind or another.

III. Deuteronomy This reading comes from the final section of
    30:10-14   the third and last great discourse by Moses to
    1st reading   the people (Dt 29-30). The legislator wants
    3rd cycle   his people to make a deliberate choice be-
                     tween the "two ways" of good and evil, one
leading to happiness, the other to misfortune. To add zest to the
choice, he points out that, while God because of his holiness is
demanding, his goodness is such that we can believe him very
close to his people.

The author is pointing out how God's holiness and transcendence are tempered by his *nearness*. We do not have to become
pilgrims of the unattainable and seek him at the ends of the earth
(vv. 12-13). God is close to man. He has made man in his image
and is preparing, through his Son, to dwell with man (v. 14).
The transcendence of God has become word and is human, so
that it be seen and lived by men.

Verse 14 is one of the first scriptural texts to personify the
Word of God. It becomes then the source of the "Word" doctrine
that will find expression successively in Proverbs 8:22 and Wisdom 7:22, and culminate in the theology of John's prologue and
the "word of faith" theme of Saint Paul (Rm 10:6-8). The mysterious thing about this word is that it is simultaneously in the
mouth and in the ear (v. 14), a word that must be heard, and a
word that must be professed. That is why Jesus gives a special
significance to healings of deaf-mutes (Mk 7:31-37). He is demonstrating that one is only mute because one is deaf, unable to
hear. The God of the law then is not an authoritarian God who
transmits by his word some transcendent will. He is the God of
dialogue, who desires exchange so that he can be heard and
evoke response.

The evangelic law is the greatest fulfillment of God's Word,
and does not exceed human powers. The person who is open and
listens, who receives the Word come among his own, will find

the yoke of the Word light. The interval between hearing and fulfillment, between the ear and the lips, will be exceedingly brief.

IV. Romans
8:18-23
2nd reading
1st cycle

In one of the noblest passages in his letters Paul replies to the eternal question of many Christians, "How can suffering and failure continue to affect us, who have been reconciled by baptism and are sons of God?" (Rm 6).

Christians could find very little light on the point in biblical tradition. The sages, who were limited to observation of nature and present time, either frankly affirmed that it was presumptuous to look for a clear view (Jb 38), or concluded that the universe was absurd (Qo 1:2-9). The prophets foresaw some solution. But it was connected with the eschatological future, that would succeed a catastrophe destined to put an end to actual creation and humanity (Is 51:6, 65:22-23; Ps 101/102:26-27).

The main excellence of Paul's treatment is the manner in which these trends of thought are synthesized, by insistence on man's solidarity with nature. Human hope for a new world is crucial also.

a) He begins by considering sapiental thinking and the conclusions reached. Our body belongs to the *present world* (v. 18) and is thus subject to suffering. Creation, the material world that is, with which our bodies are so closely linked, is subject to vanity (v. 20)—the term would be absurdity in our idiom. The reason for this is not human sin, as commonly alleged. The very laws of the universe (Is 40:26; 48:13; Ba 6:59-61; Si 16:26-28) impose on it endless rebeginnings and cycles (Qo 1:4-11). It is confined within limits too narrow for its energies (Jb 38:8-11; Ps 88/89:10-11; 103/104:6-9).

b) But Paul immediately passes to a more prophetic vision of the totality. As he sees it, nature feels constrained by those very laws and limits (vv. 19-21). There is a *cosmic hope** which is not empty; involvement of the human body and the cosmos in suffering and decay is tempered by this hope. Our bodies hold the secret of the hope; they already possess the earnest of future glorification (v. 23) which will extend to the cosmos (v. 21).

In this whole notion of joint hope for a new world Paul is faithful to biblical thinking (cf. Is 65:17-25; 11:6-9; 55:13). But he introduces important modifications. No longer is the paradisal state promised to the universe confined to salvation for the Jewish people, as in the Old Testament. It is linked to the revelation of our divine sonship (vv. 21-23). On the day when this becomes a reality for all humanity to the point of transfiguring their bodies, all nature too will be transfigured. So that it may be conformed to the new state of humanity, it will be delivered from the slavery of "vanity."

Paul then does not base his hope, like the Greeks, on some vague immortality for the soul as distinct from the body and the universe. Nor does he, like the gnostics, remove it to a region beyond the actual world and actual life. He defines Christian hope in terms of the here and now. The object of our hope is not on the other side, but here. If we wish to attain it we must live out life in this world. By reminding the Christian that he has already died in baptism, he has stripped away all mystique about "the other side" after death. The Christian is in a certain sense already on that "other side," and can actually feel that the more intensely his life here below is lived.

V. Ephesians **1:3-14** *2nd reading* *2nd cycle*	With this passage we begin the series of readings from the letter to the Ephesians that will continue for some Sundays. Apparently the letter was written from Rome between 61 and 63, during Paul's first captivity. Subsequent to

*See the doctrinal theme: *hope,* p. 180.

the great classical letters, the apostle had widened his horizons and deepened his thought. This letter gives us the fruit of all that. It is marked particularly by polemic against the Jews, and the syncretists of Colossae and Ephesus.

The tone is extremely meditative. Two parts can be distinguished, a liturgical (1:3 — 3:21) and a paraenetic (4:1 — 6:20). Both are characterized by contemplation of the mystery of reconciliation of Jews and Gentiles in the Church, which is Christ's Body and a sign for all humanity.

Our reading today gives us the "blessing" with which Paul opens the letter. It can be divided into the introduction (v. 3), a first strophe (vv. 4-6) which culminates in a refrain about God's glory, then a second strophe (vv. 7-12) culminating likewise in a reference to the divine glory.

Quite probably the whole piece is inspired by a daily Jewish ritual prayer where we find identical themes: divine fatherhood (v. 3), election (v. 4), phrases like "richness of grace" (v. 7), "praise of God" (the refrains in vv. 6, 12, 14), "in love" (vv. 4 and 6). The differences between the two prayers are important. Where the Jewish ritual thanks God for the gift of the law, Paul gives thanks for the gift of his Son (v. 6).

a) The introductory strophe at once defines the dominant themes not only of the prayer, but of the whole letter. Thanks are being offered for salvation (here presented as a blessing), which is willed by the Father, merited by Christ, and realized by the Spirit.

The salutary *blessings* for which God is praised are: the death (v. 7) and glorification of Jesus (Ep 1:10); the beginnings, through faith and baptism, of divine life among men (Ep 1:13); and throughout the world, thanks to the Lordship of Christ (Ep 1:10). The phrase "in the heavens" which characterizes these blessings designates everything which is neither "flesh and blood" (Ep 6:12), nor the "celestial powers" supplanted by Christ (Ep 4:7-16; 5:23). The phrase "in Christ" is meant to indicate the mediation by which the blessings of the Father are conveyed. In the order of salvation Christ has been substituted for "flesh" and "spirits."

b) The next strophe (vv. 4-6) explains how God's blessing aids man, who has been called to holiness by Christ. This blessing is the *election* made by the Father's love; it transforms men into children of God, "heirs" of the privileges that have been hitherto connected with observance of the law (Ga 3:18): it links them with the renewing presence of the Spirit (Rm 8:14-17). First among the privileges is holiness. This is the communication of God's very life (Lv 19:2) through the channel of his love, which reaches its culmination in man's adoptive sonship (v. 5).

c) In the third strophe (vv. 7-12) the advantages accruing from the work of Christ are enumerated. The first is *redemption*, where grace abounding is combined with the remission of sins (Rm 13:21-26; Col 1:14).

"Redemption" in these terms, or "remission of sins," is the possibility offered to every man of union with Christ, of transcending his limits and shortcomings, while he searches for greater depth, for something beyond the pole of banality. "To him who demands your cloak give also your tunic."

The second advantage is *knowledge* of the mystery (vv. 8b-10). It is called "intelligence," that is to say elucidation in depth and "wisdom," or again religious appreciation. The object of this knowledge is the salvific will of God towards all men (cf. Ep 3, 5, 9; Rm 16:25-26). It is a will that has remained hidden for long, but is now revealed in the person of Christ. It is in Christ that every being and every thing finds meaning. The knowledge is knowledge of God's plan: when we cleave to that plan we enter the "universal recapitulation" that Christ accomplished.

d) The *recapitulation* in Christ of all things (v. 10) is the most significant detail in this strophe. Some commentators give "recapitulation" a rather weak interpretation in this context, its purely philological sense that is of summing up (as the law is summed up in one commandment: Rm 13:9). Others believe that

Paul is investing the word with his ideas about Christ the Head and the Mystical Body (cf. Ep 1:20-23). In this view what we have is an affirmation of the "taking up" of all things in Christ, in whom they have been created, and in whom they are now reconciled, since he has been proclaimed "Lord" and "Head" of the universe (Ph 2:9-11). It is a cosmic restoration, where all creation recognizes Christ as Lord and lives by the very life of Christ. All things belong to God, and return to him through this lordship of Christ. The recapitulation is accomplished through stages. Gentiles are associated with Jews (vv. 11-13), "terrestrial" men with celestial beings. All together will enjoy the same rights and the same life.

From this notion of the solidarity of all being under one and the same head, by now another idea is beginning to take shape. No longer can some be regarded as subject to others in some sort of dependence. No longer are Gentiles inferior to Jews (Ep 2:11-12), or men subject to angels (Ep 1:20 - 2:10; cf. Ep 4:9-10).

In verses 13-14 we have the final strophe of the blessing, with particular reference to the Christians of Ephesus. The chief stages of *initiation to faith* are mentioned: evangelization (v. 13b), the salutary content of this missionary gesture, conversion, the sacramental reception of the Spirit's seal (v. 13b), and finally the presence of this Spirit, the pledge of life eternal, in the whole texture of life. The strophe is designed to reassure Paul's correspondents that they do share in every truth in the spiritual blessings that have been celebrated in the early portion of the hymn.

VI. Colossians 1:15-20
1st reading
3rd cycle

The subject of this passage is the primacy in lordship of Christ. It is presented in a hymn composed of two couplets: 1) Kingship over the created world (vv. 15-17); 2) Kingship over the re-created world (vv. 18-20). Both couplets follow a structural scheme that ensures correspondence:

v. 15	He is . . . First born of all creation	v. 18b	He is . . . First born of all the dead
v. 16	In him . . . All that is	v. 19	In him God . . . all perfection
v. 16	In the heavens and on earth	v. 20	In the heavens and on earth
v. 16	Created for him	v. 20	Created for him

a) The piece seems to paraphrase an ancient liturgical hymn (possibly a baptismal hymn). The first strophe concludes with an enumeration of the supposed lords of creation: thrones, lordships, dominations, etc.; the second with a mention of the cross, the symbol of the new lord. Both strophes are concerned not with the divine word, but the Word incarnate.

He is "first born" of all creation, not in a chronological sense, but in a causal. In creating the world God used Christ as a model (cf. Pr 8:22 on the topic of Wisdom).

He is also "first born" (chronologically this time as well as causally) in the supernatural order.

It is the preexisting Christ that is envisaged, but he is seen in his historic personality as man-God.

The *primacy of Christ* is expressed in three images: first born, head of the body, and plenitude. These are important notions in the theology of Paul. As he sees it, Christ's resurrection places his human nature at the head and front of regenerated humanity and of creation itself (Rm 8:19-22; 1 Co 3:22; 15:20-28; Ep 1:10; 4:10, etc.).

b) The passage should be taken not so much as a precise doctrinal statement. It is rather a passionate and existential *profession of faith* delivered with the gnostics in mind. The one

essential is the primacy of Christ; all else is fantasy. Gnostic discussions about the existence of a creator God are futile; Christ
does all. Even Adam is stripped of his title as first man in favor
of Christ. Equally futile are discussions about the existence of
angelic beings; Christ is, and that suffices. Paul is actually using
gnostic vocabulary to combat gnosis: there is no question of
indiscriminate importation of gnostic ideas into Christian doctrine.

Two principles then are of importance in the hymn. The Risen
Lord is head of the faithful who wish to follow him by sharing
the life of the Church. But the resurrection also firmly establishes him in absolute preeminence over natural creation. His
preeminence arises not only from the fact that he is creator, but
also, and chiefly, from the fact that he is Lord, because of the
resurrection. According to Pauline cosmogony angelic powers
and dominations had usurped a power over creation that Christ
was able to recover through his resurrection.

The danger might arise of regarding Jesus' lordship in the
same way as that of the angelic powers, a dominance which
would deprive man of free choice in his destiny. This is not so.
Alone among Lordships, that of Christ means no alienation for
humanity or for creation. It was something accomplished in the
context of a human life. It is exercised in the context of human
toil, that "recapitulates" creation and gradually spiritualizes it.
The relationship to nature is essential to it, and the dominance
by Christ over all things.

Christ then is Lord of a creation that finds its harmony in a
restored humanity. If the basis of his Lordship be the mystery of
his resurrection, that is because resurrection provides the ultimate
reconciliation between body and soul, matter and spirit, earth
and heaven. The eucharistic celebration which follows a reading
such as this should seem the victory here and now of spirit over
matter and "flesh."*

---

*See the doctrinal theme: *lordship,* Eastertime volume, p. 90.

VII. Matthew
13:1-23
Gospel
1st cycle

Three problems are posed by the parable of the sower: First, the original meaning of the piece as spoken by Jesus (vv. 1-9): second, the emphasis given by Matthew in inserting it at this point in his gospel: third, the significance of the interpretation given by the primitive Church (vv. 18-23).

a) Between a mention of sowing (v. 3) and harvesting (v. 8), we have four successive scenes in the actual parable, and the main point is the fate of the seed in each of the four terrains. The general tone is optimistic, culminating in the extraordinary yield from the *seed*.

The harvest theme, as an image of the final times was traditional in Israel (Jl 4:13). The new emphasis here is the insistence on the toil of the sowing. So that Jesus is actually modifying slightly the eschatological aspect of the coming Kingdom (harvest) by turning attention to the rigors of realization. He does proclaim the coming of the Kingdom, but is quite insistent about the slowness of fulfillment and the arduous process of growth.

b) Matthew's particular context gives the parable a christological interpretation. We have Jesus reflecting about the failures and obstacles of various kinds that beset his mission: the scribes' blindness, the superficial enthusiasm of the crowds, his relatives' misgivings, etc. He seeks to give meaning to this incomprehension, and finds it in the contrast between the partially fruitless toil of the sower, and the very rich harvest after all. His troubled *mission* is analyzed in the light of the judgment that is coming. The judgment is implicitly delivered in the understanding his disciples seem to display (vv. 10-17). This compensates for the indifference of the others.

The primitive communities came to develop their own interpretation. The main point for them was no longer the mission of Jesus, but the motives for conversion. They did not fear the final harvest, but rather the daily difficulties arising from persecution (v. 21).

Subsequently came an allegorizing trend. Each scene of the parable was seen as a description of a *type* of conversion. The sowing did not matter very much, but the manner in which the seed was received. Even the eschatological significance became obliterated in favor of largely psychological and paraenetic considerations (v. 24). Where Jesus was optimistic about his mission, the primitive Church seemed tense and worried.

VIII. Mark 6:7-13 There is no need to recapitulate here the
Gospel exegesis of the important mission discourse,
2nd cycle which has been already given for Matthew
9:35 - 10:8 (11th Sunday) and Luke 10:1-11
(14th Sunday). It is sufficient to note that Mark gives us the shorter version (parallel to Luke 9:3-5).

IX. Luke 10:25-37 There are three distinct portions in this pas-
Gospel sage. 1) An affirmation of the happenings of the
3rd cycle apostles who see and hear what the kings and
prophets wished to see and hear, and who
assist at the realization of God's plan. 2) A discussion concerning the greatest commandment which Luke inserts in this context, but which seems to have taken place after Jesus' entry to Jerusalem (Mt 22:33-40). 3) The parable of the good Samaritan, peculiar to Luke.

The second portion breaks the unity of the narrative. Actually to the question "*Who* is my neighbor?" Jesus replies with a parable concerning *how* one should love another. There is no continuity. Doubtless Luke inserted the discussion about the greatest commandment at this point so that the parable of the good Samaritan would provide the moral conclusion. If we consider the parable apart from the discussion everything becomes clear. It is a parable of the Kingdom in the same way as that of the good Shepherd, or those about sowing.

a) Indeed there are some concrete phrases in the parable which preclude a purely moral interpretation. In verse 33 the Samaritan is "moved to compassion." The Greek word is used to indicate the compassion of God only, or Jesus (Mt 9:36; 14:14; Lk 7:13; 15:20). So what the Samaritan feels is a divine sentiment. He is an image of God, the revelation of *God's love* for man. Another detail is equally revealing. Verse 35 mentions the "return" (*Epanerchesthai*) of the Samaritan. If the purpose of the parable be merely moral or edifying, this is meaningless. Surely what is contemplated is Christ's return at the end of time. This view is reinforced by the fact that the word is found in the New Testament in one other instance only, and that it has precisely this significance (Lk 14:21).

Indeed the parable is curiously similar in structure to those of the Good Shepherd and the master of the vineyard (Jn 10; Lk 20:9-18). The Good Shepherd comes to save the sheep who have been maimed and left to die (Jn 10:10). The son of the master appears on the scene after the prophets have come in vain. So, after the priests and levites who neither would nor could save the wounded man, comes the good Samaritan. He reveals God's love for man. He tends man with the sacraments of oil and wine and places him in an inn which is the Church. In this interpretation the introductory portion of our passage is clarified too. The apostles are blessed because they at last witness the manifestation of the love of God, because they are destined to be more efficacious harbingers of it than the Jewish priests and levites.

b) The parable should be regarded too of course, like the other great parables of the Kingdom, as a reflection on *salvation history*. Christ comes in the guise of a Samaritan, a despised person that is to say (Jn 8:48), to reveal God's love, just like the master's son; because all Gentile and Jewish efforts at salvation have failed. Conceivably, 2 Chronicles 28:15 may have inspired Jesus' parable. In that text we have the Samaritans showing a similar charity towards the Jews. We have mention of Jericho, a refuge for those who have survived a massacre, provision of mounts for those who are disabled, the provision of "shelter."

c) The reason for prefacing the parable with the discussion about the greatest commandment may have been the wish to indicate that, since Christ, *charity* has become demanding in a new way. It is no longer sufficient to love one's neighbor as oneself. We must ask ourselves how we can be close to our neighbor and love him as God loves him. This is the import of the new commandment in the discourse after the Supper. We must love the other as we have been loved (Jn 13:34). We must be aware that he belongs to a humanity that is wounded, left half dead by the roadside, that Christ has come to save. Charity now is more than just a moral obligation. It is the reflection of God's own love. It is a sign of the last times where the Jewish means of salvation have been replaced by divine mercy. By his deliberate interference with the context, replacing the discussion here, Luke is furthering the doctrine of charity (note the contrast between his account and Mt 22:34-40; Mk 12:28-31) and preparing the way for John's concept.

B. DOCTRINE

1. The Theme of Hope

The strongest objection of modern man to Christian teaching is that it is alienating. By recommending man to place all his hope in God, we are, it is alleged, turning him from human responsibility towards this earth. We are destroying in him human hope.

The accusation is a grave one. Is it, we may ask, brought about by essential Christian teaching, or merely by the short-comings in the application of this by us Christians, as we stand on the threshold of a new world? We should have to admit that some religious attitudes do really indicate evasion of worldly responsibilities and human tasks. But are these integral to Christian faith? Do they not rather spring from a distortion of it?

It is of the highest importance that the answers we provide to these questions be in full conformity with Christian truth. If we assert that the teaching criticized by modern man as alienating is really a truncated Christianity, we must be ready to indulge in self-criticism and to make corresponding adjustments in attitude. Otherwise the faith would be jeopardized, and, worst of all, questions would arise about the evangelization of the world.

The whole matter then of our reflection on this Sunday will be "Christian hope and human hope." Our purpose will be a better understanding of modern criticisms and a deeper insight into our responsibilities in the world of today.

Israel's attitude to earthly goods

The Jews were too realistic to be indifferent towards earthly prosperity. While fully aware that this life is for the most part a vale of tears, they fixed their gaze on an abundant future. On a new earth, temporal prosperity would be man's destiny, side by side with knowledge of God, conversion of hearts, conversion of the nations, and a perfect cult. Jewish hope, true, was concentrated on Yahweh and his universal reign. But this did not lead the believer to turn his eyes from the actual world. Rather, he awaited its renewal, when the obstacles to temporal prosperity would be removed.

Did this attitude to material prosperity imply a genuine human hope, in the modern sense? Was there some idea of rebuilding a better world by the fullest use of human resources? The answer to these questions has to be qualified. In the Jewish view, temporal prosperity was above all a divine blessing, bestowed gratuitously. Yet it was at the same time the normal product of human toil. Furthermore, their dream of dominating all nations could only come through an all powerful intervention by Yahweh. Yet they were by no means averse to the use of human means towards that end.

Experience however had shown them that temporal prosperity was impossible in any real sense in a world dominated by suffering and death. An earth that bore the mark of sin was inevitably maimed. So, the salvific intervention by God had to be awaited. It would free man from sin, bring to birth a new earth, a terrestrial paradise more marvelous than the first.

To this extent there was no element of evasion in Jewish hope. It bore no resemblance to Greek ideas about the ascent to God of an immortal soul, once the yoke of the corruptible body had been shaken off. On the other hand, it was not the sort of hope that implied genuine human hope, or inspired it, in the modern sense. For that we must wait for Jesus of Nazareth.

Jesus of Nazareth and the true visage of hope

Jesus proclaimed, as Messiah, that the Kingdom of God had come. Contrary to Jewish expectation it had come without fanfare; nothing on the face of the earth had changed. All seemed to go on in the old way. This Kingdom that was not of this world began imperceptibly, like the tiniest of seeds. Gradually, it would grow. When the shoot had grown to proper height, the end would come. Jesus would return the Kingdom to his Father.

All this was a profound challenge to Jewish hope. Everything was so contrary to expectation: a Kingdom that did not mean any change in the universe, that was insignificant, that did not affect in any way Israel's status *vis-a-vis* the nations. Up to the moment of the ascension Jesus' own disciples were so uncomprehending that they could ask the question "Lord, will you at this time restore the kingdom to Israel" (Ac 1:6).

To understand Jesus' viewpoint one had in fact to begin by taking a new look at the terrestrial condition, one that differed considerably from the customary Jewish view. Our earth, where man is constantly confronted by suffering and death, is not the result of sin. Jesus, who is sinless, has confronted both, like every other man. The real result of sin is the meaning given to suffering and death by sinful man. They appear to the eyes of pride to be insurmountable obstacles. But by confronting them in obedience to the creatural condition, with the renunciation of self that this implies, Jesus reveals the true meaning. Death in particular becomes the point of greatest self-giving. Here the double love, for God, and for all men, shows itself most unmistakably.

And now we see the real nature of hope in God. Its object goes beyond any terrestrial vision. The Kingdom that Jesus inaugurated is not of this world; it is the Family of God's children. The happiness it brings can never be coterminous with mere material well-being. The avenue of approach to it, for humanity and for creation, is through death, after the example of Jesus and in association with him. Yet the Kingdom in another sense *is* here below; it is rooted in the man-God. It must gradually grow by means of human cooperation. The cooperators will follow Christ along the road of his obedience; they too will manifest the double love, for God and for all men. Genuine human hope can be rooted in a proper soil.

The Church and hope: the dynamism of history

It is instinctive to consider the lesson of Church history. In the primitive community the old eschatological hope, the expectation of a Kingdom that would descend ready-made from above, yields to intense missionary activity. The role of Saint Paul was crucial. In Jesus Christ the promises had been fulfilled; the hoped-for glory was here and now realized. What remained was to fill up "that which was wanting" in the Passion of Christ. All men were called upon to work as Christ's partners in building the Kingdom.

Then it grew apparent that universal mission, which Paul had originally thought to be a task within his competence, was something of very great complexity. It was always urgent, but could only go forward very slowly, and called for infinite patience. Being as it was an approval to man in his search for salvation, it called for reestimates of the whole tenor of secular history. It was an expression of universal brotherly love, claiming a dynamism capable of renewing the face of the earth. Simultaneously with the summons to enter the family of the Father, it appealed to man to muster all his creatural resources. Freed from sin, humanity would become aware of earthly responsibilities. The love which builds the heavenly Kingdom becomes on earth a dynamism capable of making the world new, more human, ever more in harmony with gospel principles. Mission, in belief, by affirming man's divine destiny, clarifies his terrestrial destiny.

This ecclesial awareness of the terrestrial implications, in terms of human progress, of Christian hope, did not come about overnight. It took time, a great deal of time, before people realized all that belief in Jesus Christ involved. Many Christian generations had to live this faith and discover, by experience, where it pointed.

Proclaiming Christ now, and sharing human hope

Given the truth of what we have just said, how is it that the aspirations of the modern world get a cool reception from Christians, particularly Catholics? How did the accusation of religious alienation come about? How was it possible for the 19th century Christians to preach resignation to the workers of the industrial revolution, though they were manifestly victims of exploitation?

The reasons were various. The Church inherited that interpretation of Christianity which regarded human beings as people who needed to be sheltered. It suspected modern man of resuscitating the Promethean dream. The campaign for a perfectly legitimate autonomy seemed to mask, in the guise of a power over nature that science, and soon technology, were to provide, a challenge to God. It is undeniable too that Christians, and even people estranged from the Church, tended to regard Christianity as the best sort of bulwark for an established order, that had developed in a Christian social *milieu*. In countries where Christianity was the religion of all the people, the intensity with which it was lived varied of course among various groups. One can detect elements of paganism, or at least of Judaism, in Christian ethos that merited the criticism of religious alienation.

The proclamation of Christ in the modern world, we are coming more and more to realize, requires the purging of these elements, a heritage from the past that never ceases to constitute a threat unless we are careful. In fact we can be much assisted in that task by the very keen modern consciousness about power over nature. It is this very power which gives human hope its most vigorous *elan*. In any case, when we examine it closely, there is no reason why it should necessarily mean a Promethean temptation. The more we understand about human hope the more clearly we should see the divine hope in which it is rooted. Both are radically distinct, but at the same time closely articulated. The essential love of man is a single entity. His divine hope and his human hope are neither juxtaposed, nor superimposed one on the other. They are just two different dimensions, both necessary, of human activity that is conformed to the divine plan.

The eucharistic celebration: a blending of the two hopes

We have reiterated over and over again that the eucharistic celebration is quite pivotal in salvation history. This is the moment, above any other, when divine hope takes concrete shape. It is the memorial of Christ's cross, "until he comes," and provides the best basis that is for hope. Hope of course is concerned with the building of the Kingdom, and this Kingdom, though it is not of this world, has to be built in this world where believers are called upon to follow the footsteps of Christ in his Passion. The Kingdom awaited in the eucharistic celebration is the Kingdom we must build, in imitation of Christ. Our hope is firm because it is based on the victory won by Jesus once for all when he died on the Cross. If ever the Eucharist is taken as an excuse for evasion, as merely an exercise in spirituality, that would be a complete deformation. Essentially, it is something that summons the faithful to action; it is indeed the most serious action that a man can perform.

Because it reveals the true visage of hope, the Eucharist will always be the best focus of reconciliation between theological and human hope. It summons man to build the Kingdom; it liberates him from sin, and points the way for the most lucid deployment of natural human resources. It invites us all to construct a human city that will bear the fullest possible witness to daily victory over death. This will be the city worthy of human kind, where love will be constantly reversing the tide of divisiveness and hate.

2. The True Meaning of History

Christians of our time who share the legitimate aspirations of modern man are frequently disconcerted by what seem to be the limited horizons of Christianity, the Christianity they know at least. They are almost ashamed of being believers. Whether or not they manage to adapt themselves, they feel a sort of cleavage in their lives between the sacred and the profane. If they be loyal to religious practices it is because theoretically they realize the importance of this, but their main interest is in profane activities. These constitute the really serious element in their lives. This sort of divorce between the sacred and profane is evidently detrimental in both fields.

To confine ourselves to one area only. Modern man differs from his ancestors in believing that he is the first to have a proper estimate of history. He rejects any notion of recurring cycles, and uses the formidable power over natural resources that he possesses to transform and hominize the earth. He does not see history as ready-made, something that has to be endured and accepted for better or worse. Rather is it a task to be accomplished, a chronicle of gradual triumph over the obstacles that stand in the way of earthly happiness for man. Modern Christians share this view of history. Unfortunately they seldom pause to wonder about the connection this might have with salvation history itself.

Being believers, we must raise a fundamental question. Is the modern estimate of history a valid one? What exactly is this estimate? Is it just another human attempt to cancel history, this time by making man master of developments instead of having man evade them? It becomes more than ever imperative for the Christian to deepen his faith and seek there the sort of view of history that he should nowadays put forward. If it is true that Jesus Christ clarified the humane dimension of history in its essentials, ignorance of that on our part would be unpardonable.

The Jewish view of history

Throughout that period of history that can be described as prescientific, man's natural reaction to the march of events was one of evasion. He was looking for salvation, because man needs security. Insofar as events denied him that, unpredictable as they are, he would refuse to recognize them, simply cancel them. What then remained? He would try to evade the profane world of actuality, and touch the only world that could fulfill his aspirations, the sacred. In his experience this was represented by all that seemed solid, stable, cyclic. To avoid the absurdity of existence, he had to feel himself involved in the activity of the Gods, something that transcended suffering and death, and the vicissitudes of history.

Jewish man was different. Taught by the prophets, he met the event face to face. Very often he had to recoil, because he suddenly felt deprived of the security he once knew. The salvation he envisaged could only come from the initiative of a Totally-Other God, and fidelity to this God was the only security he could depend on. Confronting events with a mentality like this, he began more and more to develop interiorization. He began to discover the mystery of human liberty. Man does not realize his destiny by possession, but by openness and giving. Gradually he began to learn from the event that the *conditio sine qua non* of fidelity to his state is poverty. If God intervened in the event it was in order that man might be stripped of all illusion.

Thus, while arriving at a proper estimate of the event, Israel, in the course of her arduous pilgrimage, did not succeed in making the next step, the proper estimate of history itself. The truth is that one dimension of the event always remained for her an insurmountable obstacle. That is, death. Sinful man indeed could not have any other view, because acceptance of death as an integral element in the human condition means, deep down, a rejection of sin. It is easy then to understand how Jewish hope was turned to a new heaven and a new earth, the work exclusively of divine intervention, on the day of Yahweh. History however was destined for cancelation once again.

A definitive estimate, in Jesus Christ, of history

The whole of Jewish eschatology was changed by the intervention of Jesus of Nazareth. He inaugurated the Kingdom, but did not bring about any transformation in man's earthly condition. His Kingdom was just the planting of a seed, the smallest of seeds, though it was destined to grow until all humanity would be involved. He laid the first stone, the cornerstone on which the whole edifice would rest. All other men are called to co-operate with him in the building.

What happened was that Jesus pushed to the limit the realistic confrontation of the event. Sinless as he was, he realized the true meaning of this death, with which the event is always burdened. If it be confronted in obedience, human liberty is then restored to its highest level, because a man is led to absolute openness, and to awareness that his liberty requires an outside source to fulfill itself. Death is the moment for the greatest poverty, the most total renunciation of self. When Jesus encountered death he saved man, because he was man-God. His act of creatural poverty was also the response of the Son to the Father's antecedent initiative. This is the wonder of human salva-tion. Grace makes human liberty capable of blending with the divine initiative while still remaining creatural. With Jesus, history finally gets its full and proper evaluation. It is shown that, in the very act of living the event in obedience, the King-dom of God is gradually being constructed. The real history of man is a salvation history and its great architect is Jesus, the final ages, that were so eagerly awaited by Israel, open up the ultimate pages of that history.

It is a history that must always be worked out under the aegis of love. The death of the Cross, encountered in obedience, shows death to be the focus of the greatest love. It is filial love of the Father, a sharing in the very life of God, which builds the Temple of universal brotherhood in the unity of the Holy Spirit. It is love of human beings, which musters every human energy for the task of accepting, with full recognition of their otherness, one's fellow men.

The Church of the last days and salvation history

The apostolic community was fully aware of its role in in-augurating the "last times," that had come about in such unforeseeable fashion. Yet it was only gradually that the primitive Church came to realize the full extent of the change that had been wrought in Jewish eschatology. One urgent task confronted Christians before the end: mission to the very ends of the earth. The time of the Church properly speaking is the salvation history of the last times. Jesus Christ is the architect of this. The value he gave the event, by his confrontation with death, becomes now the task of the members of his Body. In baptism they all receive the power to provide a particular stone in the building of the Kingdom.

The motive force in the salvation history is of course charity. It was so for Jesus; it is so for us. All salvation history is a true history of love, but it found in Jesus its greatest perfection. The parable of the Good Samaritan (Gospel, 3rd cycle) teaches us the sort of behavior that should characterize this final stage of human history. The Samaritan places the essential value where it ought to be. He is absolutely open to the experience of God to be found in his brother, wounded by the roadside. Nothing is allowed to impede this encounter, not even the fact that the man is a Jew, a natural enemy. True love does not accept persons; it goes the full length in self-giving.

Under the influence of this sort of love the Church today could develop a new dynamism for her mission to the modern world. Salvation history, once we understand it properly, the history of the children of God, will clarify the true meaning of what we call, for want of a better term, profane history. Man's creatural destiny is really integral to his salvation. The exercise of filial love, as children of God, will lead us to muster all the energies we have for the enterprise of civilization. This is the task in which human liberty will find its most authentic expression.

Missionary witness and the meaning of history in the modern world

When modern man maintains that he has the meaning of history, what does he mean? He is asserting that the increasing mastery he possesses over the material universe, thanks to science and technology, gives him the power to transform it to his standards. He differs from his predecessor in not seeking to evade this universe. On the contrary he confronts the unpredictable event with confidence that he can master the unpredictability, and control it as he wishes. In every age man has had to meet challenges from nature. But modern man feels himself capable of taking the measure of these, and disposing of them. We do not yet have the order that will provide man with the happiness he seeks. We have to establish it.

The truth is that, far from being a true estimate of history, this modern attitude, in a new sort of way, denudes history of its true humane dimension. True, man is transforming the earth and making it, in a sense, more habitable. Yet despite the growth of security in every domain, somehow human liberty fails to find adequate terrain for expression. In a cultural environment where the event loses the dimension of unpredictability, nothing seems to happen that engages fully the free man. Freedom somehow loses the key to its own mystery, and withers away. If the peace that we have to work towards becomes merely a matter of political, social and economic structures, it ceases to be the peace of free beings, who accept the otherness of fellow men. It becomes bewilderment. Pride remains; and nations continue to oppose one another.

In a world that runs the risk of becoming a concentration camp, we Christians carry a grave responsibility. The tasks of modern man are ours too, but we must approach them with a lucid appraisal of both event and history. Where securities are multiplied, instead of denuding the event of its unpredictability, man could be brought to a valid estimate of this unpredictability. It will be our business as Christians to bear witness that human liberty, if it be not altogether blended, must continually encounter death. It must face the impossibility of realizing its aspirations alone. Only under such circumstances will true encounter with others become possible, and true human progress. Then and then only will there be a valid estimate of human history. It will be the arena, not of some predictable project, but of high spiritual adventure. The adventure that is of free men, who are prepared to accept fellow men, in all their otherness, as brothers.

The eucharistic celebration and the meaning of history

Someone has said that every Mass is a major event in salvation history. That is true, but not in an absolute sense, especially when we consider those assisting at the Mass. As the act *par excellence* of Christ it continues to accomplish the Father's will, and to associate others with him in building the Kingdom. Insofar as he is the principal agent, the eucharistic celebration will give full meaning to human history; it is a reenactment of the Cross-event. However the role of the faithful in the celebration is no less essential. They are required in turn to take up the work of the cross. The extent to which they do this will determine how effectively the celebration becomes an event in this history.

The importance of the liturgy of the Word in this context cannot be over-stressed. Its whole purpose, and this includes the homily, is to influence ever more deeply the hearts of the faithful towards imitation of the obedience and love of Christ. The Word in this sense is always a challenge to conversion. It detaches us from illusory securities, and makes us ready to see the living God in the daily event.

SIXTEENTH SUNDAY

A. THE WORD

I. Wisdom
12:13, 16-19
1st reading
1st cycle

At the time this text was put together the Jewish nation had achieved a certain autonomy, but it continued to be distrusted among the other nations. Most Jews moreover were dispersed among the Gentiles, and found themselves in a situation not unlike that of their ancestors in Egypt, or the descendants of the Canaanite patriarchs. Stringent laws against defilement sheltered them from the surrounding promiscuity, but nevertheless they felt continually disturbed. How could God tolerate such things; why did not his thunderbolts fall at once on the impure and the idolatrous? It is an eternal question which the apostles would in their turn pose to their Master. He replied with the parable about the wheat and the tares.

The reply of the Wisdom author is indeed a foreshadowing of that of Jesus. God's power is very actual, but instead of using it for destruction, he masks it with tolerance and *moderation* (vv. 16-18).

There are two reasons for this moderation. First, the respite allowed by God gives man the opportunity to overcome his egoism and be converted. Second, Jewish people are required to become more humane (v. 19). They must learn to live not only in the inbred atmosphere of the ghetto, but among their fellow men with mutual respect and tolerance.

In reading this Wisdom passage one tends naturally to reflect on the lessons provided by the Second Vatican Council. Doors of Christian tolerance were opened to all men, of whatever religion, even of no religion. Tolerance of this kind does not necessarily have to seek justification in the providence or moderation of God.

A belief in the dignity of the human person, and in the traces of God's image to be found in human liberty, is sufficient basis.

The whole notion of tolerance is bound up with the meaning of the Church in the world. Judaism, even the Judaism of the Diaspora, was generally recessionist and suspicious. So often the Church has tended to be the same. Is there not something in her very nature that ought to preclude such isolationism?

It is through her that Christ must be re-presented to humanity. This is accomplished through Christian attitudes toward one another and toward their fellow men. She is also the focus of human progress, to be gradually accomplished in Jesus Christ. She can never afford to be distant from the world, in that it is through her that Christ enters into solidarity with the world and represents it before God.

She can never thus become a ghetto, or a Noah's ark, from which to issue proclamations of destruction. Nor can she become a cenacle of refuge, where ancient glories like the Christ-event are remembered, and the sacramental instruments of grace stored. She is the center, as yet partial and hidden, of union for all men in Jesus Christ. This is the reason why she imposes tolerance on her members, and absolute solidarity with all humanity.

II. Jeremiah 23:1-6
1st reading
2nd cycle

Nabuchadnezzar has just administered a severe rebuke to the kingdom of Judah for too flagrant friendship with Egypt. The davidic king had been removed, and an insignificant creature of the Babylonian king, Sedecias, was reigning in Judah.

The majority of professional prophets, true to the tradition of court clergy, and royal counselors were calling for a resurgence of nationalism, the renewal of alliance with Egypt, and revenge for the actions of Nabuchadnezzar.

Jeremiah's pessimistic temperament enables him to see the hollowness of this nationalism. A realistic estimate of the international situation and of Judah's current resources counseled moderation. The kingdom no longer had the power to justify grandiose pretensions. It would be better to acquiesce in the tutelage of Nabuchadnezzar, which was not for that matter so insupportable.

He reminds the royal counselors where their nationalist policy had led. The northern kingdom had been entirely dispersed, and in the south the *elite* had followed the king into exile (vv. 1-2). Despite their pretensions to the title, they had not proved themselves true *shepherds.**

Jeremiah however is no defeatist. His Yahwist faith leads him to the affirmation that the false shepherds will be replaced by Yahweh himself. By means of competent leaders from the davidic dynasty (vv. 3-5) he will shepherd the people. Here Jeremiah shows himself a follower of the royalist loyalties of Isaiah.

The "nationalism" of the false shepherds of Judah never quite dies. It manifests itself again and again in Church history and in all history. Outmoded institutions will fail to diagnose in time the exigencies of particular situations and make the necessary adjustments. There will be a tendency to live in the past, where people really ought to be witnessing for the present and the future. Such enclaves stand in need of prophets who have a lucid vision of the actual situation, and can indicate the task for which God is seeking cooperators.

III. Genesis 18:1-10
1st reading
3rd cycle

In pagan circles there have been numerous legends which tell of gods and goddesses walking on earth. They would be received by privileged human beings. According to the measure of hospitality blessings would be multiplied. Legends like this were probably altogether too naive for acceptance by the Yahwist cult. In most cases they were connected

---

*See the doctrinal theme: *pastorate*, Eastertime volume, p. 127.

with the origins of some holy place (in this instance Mambre).
Nine or ten centuries before Christ, the most Hebrew religion
could accomplish was the adaptation of such stories to strict
monotheism. Thus the legend of three gods being received at the
oak tree of Mambre by a human being becomes the visit of God
himself, accompanied by two angels.

The final chronicler however in this instance had great difficulty in giving the old story a monotheist coloring. In verse 18
we have Yahweh, but in verse 2 three men. In verse 3 someone
called "Lord," in verses 4-9 several people. In verse 10 a "quest,"
in verses 13-14 Yahweh. In verse 15 a person, in verse 16 "men."
In verses 17-21 Yahweh . . . and so on, to the end of chapter 19.

Clearly, the whole story has several tangled sources, which
only the greatest ingenuity could sort out. Indeed it is possible to
distinguish there some distinct themes. Chapter 18 has two parts.
The first tells of the foundation of a sanctuary where there had
been a theophany (vv. 1-8). The meal under the tree offered to
several people is important. Then we have an "annunciation" of
Isaac (vv. 9-15). There is only one person invited. There is no
question of a sacred tree, and the dominant theme is etymological
(concerning "laughter").

a) Abraham is a signal example of *monotheistic faith*. He sees
three people, but, in the final redaction anyhow, he knows that
there is only one God among them (v. 3). The legend, originally
pagan, is part of inspired scripture and of revelation not so much
because of its content, but because of anxiety on the part of
Yahwists to supplant polytheistic views of the universe by unitar-
ian. The world is not the plaything of gods or chaotic forces. One
single will directs it; all events lead towards a single end.

Abraham becomes host to the one and only God. As a consequence he comes to know God's view about history and is concerned with the fulfillment of this. He is destined to provide the
world with the first fruit of the promise (vv. 9-10).

b) It is rare for the Bible to depict Yahweh in an atmosphere of such great *familiarity* with men. God was never seated with man eating his meats (vv. 4-8), not even in paradise. Doubtless the impact of pagan legends was required to introduce into a book preoccupied with transcendence above all such a familiar image of God. The Bible accepted and absorbed this. God is not far from man (v. 3). Perhaps his real transcendence consists in being near to man.

c) To the theme of God's familiarity that of Abraham's *hospitality* is closely related. If one is to enter into the mystery, one must kill the fabled calf for the stranger. To "receive" a guest, one must be ready to "give"* everything.

God's familiarity with man, who becomes host and welcomer, prefigures the incarnation. God is the architect of history, but it is with man that he moulds history. Our account today is anthropomorphic, but it is a forerunner of the man-God's incarnation, and, at a further remove, of the Trinity doctrine itself.

All men, like Abraham, are simply asked to welcome God. Welcome will gradually reveal the personality of the guest. Abraham was the first to have the experience of receiving the one and only God in the whole mystery of his personality.

So it is with those who have faith in the Lord Jesus. They have confidence in his person and his message; they accept at the first encounter all that Christ will reveal of his union with the Father and the Spirit.

IV. Romans 8:26-27
2nd reading
1st cycle

Chapter 8 of Romans has received particular attention in the new lectionary; it is put forward in the readings of several Sundays. To the Jewish or pagan concept of a law or rite that gives security, something that he designates as "flesh" (Rm 8:1-10), because man in these circumstances has recourse to overly human means, Paul opposes the Christian

---

*See the doctrinal theme: *hospitality*, p. 210.

notion of life in the Spirit. It is something brought about by divine intervention, but it comes to fruition and accomplishment in human activity (Rm 8:11-17). The things that militate against life in the Spirit are numerous, suffering and death above all (Rm 8:18-23). Yet, for Saint Paul, there can be no doubt that victory over death has been definitively achieved by man and by creation.

At this juncture the apostle is dealing with another difficulty. If the believer has the Spirit of God in him, why does he encounter such difficulty in prayer (vv. 26-27)?

To physical suffering then is added the spiritual suffering experienced above all in the domain of *prayer*. Some pharisaic spirits sought solace for this in a flood of language (Mt 6:7; Lk 18:10-12). The believer in Christ consoled himself with the certainty that the Spirit dwelling in him guaranteed his spiritual life.

The issue does not concern knowing how to pray; having subjects for prayer is sufficient for this. Nor does it concern knowing how to speak, a quite common accomplishment. What is important is praying "as we ought" (v. 26). Only the Spirit can bring this about, because only the Spirit knows God's plan (v. 27). The most authentic prayer then will spring from the petitioner's deep disturbance, combined with certainty about the Spirit's role. The essential role is that of intercessor (v. 27) and interior mover, enabling a man to realize his greatest potential, his full status as child and heir of God.

Agony in prayer is a normal characteristic of the interval between our justification in baptism and its full realization in the glory of God. Spiritual life now is no longer just the product of human effort, but the progressive expansion in us of the life of the Spirit (v. 26). This expansion becomes perceptible, when we deepen the roots of our faith, and try to purify the words that spring to our lips in the light of God's plan.

Paul's insertion of this piece about prayer in the context of a larger reflection concerning the meaning of the universe is not without deliberation. It indicates that prayer cannot be considered some sort of escape to God, but rather joint recognition by God and man of involvement with the universe. It is a supremely realist act, of which only the mature Christian will be capable. He will be God's partner, toiling and struggling with him in a universe that is sometimes malleable, sometimes recalcitrant.

V. Ephesians **2:13-18** *2nd reading* *2nd cycle*	Here we have the culmination of the author's treatment of one of the principal fruits of the redemption: the reunion in the one and only Church of God of Jews and Gentiles.

Christ is *peace* in a double sense. He has inaugurated a new humanity in which the differences between Jews and gentiles are wiped out (vv. 14-16). He has also, by his death on the cross (v. 16) and his gift of the Spirit (v. 18), made peace between God and man.

He proclaimed the peace that was foretold and preached by the prophets (Is 57:19). He restored normal relations between men, and between them and God, so signally that his message reaches even the most estranged.

This great insight is manifestly relevant when we ask ourselves about Christian obligations in the struggle for world peace. How do we make the peace of Christ reign?

There is really no difference between the peace of Christ and the peace of men. There is just peace, the pursuit of which is well worth anyone's lifetime. We do not have to invoke the kingdom of God in seeking world peace. Mere "living together" demands this. But the very quest will demand the exercise of powers that are deeply hidden in us. What is often described as peace is something that muzzles its victims. We have supposed states of coexistence that are no more than superficial. Even at the core of pacificist movements we find so much egoism and ambiguity. The Christian will have to depend on his faith alone if his peace-making activity is to be really inspired by the Spirit of God. He will reach this detachment only gradually, having plumbed the depths of merely human effort, and learned to live with its limitations.

VI. Colossians 1:24-28
2nd reading
3rd cycle

Colossians is really no more than a rough draft of the letter to the Ephesians. In a previous instance (Col 1:21-23) we have seen how the ideas of the Colossians passage are found in the Ephesians parallel. This Sunday it is the same. Our reading has the same themes as a corresponding Ephesians passage (Ep 3:5-12): the mystery of God, that is (v. 26), and its revelation through preaching (v. 25).

There is however a special emphasis here on the theme of *suffering*. Paul reveals the mystery not only by his preaching, but also by the hardship inseparable from his ministry. Another idea too, that of richness (v. 27), is peculiar to Colossians. Doubtless this conjunction of the two ideas, suffering and richness, poverty and glory, in a sort of antithetic structure is quite deliberate.

Though most translations give us this meaning, it does not seem that Paul contemplates a completion of "that which is want-ing" in the sufferings of Christ (v. 24). He is expressing a wish to share the agonized *(thlipsis)* destitution *(haterema)* of Christ. The two words are borrowed from the vocabulary for the poor of Yahweh (Ps 33/34:7, 18, 20; Ps 43/44:23-25). With the mystery of the cross before his eyes, before passing to a consideration of the undreamed-of riches of the Risen Christ, he returns to the source, the poverty and anguish of calvary (cf. 2 Co 8:9; 13:4; Ph 2:5-8).

Charged as he is to proclaim salvation by means of the cross, he must himself live its mystery. He must endure in his body its weakness and poverty in order to experience the power and richness of the resurrection. In this way his preaching will be more credible (2 Co 13:3-4; 4:6-12).

Later, in the letter to the Ephesians (Ep 3:5), he will repeat this affirmation indirectly by noting that the proclamation of the "richness" of God's plan has been entrusted to the "least" of the apostles.

All this could very well be taken as the Pauline commentary on Christ's teaching, where he tells the apostles that their poverty will be rewarded a hundred fold (Mk 10:21, 28-31). Christ had revealed the richness of God by the poverty of the cross. So, the apostle is a vessel of clay filled with the richest treasure.

There is an attitude towards suffering, described as religious, which implies recoil from reality and refuge in a God "on the other side," who can put an end to pain. That is not what Paul is talking about. Suffering for him is holy because God by entering our world endured it; the method found by Jesus of disclosing the face of God was none other than silent suffering. He knows that suffering molds a person into the image of God. We have only to accept the human predicament, endeavor to fulfill our liberty and understand its mystery, in order to find side-by-side with suffering certainty of God's presence.

Such is the believer's view of suffering. It is not some sort of springboard for eternity. Nor is it something to be embraced masochistically. It becomes a secret assurance that, in Jesus, we are communing at once with both God and the world.

VII. **Matthew 13:24-30, 36-43** *Gospel 1st cycle*   Like most of the parables, the one about the tares in the wheat should be subjected to precise laws of interpretation. We have to distinguish the precise meaning of Jesus from multiple rereadings. The common synoptic tradition, for instance, as well as the individual attitudes of each evangelist, and parallel, noncanonical traditions like the gospel of Thomas. It seems certain that there was a general tendency on the part of the evangelists to make an allegory (where each detail has a special meaning) of something that was intended by Jesus to convey merely a single general lesson.

a) The meaning of Jesus becomes clear when we compare the long version in Matthew with the brief one in the apocryphal gospel of Thomas.

The patience shown by Jesus with his enemies the Pharisees, and those disciples who were vacillating, troubled the apostles, who feared the opposition of the first group (Lk 9:51-56) and the defection of the latter (Jn 6:60-71). When they press him to make his followers a sect of the pure, he shows them the *patience* of God, who delays the judgment (vv. 28-30) in order that sinners will have time to repent, and who forbids men to usurp divine prerogatives by judging others (v. 30b). The last times have indeed been inaugurated, but they are not times of power and judgment as the Jews thought. They are times characterized by gradualness and tolerance (cf. 2 P 3:4-9; 1 P 3:20; Rm 11:25-27; 8:1-18) where God is cooperating with the frail liberty of man.*

b) Matthew adds some special nuances to the primitive account. The tares (v. 26) are unusually numerous. They have been sown by the "enemy" (v. 28). They are gathered first and tied in bundles to be burned (v. 30). He also gives a good deal of attention to sorting the wheat from the tares. His view is not quite that of Jesus. He is less concerned with explaining the reasons for gradualness in the Kingdom and God's patience. He is giving a small eschatological treatise to describe the fate of the just and the wicked at the last *judgment.* Later (vv. 36-43), in the explanation he provides, he will reinforce further the eschatological lesson.

---

*See the doctrinal theme: *patience,* p. 206.

VIII. Mark   This reading opens Mark's treatment of that
6:30-34   portion of synoptic material that has come to
Gospel   be called, for convenience, the "section of the
2nd cycle   breads" (Mk 6:31 — 8:26). It is built around
the account of the two multiplications. Of the
three synoptics, Mark's handling of this material is the best. He
introduces it in anecdotal style, uses the central theme of bread
to give unity to the different elements, and makes the whole
section a summary as it were of Christian life.

Our reading gives a series of seemingly anecdotal incidents
that are designed by Mark to effect the transition between two
portions of the gospel, and bring Jesus to the desert. We have
the return of the apostles (v. 30), their resting (v. 31), the im-
portunity of the crowds (v. 31b), all details peculiar to Mark
which provide an explanation of Jesus' being in the desert (v.
32), surrounded by a hungry mob (v. 33).

Verse 34 however, which describes the terms of Jesus' preaching is more revealing. The image of sheep without a shepherd is
taken from Numbers 27:17, where the reference is to Moses'
anxiety for a successor so that the people will not be without
direction (Ez 34:5). Christ then is presenting himself as successor to Moses. He is able to take charge of the flock, nourish it
with the food of life and lead it to proper pastures. The whole
section of breads is designed to put Jesus forward as the *new
Moses* who provides the true manna (Mk 6:35-44; 8:1-10). Like
Moses, he triumphs over the waters (Mk 6:45-52), liberates the
people from the legalism to which the pharisees had reduced the
law (Mk 7:1-13), and offers even to the Gentiles entry to the
Promised Land (Mk 7:24-37).

Moses' career as legislator was against the background of a
society founded by Abraham on faith and the promises. This
meant that his law had meaning to the extent only that is fostered

the faith of Abraham, leading to the discovery of a totally other God.

It was wrong to reduce it to a moral code without reference to the salvation events which provided its context. Its true use was as framework for the exercise of faith. Divorced from that, it inevitably became deformed.

Christ could claim the title of new Moses, because, in his personal life, he restored legal observance to its proper climate of faith and attachment to the Father. Incarnate in the body, he demonstrated the sort of fidelity that was required by the covenant, and became an example for all humanity. Inevitably, under the impact of a fidelity so intense, in obedience so deep that death itself became its sign, something had to give in the old law.

Christ does not manifest himself to the world through the moral "good example" of Christians. Atheists can lay claim to ethics as well as Christians. The true sign of the presence of this new Moses in our world will be the faith with which the Christian clings to the "Totally-Other." He will show that by his attitude to daily trials, to the challenge of death, and to the massive problems of war, hunger and social injustice.

The Eucharist is the great source of replenishment for our moral life. It brings us into touch with the major event, in which the new Moses showed his fidelity to his Father's mysterious design.*

IX. **Luke**	Too often this anecdote has been made into
10:38-42	an allegory where Martha stands for action
Gospel	and Mary for contemplation, the idea being to
3rd cycle	show the superiority of the latter.

What we really have is a story from the collection made by Luke among the disciples, principally the women. They have often been curiously interpreted.

*See the doctrinal theme: *law and moral life,* Lent/Easter, p. 80.

a) The family of Lazarus and his sisters is the object of three important gospel traditions (Lk 10:38-42; Jn 11:1-44; 12:1-8). Each time Mary and Martha appear in the roles that Luke allots them here, following doubtless the family custom of the time, Martha does the domestic tasks while Mary is occupied with caring for guests. It was a division of household responsibilities meant for the comfort of guests. All the three accounts where we find the sisters indicate that the purpose of the arrangement was to provide the highest degree of *hospitality*.

b) Yet the anecdote was destined to have different interpretations among the primitive communities. The first related it to the time of *eschatological waiting*. Time has become too pressing to allow any concern about material things. Martha's purpose of course in cooking a special meal is to honor her guest, but things turn against her, and she has to seek help from her sister (v. 40). Jesus intervenes and tells her not to be troubled about food (one dish is necessary: v. 42). "Few are needed" (v. 42a). Luke attaches great importance to this teaching. Because the Kingdom is close at hand (Lk 12:22), there should be no preoccupation with affairs of this world. Indeed one wonders whether Luke here is not reflecting Pauline teaching. There is a similarity in vocabulary between Luke 10:38-42 and 1 Co 7:29-35.* The virginity of the sisters (they were destined subsequently to be regarded as virgins) enabled them to await the approaching Kingdom without being preoccupied with marriage obligations.

c) Luke shows great preoccupation with poverty as a sign of eschatological waiting, and he attributes similar importance to *hearing the Word* (Lk 11:27-28). In another context he contrasts with Jesus' family, who were concerned about livelihood (Lk 8:19, clarified in Mk 3:20), those who choose to hear the Word and practice it (Lk 8:20). This does not mean that Jesus made contemplation superior to action, but rather that concern for the Kingdom (here represented as a Word; cf. Lk 8:11-15) must not

---

*See the doctrinal theme: *hospitality*, p. 210.

be impaired by too exclusive a concern for mundane matters. In any case, for Saint Luke hearing the Word had nothing to do with inactive contemplation. It was meant to lead to concrete and immediate action (Lk 8:15).

B. DOCTRINE

1. The Theme of Patience

Our natural tendency is to classify men in two categories, the good and the bad, ourselves generally in the first category, and others in the latter. This is something characteristic of nations as well as individuals, and presents a crucial problem among some groups.

In the great search for security, men, instead of being molded by values, will want to mold them. They will be blind to relativity, and will absolutize all their own concepts about everything. The other is always a threat, to the extent that he does not become like us. So that naturally man is sectarian and intolerant. We find these characteristics just as frequently among progressives as among conservatives.

Religion of course is liable to give final rigidity to these attitudes. As men seek final security by touching the world of the sacral, they will invoke divine judgment. They want God's blessing for themselves, their family, their people, their projects, but a curse should fall on others, on enemies, on opponents. This will settle matters once for all.

The Old Covenant, the time of divine patience

Israel's infidelity to the obligations of the covenant provoked divine wrath. The prophets did not fail to see the evidence of this in the catastrophes that befell the chosen people. Even the nations might become instruments of divine vengeance.

However the prophets never rested content with just this version of things. Anger is not the final word in divine manifestation; always there must be pardon. Yahweh is rich in grace and fidelity. He is always ready to withdraw his threats provided Israel turns again to the path of conversion. Divine patience extends even to the Gentile nations where sinners are concerned, as the history of Jonah demonstrates.

Israel nevertheless did not perceive the full consequences of this revelation. Even the choice element in Israel, the poor, becomes impatient. Under the old covenant they are ready to invoke divine vengeance on their enemies, of which they had many, from gentiles to inadequate fellow citizens. They are disturbed when God delays his manifestation.

The patience of Jesus, the incarnation of divine patience

Jesus inaugurated the Kingdom of the final times. However, instead of appearing in might as the judge who separates the good from the wicked, he presented himself as the universal shepherd. He has come above all for sinners, and all men of whatever kind are invited to accept him. No one is excluded from the Kingdom. Throughout all his life he was the incarnation of divine patience toward the sinner. No sin could snatch man from the merciful power of the Father. Divine pardon is limitless.

The secret of Jesus' patience was love. He loved the Father with the same love with which, as Son, he was loved. And his love for men was the same as the Father's love for men, a love that is absolutely universal. Thus he found patience to be one of the greatest expressions of himself.

Love begets dialogue, perfect reciprocity. Jesus' love for men is an invitation to them, with profound respect, to respond freely as partners. Such a unique response requires time. It is developed little by little through an arduous spiritual pilgrimage where advance is punctuated by retreat, the giving of self by return to self. Jesus' love for men is a patient love, because the other is respected even in his otherness.

It goes further still. For him loving men means loving them even in their sin, even in their rejection of God's plan. It was human sin that led him to the cross. The greatest proof of love is laying down life for the beloved. Sin indeed struck down Jesus in death, but his love persisted, deepened, and asserted victory. Here, in the Passion, the plenitude of his patience became evident. The supreme moment of fulfillment of the divine plan, which man had seemed to threaten, is one of love and mercy for man: "Father, forgive them, for they know not what they do."

This sort of patience can provoke criticism, because it arises from a double love of God and men that demands absolute denudation of self. If we are to love as Jesus asks us to love, we must accept this condition of becoming radically poor. We fear such denudation; we think that we are losing all. Yet that is the lesson we must learn from his life and death. That is divine patience.

The Church and the universal tolerance of love

Being his Body, the Church is charged with the task of incarnating among men the patience of Jesus. His mission is not to sort out the good from the wicked, but to present a genuine visage of love. On this earth the wheat is always mixed with the chaff. The line that divides them is a line that cuts through the center in us all. Sorting cannot take place until after death (see Gospel, 1st cycle).

The Church's patience then, founded on love, requires us first of all to show absolute respect for the other person, whether he is a believer or not. She does not coerce; she looks for willing recruits in the love of Christ. She invites each man to place his irreplaceable stone in the construction of the Kingdom, to give his mite of cooperation in the accomplishment of salvation history. The essential note of respect for the other is associated with patience, because the element of time is involved. It may take considerable time to perceive the precise role in which the other is destined to make his pilgrimage to God. It may take considerable time for us to achieve the selflessness we need to accept the other as he is. Experience has often demonstrated this; we are so prone to proclaim as absolute Truth our own particular version of it. There have been many intolerant Christians.

Patience in the Church, we must also realize, will bring her tribulation, as it did Jesus. Man is very attracted by the notion of universal brotherhood, but he does not easily achieve the sort of love that annihilates barriers, when acceptance of the other will mean loss of all human security. For that, the one and only possible basis is God. The Church will meet with no more acceptance than Jesus did. Most often the world will seek to use her; if she resists it will persecute her. But here lies her true destiny. When she endures apparent failure with patience, she is bearing witness to the truth that love actually *has* conquered sin and death once for all.

Mission and gradualness in the Kingdom

The very peak point of ecclesial patience is of course mission. He who performs mission is actually putting into practice, on the human level, the mystery of fraternal charity. It is a work of love, with all the demands of love. If it is not carried out in that spirit, it becomes mere propaganda or coercion.

Both in theory and in practice, furthermore, it is a task of great complexity and great gradualness. The translation of the mystery of Christ from a Christianized environment to one not yet Christianized raises severe problems about encountering the other, particularly on the collective level. It is only very gradually that missionaries can come genuinely to share the life of the people they evangelize, just as it is only very gradually that the Spirit leads these people to the encounter with Christ. In either case, the whole being has to be engaged.

Mission is also a work of patience for a deeper reason. Because it proclaims universal communion through denudation of the self, it must always be a stone of scandal for men. If patience in trial be required of the whole Church, so that she be conformed to the image of the Head, this is especially true of missionaries. Jesus came to fulfill the destiny of Israel, and he was nailed to a cross. A like fate may well be that of those whose role it is to fulfill the spiritual destiny of non-Christian peoples.

The Eucharist, an efficacious sign of Christ's patience

None of us can hope to imitate the patience of Christ unless we are nourished by the Word and the Bread. This patience is not a moral virtue; it is the expression in time of the love with which he loved men to the limit.

When we share the Bread we are constantly renewed interiorly. We join Christ's thanksgiving when he gave himself over to love in the poverty of the cross. We receive the guarantee of that decisive victory over death. Hearing the Word is no less essential. Its power penetrates us, and molds us gradually towards the patience of Christ.

2. The Theme of Hospitality

Hospitality has always been highly regarded among human beings. Yet, nowadays, one gets the impression that, instead of increasing, it is on the decline, at least in those areas of the world that could be described as most modern, above all perhaps in the older societies of Europe. One has only to travel to notice that one is liable to meet the best reception in those areas of the earth that are still poor. The next step would be to assert that Christians are actually the least hospitable of people. Could there be truth in that?

In a modern society actually the stranger tends to be looked on as an intruder. Hospitality is practiced indeed, but usually it is interested hospitality. Tourists are welcomed because of their money, foreign workers because their labor is needed, but that is the extent of it. As long as the community's security is not threatened, everything is fine. If it is, the stranger will very quickly find himself at the frontier. Have people forgotten the meaning of gratuitousness, and hence the true meaning of hospitality itself?

These are serious considerations. If developments in the modern world are really leading to a loss of the sense of hospitality, the future would seem grim. Interested hospitality is not hospitality. On a closer view, the situation may not be quite that bad. It could be that hospitality has just become impracticable unless it

is true hospitality. The sense of hospitality may be like the sense
of God himself. Modern man does not naturally have a sense of
God. When he does have it, it is probably a more authentic sense
than men used to have. The truth is that a sense of God, a sense
of the gratuitous, or a sense of hospitality are not spontaneous
human attitudes. Whenever they seem to be, they are colored
by many ambiguities.

Some doctrinal reflection about hospitality will show us how
closely the virtue is connected with living faith. It is an area
where modern Christians find themselves vigorously challenged.

Yahweh, the Totally-Other, the quest of Israel

Among ancient peoples, particularly nomad peoples, hospitality
was a strong tradition. The passing stranger was much respected
and could count on food and lodging. In fact, the respect was a
religious respect. The entry of an outsider into the daily routine
seemed like a visitation from the sacral world. The stranger could
be someone associated with the gods. He was mysterious; his
welcome might win favor with the gods. And one never knew,
the gods themselves might visit.

In Israel, there was a change, under the regime of faith. A
stranger's unexpected arrival was an event, consequently some
sort of intervention by Yahweh, which concerned fidelity to the
covenant. In the first place such a person was a living reminder
that Israel once, in Egypt, was herself an enslaved stranger. In a
broader sense he was a reminder that we are all strangers here
below. Whenever Yahweh intervened, moral obligations arose.
Hospitality, for the Jew, was more than just an opportunity for
touching the sacral world, which it was for the pagan. It was
above all an imitation of God's own activity. The stranger should
be loved, because God loves him (Dt 10:18-19).

The account of Abraham's hospitality (1st reading, 3rd cycle)
opens up a more important aspect still, on the religious plane.
The stranger is not any longer that mysterious being whose reception may lead to favor from the gods. He is the "other," sug-

gesting immediately the Other *par excellence,* who is Yahweh. The God of faith is the Stranger, the Totally-Other. His intervention in the life of his chosen people will invariably be unexpected. It will not reinforce Israel in security; on the contrary it will denude her. The greatest interventions led her to the desert or to exile, and these were the times when her faith became deep and firm.

Abraham's hospitality was destined to become standard. Its implications were a direct preparation for New Testament revelation. Hospitality came to be understood as reception of the other, and thus a way of encountering the God of faith. With the gospel, the full meaning of hospitality will become clear.

Jesus of Nazareth, the stranger

The gospels show us Jesus, the Messiah, as a guest who is received well, or badly, or not received at all. He is never the host. This seemingly accidental circumstance has really a deep meaning. The hospitality he received, and his judgment of it, tell us a good deal about his message and his personality.

He was often invited by publicans and sinners. Invariably such hospitality seems to have been impulsive and disinterested. When he was criticized for accepting such invitations, he said that he had come, not for the just, but for the lost sheep of Israel. Among sinners, he was among his own, but his presence was a summons to conversion. The fact that this summons was obeyed (consider the Zacchaeus episode, Lk 19:5-10) shows that a condition for entry to the Kingdom was the awareness of sin and the desire to repent.

His reception by the Pharisees was different. This sort of messiah was clearly not according to their idea. They did not want to be put out of countenance by him, and consequently could not receive him impulsively. Indeed it was in contrasting the two sorts of hospitality he had received, the Pharisee's and the sinful woman's (Lk 7:44-46), that Jesus revealed the true nature of love, and the meaning of his intervention in the world ("your sins are forgiven" v. 48).

Even when entertained by friends of long standing, as at Bethany, by Martha and Mary (today's Gospel, 3rd cycle), he does not react like an ordinary quest. He directs attention to the essential thing: his message and his person. In this sense he is always the stranger, someone unexpected, someone who undermines all security and requires total renunciation, someone who sets up a love relationship based on acceptance of the other as different. It was this stranger who came amongst his own, but his own did not receive him (cf. Jn 1:11).

He was never more the stranger than in dying on the cross, rejected by everyone to whom he turned. He is still so much the stranger after the resurrection that the disciples do not recognize him on the road to Emmaus. They do, when he becomes their guest (Mk 24:28-32).

Hospitality as an exercise of faith

Christian hospitality is one of the signal manifestations of fidelity to the new commandment of love without limits. It is essentially an exercise of faith, because it is welcome of the other who differs from us. Not the welcome we give our own, our neighbor, our friend: do not even the Gentiles this? But our welcome of the stranger in the other, the one who challenges and disconcerts, the always possible enemy. This welcome requires total renunciation of the kind that makes us truly love others. This sort of hospitality is an encounter with the event; it is not natural impulse; it calls for vigilance.

If Christian hospitality is this essentially, it follows that the people who benefit from it should be the poor and deprived above all. Those people that is, whose very existence challenges our security, and spurs us to muster every energy for the building of a better world. Jesus himself shows us what is the ultimate challenge by listing precisely those proper recipients of Christian hospitality: the hungry, the thirsty, the naked, the stranger, the sick, the prisoner (Mt 25:35-36). In receiving them we receive him. We should note the continuity between the hospitality required by Jesus from his own in his earthly career, he the Stranger who had nowhere to lay his head (Mt 8:20), and that required from the disciples by the Risen Lord. It is a tradition that extends throughout salvation history, a constant concern for the other, particularly the poor. Here we are at the very heart of the New Testament. If we receive Christ in the other in obedience to his word, we are receiving the Father too. "If anyone loves me, he will keep my word, and my Father will love him, and we shall come to him and make our abode with him" (Jn 14:23). Then comes the reversal of roles. Those who welcome divine guests discover that it is they who are the guests.

At the outset of this meditation we said that hospitality seems to be on the wane in the modern world. What we have just now said about Christian hospitality is sufficient to show that, due to certain circumstances, hospitality of this kind was in fact not practiced. Our modern world has at least the merit of dispelling illusions. The claims to our hospitality now of the stranger and the poor are quite imperative. In giving it we shall not be laying our conscience to rest. We shall indeed never again be at rest, because it will demand our total selves.

Christ's envoys, in search of hospitality

Those New Testament passages which tell of the mission of the Twelve or the seventy disciples stress similarly the theme of hospitality. "Whatever town or village you go into, ask for someone trustworthy and stay with him until you leave. As you enter his house, salute it, and if the house deserves it, let your peace descend on it; if it does not, let your peace come back to you. And if anyone does not welcome you or listen to what you have to say, as you walk out of the house or town shake the dust from your feet" (Mt 10:11-14). Previously, Jesus had given the Twelve this direction: "Provide yourselves with no gold or silver, not even with a few coppers for your purses, with no haversack for the journey or spare tunic or footwear or a staff" (vv. 9-10). His envoys then are to be as he was, bearing the badge of poverty, of the stranger seeking hospitality. The synoptics are unanimous about this, and in Saint John we have this saying "He who receives him whom I send receives me" (Jn 13:20). It is because he identifies himself with his messengers that he requires his own behavior from them.

It is remarkable that in the theme of hospitality in this context, the roles are reversed. He does not require his envoys to practice hospitality, but to seek it. In the texts we treated earlier the practice of hospitality was the great sign of faith. In a way we should expect a similar injunction for missionaries. The missionary of course is not forbidden to exercise hospitality, but it is the other aspect that is stressed.

The detail has a moral for our meditation. The fact that Christ's envoys approach men in search of hospitality indicates that they want to come empty-handed, ready to listen and accept, ready to be with men as men are. In other words they seek in men something that is already a movement toward faith. When pagans welcome missionaries, it is a sign that they have already embarked on the pilgrimage of which only Christ can provide the goal. They are ready to be addressed by that stranger whose role it is to enlighten every man that comes into the world (cf. Jn 1:9).

Christian initiation to hospitality

The two aspects of hospitality we have been mentioning are actually interwined. One cannot exercise this sort of hospitality towards the poor, the deprived, the stranger without coming to see in the other a person one needs, needs to be received by. The guest suddenly becomes the host, the Master. Christ is inviting us to his own table. Likewise, we cannot as bearers of the Good News, of Christ that is, beg hospitality from others without ourselves being hospitable. It is all an expression of living faith, and consequently something we can be always deepening.

The best place to do this is the eucharistic celebration. Here, each of us should be eager to give hospitality, to receive the others as brothers, and, in them, Christ who is sharing himself with us. But as we give hospitality, we discover we are receiving it. The real initiative comes from the other, the stranger, ultimately from Christ himself.

Very evidently however all this does not happen automatically in the eucharistic celebration. To bring it about, there are two minimal conditions. In the first place the assembly must actually be open to "others" and concrete steps should be taken to achieve this. In the second place the celebration should be regularly so organized that each member can actively share the welcome and the openness. This meditation should lead us to question ourselves on all these issues.

SEVENTEENTH SUNDAY

A. THE WORD

I. 1 Kings
3:5, 7-12
1st reading
1st cycle

From its beginning Solomon's reign was on a level other than that of David. The period of conquest was over, and the new king turned his attention to problems of organization and development.

Solomon goes to Gabaon to seek the *wisdom* of Yahweh. There is no question here of divine wisdom as it will be understood later in sapiental literature, but of practical wisdom. The king is young as yet (v. 7); he has never exercised authority, but his position implies above all a capacity to distinguish between good and evil (v. 9a; cf. 1 K 3:16-28). Furthermore, the kingdom over which he has power is not his, but God's (v. 9b).

His prayer reflects his great disquiet as he confronts his charge; it is inspired by the humanity of a man who realizes he is being made the plenipotentiary of Yahweh. It is all very well to swagger and flaunt power, but so often, in the moment of truth, one realizes that one is alone and insignificant. In those moments prayer is the only recourse.

II. 2 Kings
4:42-44
1st reading
2nd cycle

The biography of Eliseus is made up of traditions that antedate, in a large measure, the 18th century BC. The compiler is principally anxious to mention episodes in the prophet's life that show him to be the equal in charisms and power of his master Elias. The Elias cycle of traditions included a multiplication of loaves (1 K 17:1-15). Consequently a similar miracle is attributed to Eliseus. It is the topic of today's reading.

The chief interest of the multiplications by both prophets is the emergence in the accounts of some themes that will be important in subsequent Jewish eschatology.

Elias was concerned mainly with the misery of the poor. The chief emphasis in the account of Eliseus' miracle are the abundance of the loaves, the importance of the fragments and the prodigious nature of the incident (vv. 43-44).

In the eschatological meal of Third-Isaiah (Is 53:1-3; 65:13; cf. Pr 9:1-6), a banquet of *abundance* offered to the *poor*, both traditions are fused. For this meal in fact an attitude of spiritual poverty in the guests is presupposed. One must be hungry to participate (Lk 6:21), hungry for bread and justice, and one must be spiritually and materially poor. It is a meal of abundance. The guests cannot exhaust the menu; the fragments that remain are infinite (vv. 43-44). Such profusion is symbolic of the riches of the Kingdom, that surpass any human resources.*

III. Genesis 18:20-33
1st reading
3rd cycle

Chapters 18-19 of Genesis are fairly composite. The primitive account doubtless was composed of Genesis 18:1-16, 20-22a, 33b; 19:28, 30-38, etc. It would include some verses of today's reading. At a later date (postexilic?) verses 22b-33a were added. Stylistically, they fit well, but contextually, no. Abraham's interlocutor is no longer one (or more) angel(s), but Yahweh himself (v. 22b). Lot is saved by Abraham's intercession, whereas in the primitive account he is saved by his hospitality (Gn 19:1-16). Then, according to the primitive version (cf. v. 21), God comes down to Sodom to see whether its bad reputation is justified. But the other has him decide irrevocably to destroy the city.

a) We have three doctrinal themes in the account. The first seeks to prove that according to the promise (Gn 12:3) all the

---

* See the doctrinal theme: *bread for the poor*, p. 239.

nations are blessed. They find, that is, in Abraham the source of happiness. Even Sodom and Gomorrha can profit by the divine blessings promised to the Hebrew patriarch, if they display a minimum of faith and conversion. If they become hardened and rely on themselves, they cannot.

b) The second is the theme of *intercession.** It prepares the people for an understanding of the Messiah's function as mediator. The prophets and men of God were the first to undertake the task of intercession: Samuel (1 S 7:15; 12:19-23; 15:11; Jr 15:1), Amos (Am 7:1-9) and Jeremiah (Jr 7:16; 11:14). Moses however was the greatest of all mediators. Numbers 11:2, 11-15; 6:20-24; 14:13-19; 21:4-7; Exodus 32:30-34 are fairly late witnesses to this tradition. They demonstrate very well however how postexilic concepts of leadership were more and more concerned with someone given to prayer and a spiritual relation with God. This sort of concept too goes into the making of the suffering Servant image, the mediator *par excellence* between God and men (Is 53:12).

Primitive traditions however had never presented Abraham as intercessor. What we have here is a transposition to him of the prerogatives of Moses and the suffering Servant. He is a leader of the people like Moses and the Servant. He enters into personal relationship with God, and by his life and his prayer becomes the unique mediator between Yahweh and the people. Jewish thought is conjoining in one person the functions of leader and priest.

c) The third theme is the idea that the *merits* of a few just people can bring about the salvation of a multitude of sinners.

Primitive Israel was convinced about corporate involvement in sin and chastisement. Exceptions were made for a few individual just, like Lot (Gn 19:15-16), but the notion of individual responsibility, it seems, was only developed with Jeremiah 31:29-30; Ezechiel 14:14-15, 18. By the time this account of the inter-

---

*See the doctrinal theme: *prayer*, Lent/Easter, p. 185.

vention of Abraham was put together, the concept of individual responsibility itself was bypassed, and the notion had arisen of salvation of the many by the few. It is noteworthy however that Abraham does not dare think that less than ten men will suffice (v. 32). Ezechiel will go further with the concept of one just man saving a whole city (Ez 22:30). The poems about the suffering Servant, insofar as he can be regarded as an individual, will corroborate this in considering expiation by a suffering Messiah (Is 53).

Abraham then was one of the pointers that prepared humanity to understand the role of Christ, the first-born. He is the source of all blessings, even for sinful nations. He is priest, and one and only mediator between God and his people. He is the just man expiating for the sins of all. Christ, by his sacrifice and his prayer, accomplished salvation once for all in the name of sinful humanity.

The primacy of Christ as mediator gives meaning too perhaps to the mediations we have known in our modern world. The deaths of people like Kennedy, King, Torres, etc. become intercessory in the name of a humanity that has grown torpid. There must be many men whose only hope of salvation is association with some hero or some martyr. The Christian, wherever he happens to be, by his attitude and his choice, can roll together all such mediations and proclaim the solidarity of everyone in Christ.

IV. Romans   A general commentary on Chapter 8 of the
   8:28-30   letter to the Romans will be found above, 16th
   2nd reading   Sunday, p. 196.
   1st cycle

The thrust of the cosmos, and of humanity, towards glorification will carry the plan of God to fulfillment. Corruptibility in one, or spiritual weakness in the other, can never jeopardize the project of a God who is faithful to his purpose (v. 28), and who finds in Jesus Christ a perfect partner. "Those who love God" then are assured of glory, not as a merited reward, but because they, in turn, have become his partners.

God "knew them in advance" with that biblical knowledge which is communion and sharing of life. He transforms them into children of God conformed to Jesus Christ (v. 29).

Divine *predestination* does not mean election of one and rejection of the other. It means that God is the first to know and to love. His love is realized in Jesus even before men come to it. Predestination is concerned with his plan of love and its way of operation. We are not dealing with a time element at all. A divine initiative precedes all the stages of Christian life (v. 30): the call (by preaching), justification (by baptism), glorification (by death). He calls, justifies, glorifies and, through the person of Christ and the Spirit who dwells in our innermost being, disposes all our Christian life.

V. Ephesians
4:1-6
2nd reading
2nd cycle

Previous readings from the letter to the Ephesians have indicated the importance in the whole letter of the theme of unity. It appears again, more explicitly, in today's reading.

a) Paul pleads above all for humility, gentleness and charity (v. 2). These are precisely the virtues by which Jesus established his lordship over the world, and succeeded in unifying it (Ph 2:6-11; Jn 13:14-16; Mt 11:29; Col 3:12-13). All are in *communion* with the same sources of salvation (vv. 4-6).

b) The unifying principle is described in three affirmations, each with three elements. The Spirit which animates Christ's Body and the hope it kindles (v. 4). The Risen Lord, the faith which professes him, and the baptism which makes us sharers with him (v. 5). Finally, the Father, over all, through all, and within all (v. 6).

What we have then is a trinitarian formula. The secret of *unity* for men lies in the common life of the three persons. The Father is mentioned in the third place instead of the first (cf. Ep 1:3-14), because the unity in question is built by the gradual ascent of humanity, through the Spirit and Christ, to the Father himself.

In order to show how divine life is the principle of unity not only for humanity, but for the individual person, Paul juxtaposes a theological virtue with each person of the Trinity. The Spirit sustains hope (1 Co 12:13; Ep 2:18; Rm 8:26-27). Christ kindles faith (Rm 10:8-17). The Father is "within all" to kindle love and communion (2 Co 13:13; Ph 2:1).

Theology has been guilty of so many arid analyses of the mystery of the Trinity that it becomes difficult to see it as the principle of Christian life and human unity.

Yet it is a mystery to which the key is love. It is the perfect union of three persons who remain perfectly distinct. Is not this the ideal love relationship with the other of which we all dream?

We shall be sharing the life of the Trinity if our Communion with all men is of the kind where each is only happy in his relationship with all. When Paul juxtaposes the theological virtues with the persons, he is affirming that the key is the living of our life as a gift of God, acquired in Jesus Christ.

So, without the Trinity, all enterprises of human unity are doomed. They will either mutilate individuality or swallow it whole. Related to the Trinity however, man can remain his total self.

The Christian who is concerned that everyone round him, near or far, should be taken for what he is and drawn into a harmonious union, will be the ideal witness of the Trinity. It is partly perhaps because there is an inadequate realization of the role of the Trinity in the texture of Christian life, that it has become just a dogma to be accepted, without enthusiasm and without interest.

VI. Colossians
2:12-14
2nd reading
3rd cycle

Paul comes at this point to the heart of his topic. In their search for God the Colossians accepted Christ's mediation, but they wanted to associate with that mediations that derived from different philosophies and from religious syncretism.

a) The mediation of Christ, primordial and exclusive, must be distinguished from all other mediations. He argues by first of all recalling the *primacy of Christ* in the Christian life. To this end he uses four complementary images. Christ is the root of the tree of humanity. He is the foundation of the temple constituted by Christians, which is being steadily built. He incorporates the plenitude of divinity, because in him is found all that the Colossians could ever seek or desire. Finally, he is head of the angels, because he has deprived them of their domination over man and creation. This latter is an allusion to the mythic concepts of the time, which represented the angels as masters of the universe and mediators of the law (v. 14).

However, it is futile now to regard angels as intermediaries between God and man. Paul is rejecting those Judaizing notions which still revolved about a law put forward by the angels, and gnostic notions about intermediary beings between God and man.

b) The Christian comes to share Christ's primacy over the world through *baptism*. Its principal effect is to link us with the death and resurrection of Christ, that is, with the precise act which gave him his primacy. Once that link is established, multiple fruits follow. In particular, there is no longer need of circumcision. What could it add to those who are already circumcised throughout all their flesh (who have experienced, that is, the plenitude of conversion), and who are totally pardoned for sin (v. 13)? Baptism accordingly delivers the Christian from the need for any other ritual practices whatsoever.

Christian "primacy" over the world does not mean superiority over others, but a service based on understanding of persons and things.

Let us consider for a moment the topic of man's conquest of nature. This mastery, gradually developed, by man over himself and over nature has a meaning (the spiritualization of matter for instance). To this end, man has developed methods and techniques to deal with the obstacles and alienations that stand in the way.

Christian faith however sees a deeper and more decisive meaning. God's purpose in this human mastery is the absorption of all things and all beings into the divine life itself. We believe that humanity has this destiny, by virtue of the work accomplished by the man-God among humanity. Man's primacy over nature came to have a new and unexpected meaning in him. All the obstacles to the primacy, evil, sin, death, angels, had to give way.

His reinterpretation of the whole human enterprise is continued by the assembly of all the baptized. Christians can work towards the ideal of a humanity that will be the progeny of God. They can do so to the extent that they work to liberate humanity from the alienating forces (nature itself, the sacral, sin, money-power, etc.), and for the spiritualization and humanization of all material things.

VII. Matthew 13:44-52 *Gospel 1st cycle*   Here are combined three parables of rather different purpose. We have on the one hand the parables of the hidden treasure and the pearl: on the other, that of the net.

The first two, apparently at least, convey a somewhat similar lesson. It seems reasonable to suppose that they were presented together, even though they may have been delivered in different circumstances, as the Gospel of Thomas (nos. 76 and 106) would suggest. The parable of the net however has an altogether different origin (vv. 47-50), and resembles indeed that of the tares (Mt 13:24-30). Doubtless Matthew, or one of his sources, combined the parable with the other two in order to contrast with the joy of those who found the kingdom (v. 44) the envy of those who were excluded (v. 50). In any case, while each parable seems to have its particular moral, the three in combination have a special lesson too.

a) Eastern stories generally, and Jewish traditions too, like to give us accounts of discovering treasure. The gospel of Thomas indeed, at least where the parable of the hidden treasure is concerned, succumbs completely to this genre. The discoverer becomes rich and prosperous, marries the daughter of the owner of the field, purchases his palace and his slaves, to the great discomfiture of the deprived heir (we have a similar example in a *midrash* on the Canticle of Canticles 4:12).

There is nothing like this in Matthew's version. The treasure is the kingdom of God, and the man who finds it, by chance as it were, is so conscious of his good fortune that instead of thinking about what he can purchase with this *treasure*, he reflects on the calamity should he lose it. The parable is not so much concerned with what he sacrificed for it, as with his motive. The discovery is something that must now influence the whole course of his life.

b) The parable of the pearl seems somewhat different. It sets the kingdom in relation not so much with a thing (a net or a treasure) as with a person. We have this again in the case of the Good Samaritan, the good shepherd, or the sower. In each instance the person stands for God himself, or his Messiah. The translations in the case of this parable do not normally convey the textual difficulties and variants of the Greek.

In fact, at some stage later than the primitive tradition, the piece seems to have been allegorized to represent God himself. He establishes his kingdom over humanity (represented, in the symbolism of the time, by the pearl) by selling all he possesses (divinity "humiliated" in the incarnation of his Son). It becomes, in this reading anyhow, an allegory of *divine kenosis* in search of humanity.

c) However fairly soon the allegorizing interpretation is lost sight of, and the piece becomes a simple sapiental proverb, fairly similar to Proverbs 3:13-18. The two parables, treasure and pearl, get a common interpretation. The Kingdom is so imminent that everything must be abandoned in order to gain it (Mk 1:18-20; 10:28). Selling all one possesses becomes the symbol of the *conversion* that is necessary. And Matthew slightly alters the pessimistic emphasis of the preceding parables (the sower and the tares) by describing the sentiments of the good.

d) The purpose of the parable of the net, like that of the tares, is to show that the Kingdom inaugurated by Christ must necessarily await the *plenitude* (theme of the "filled" net). The piece contains its own interpretation (vv. 49-50). Its vocabulary for the most part is that of the parable of tares (Mt 13:40-43), which seems to indicate a later redaction.

Two things then can be distinguished. The parable itself was meant to indicate the necessity of a period of transition between the foundation of the Kingdom and its fulfillment. A subsequent interpretation gave it an allegorical bias and softened the lesson by applying it exclusively to the circumstances of the last judgment.

The encounter between God and man, which is proclaimed by the treasure and pearl parables, will be fully achieved only at the final stage of world history. In the interval, patience is required. An attitude of condemnation could interfere with conversion and the growth of the Kingdom.

The combination in a simple context of two parables so different, at first sight, as those of the net and the treasure is not without point. The Church does not have the option of selecting her disciples or recruits. But every man must select the treasure of his own life. There is not any real contradiction. If the Church is ready to bet on the gospel, with all the renunciation this entails, her death to self will consist of the ambiguous allegiances and motives of her children, insofar as they remain untransfigured by the faith.*

VIII. John 6:1-15
Gospel
2nd cycle

It is customary with John to describe an incident and follow it with a discourse that explains the themes. We have this in chapter 6. Verses 1-25 describe the incident, and verses 26-66 give us the discourse. In the account of the incident however we can detect all the themes of the discourse. Consequently by devoting our attention to it, the multiplication of bread, we can hope to cover the essential message of Jesus' words.

One has only to compare the Johannine version of the multiplication with that of the synoptics to set these essentials in relief. Generally speaking it can be said that John attaches more importance to the narrative than the synoptics. They place it at the end of a day of preaching, whereas, with him, it seems as if the crowd had come to eat, and it is the principal point of interest. Jesus seems to procure food for the multitude at once (v. 5), while, in the synoptic version, he only does this when it has been established that no other solution is possible (Mt 15:32-33).

a) The first theme in John's narrative is that of *manna* in the desert, and, more generally, the desert experience itself. The initial exchange between Jesus and Philip recalls the dialogue between Yahweh and Moses, as Yahweh prepares to multiply to satiety the meat sought by the people (Nb 11:21-23). Details peculiar to John also are the enthusiasm of the crowd after the repast (v. 17) and their discovery of Jesus as the "prophet," a replica of Moses (Dt 15-18), foretold for the last times.

The care exercised by the apostles, who are specially charged

*See the doctrinal theme: *the Kingdom,* p. 232.

with the task (in contradistinction to the synoptic version), in gathering the fragments (v. 13), suggests that, unlike the manna which perished immediately, the bread of Jesus is imperishable and thus a sign of eternity.

Old Testament interpretation (Dt 8:2-3; Wi 16-28) had already presented the manna as more than material food. It was the sign of God's Word and an appeal to faith (Dt 8:2-3; Wi 16:26). The new manna of Jesus is the same, as the discourse following emphasizes (Jn 6:30-33).

b) The second theme is that of the *esthatological repast.* Jesus' question in verse 5 immediately suggests Isaiah 55:1-3; 65:13. The fact that the bread he blesses is barely bread, the food of the poor (a detail peculiar to John) indicates that his meal is satisfying the "poor of Yahweh" with the plentitude of the messianic banquet.

It is this eschatological element that will be developed later in the discourse with the ideas of bread of life and bread of immortality (Jn 6:27-50).

c) We should note too that Jesus makes himself personally more prominent in the Johannine narrative. He conducts the initial dialogue (vv. 5-10), and he distributes the bread (v. 11). Clearly the account is meant to reveal the *person of Jesus.* Furthermore, when there seems danger that his person is improperly understood, he does not hesitate to hide himself (v. 15).

In the discourse this note is made to resound, as it were, in the various "I am's" of Jesus (Jn 6:35, 48-50, 51). His meal is meant to initiate his disciples into the mystery of his person.

d) These three emphases though, exodic, eschatological and personal, are drawn together in the great eucharistic theme. Our first indication is the reference to the approaching feast of the Pasch (v. 4). The formula for blessing the bread is the one the synoptics give for the Supper (v. 11; cf. Lk 22:19).

These allusions prepare us for the unequivocal elucidation in the discourse (Jn 6:53-56). The eucharistic banquet is shown to be the fulfillment of eschatological hope, the paschal mystery, and the revelation of Jesus' person.

Does the Church still continue to be the multiplier of bread for those that are hungry? In more precise terms, when we consider the problem of world hunger now, does she have some obligation over and above the duty of reminding members of individual and collective responsibilities?

We must remember that Jesus actually did satisfy the material hunger of the crowd, and that, in revealing the bread of life eternal, he did so in the context of a material need. The bread he gives is more than the symbol of supernatural bread. That can only be revealed by genuine involvement in the great human tasks. The test of the quality of charity is love for the poor, and love of enemies. When we recognize the right of the poor to actual bread, we shall be fulfilling the deepest demands of charity. We shall be continuing the gesture he made, by a new multiplication of bread on a planetary scale.

In the Eucharist the bread of life is distributed abundantly in all its dimensions, the mystery of Christ's person, the eschatological symbol, the sacrament of the Pasch. We shall only receive this bread of life properly however, when we have reached the stage of renunciation and openness that makes all of us the very poorest brothers among human kind.*

IX. Luke 11:1-13
Gospel
3rd cycle
The beginning of chapter 11 in Luke is a short treatise on prayer. The author first gives his version of the Our Father (vv. 2-4), follows with the parable of the importunate friend (vv. 5-8), and then, as a sort of commentary, gives a series of sayings (vv. 9-13) about confidence in prayer. There is considerable unity in the whole piece, and it really becomes a commentary on one petition of the Our Father: "give us this day

*See the doctrinal theme: *bread for the poor*, p. 239.

our bread" (Lk 11:33; the theme is repeated in verse 5 and verse 11). Matthew, in commenting on the Our Father, is concerned above all with the petition for pardon (Mt 6:14-15).

a) Jesus, in giving the parable, wanted to provide instruction about *confidence in prayer* (vv. 5-8). We can recover the primitive structure by phrasing verses 5-7 interrogatively. "Who among you (a formula which suggests at once a negative response), if a friend came to seek him during the night, would say . . . . ?" He is asking his audience to witness. Could one imagine a friend who would not get up at night through hospitality (v. 6), or to have peace (v. 8), or to avoid being thought grudging, even when confronted by the inconvenience of the late hour, the single room, the common bed (v. 7)? It is unthinkable.

The conclusion follows. If this is unthinkable of a friend, it is *a fortiori* unthinkable of God. The parable is not so much one of the importunate friend, as it is often called. Rather is of the importuned friend. The central figure is not the one who knocks at the door and asks for bread, but the one who is inside. Verses 11-13 then are a perfect continuation of the parable's teaching. Here too the audience is called to witness that refusal is unthinkable. If the father of a family cannot refuse food to a child, can God? Luke in fact modifies one clause of the comparison by substituting "Spirit" for the "good things" given by God to those who ask. Here doubtless he reflects the mentality of the primitive communities. They were convinced they were living in the last times, but somewhat disturbed that they were not experiencing the blessings and prosperity foretold by the prophets.

b) Yet Luke did not understand the parable altogether correctly. In verse 7 he manipulates the first part of the phrase "who among you" so that it indicates not the person in the house, but the seeker who is more or less rebuffed. This makes the parable a doublet of the unjust judge parable (Lk 18:1-8). Attention then shifts from the friend who is importuned to the one who is importuning. He must have much patience and *perseverance*. He must continue to knock at the door; finally it will be opened.

Verses 9-10, the primitive commentary on the parable, follow this view: "ask for bread, finally it will be given to you." The beggar is persistent. He is not put off by being rebuffed. Always he will succeed in persuading his friends, however reluctant. *A fortiori,* perseverance in prayer will persuade God, who is good.

Luke then takes an optimistic view of prayer. It will be heard however importunate it may be, above all because God is good. There is an important element missing in this teaching. Prayer is not efficacious just because the petitioner is indefatigable, but because of mediation by Christ himself. On this point the teaching of John 16:23-26, which one could almost believe inspired by this Lucan passage, goes much further. It makes the unique mediation of Christ central to all Christian prayer. Oddly enough, in this cycle of readings, it is the Old Testament passage (Gn 18:20-33) that insists on the role of intercession, thus rounding out the message of the gospel.*

---

*See also the doctrinal theme: *prayer,* Lent/Easter, p. 185.

B. DOCTRINE

1. Theme of the Kingdom

There is a striking contrast between the richness of biblical teaching about the Kingdom and the jejune notions actually entertained nowadays by Christians. The word evokes no great surge of enthusiasm, and even in circles where it still has some validity it tends to be shorn of all sacral significance. Of course people continue to mouth phrases about "the Kingdom of God" and "building the Kingdom", but they tend to be no more than cliches without any real meaning.

Yet, we have only to open the Bible to realize how pervasive the theme of the Kingdom is, and how essential for any understanding of Christianity. The proclamation of the Kingdom was the primary object of Jesus' preaching; his disciples were required to accept the demands of the Kingdom. Unless we are going to reduce his message to the level of merely human wisdom, it is difficult to see how we can accept it without attempting to unravel the mystery of this Kingdom that he came to establish. Frequently the liturgy of the Word will confront us with biblical texts on the topic. Is there any way of penetrating these and forming a more precise idea?

The importance of the theme does not at all mean of course that we must use it at any cost in proclaiming the Good News of salvation. If the word, kingdom, has in fact lost meaning for people, it should not be artificially resuscitated. Indeed it is quite probable that the apostolic church itself made a different use of such terminology for Jewish and Gentile audiences. The message however always remains the same, and the only way to hear it as it came from the lips of Jesus is to use the words that he used.

The wait for the Kingdom in Israel

Man naturally seeks the absolute, and in this search he will naturally tend to absolutize the securities he possesses. He sacralizes them so that they seem in his eyes the channel of communication with the divine world.

It is very easy to understand how religious sentiment among ancient peoples would be attracted by the theme of a kingdom. Once any nation became a kingdom, it felt itself possessed of precious advantages of which the king was the living symbol: land that was inalienable, a stable and harmonious social order, political and military power, etc. Experience having shown that kingdoms were successful, it was natural that the idea should be sacralized. Royal liturgies came into being. In a kingdom it was felt that the gods were in alliance with men. The king was thought to exercise the function of intermediary, and to bring salvation.

Once Israel became a kingdom, the theme of the kingdom of God gathered momentum very quickly, but under the regime of faith there were important qualifications. True, the sources for the idea were the same as elsewhere. Israel was felt to be a stable kingdom, because Yahweh, who resided among his own, was the true king. A decisive milestone had been passed, and salvation could not be long in coming. The true witnesses of the faith however were soon to undermine such easy certainties.

To begin with, as the God of faith who is the Totally-Other, untouchable by human hand, the prophets always condemned any attempts to use God for the furtherance of political aims. Yahweh resides at Jerusalem, but the association with the chosen people is not automatic. He demands fidelity to the covenant, and this gives his kingdom a moral, not a political, character. In particular, if the kings of Israel have their royalty from Yahweh, they are obliged thereby to preserve this. The davidic dynasty was constantly subjected to prophetic scrutiny, and when it fell, the prophets did not fail to interpret this as divine chastisement. The experience of kingship however was sufficiently deep-seated in Israel to allow full development for the Kingdom of God theme after the fall of the dynasty. In their visions of the future the prophets turn to it. One day the divine Kingdom will be extended over the whole earth, and men will come from everywhere to adore King Yahweh in Jerusalem.

The gospel of the Kingdom and the foundation of the Church

The Good News proclaimed by Jesus is, strictly speaking, the advent of the Kingdom of God. By using this phrase, so full of meaning for the chosen people, the Messiah is telling Israel that her long hope has been at last fulfilled. But he is also conveying that never again is there going to be question of a restoration of the davidic kingdom. To this extent he is detaching the theme of the Kingdom from its pagan beginnings and the ambiguities this entails.

What is beyond doubt is that, if the Good News be that of the Kingdom, this is because the last times have come. When Jesus compares the Kingdom he is proclaiming with a treasure or a pearl before which everything else is as nothing (see Gospel, 1st cycle), he is in line with the great prophets. As they had foretold, the Good News is proclaimed to the poor. To have access to this Kingdom, which gives us the new and definitive Covenant, conversion is necessary and the acceptance of precise requirements.

The fulfillment indicated by this Good News of the Kingdom was disconcerting, when one considers what the expectations were. On the one hand, the Kingdom did not come with acclamation. Nor did it offer Israel any hope of the prestigious political future on which many Jews were counting. On the other hand, Jesus never ceased to liken this Kingdom to seed, to a grain of mustard, to leaven. Paradoxically, the time of fulfillment had come, but it had yet to be realized. The building of the Kingdom would have to go on gradually, by means of his disciples' fidelity to the new commandment of love without limits. So, the Kingdom is not of this world, but it has to be built in this world. It will demand the renunciation of ourselves and of all privilege, because it is universal in nature. The Father's realm is open to all human kind.

As a means of building the Kingdom Jesus founds the Church. This was the reality that confronted men who had expected a readymade Kingdom from above. What could one say? We must remember that, in trying to visualize the circumstances of the Church then, we could get a wrong impression. The Church to us immediately suggests a religious institution which prescribes different rituals for its members and urges them towards a particular moral and spiritual ideal.

It was otherwise then. What the word suggested was an assembly of all believers, summoned by Yahweh. To say that Jesus had founded was to affirm that in his person he had brought about definitive fulfillment. From now on the great assembly of human kind, founded on genuine love, had become possible. The key moment of this transformation was the cross, and the foundation of the Church was the act of the Risen Lord.

The Church and the Kingdom

These two concepts have been interwoven ever since the beginnings of Christianity. At the very origins attention was mainly focused on the theme of the Kingdom, with evidences still of Jewish eschatology. The ascension had put an end to all hope of restoration of the davidic dynasty, but the disciples continued to expect the Kingdom imminently. It could not be long delayed, because the Messiah had come. Then came Pentecost, which made the community aware that they were the messianic assembly of the final times, the true Church, that is. They were only dimly aware however, as yet, of the magnitude of their task. As they saw it the Kingdom had already come, and the great manifestation would soon take place in all its splendor, when the Risen Lord returned in glory. It was to take many years indeed before the full extent became clear of the mutation Jesus had wrought in traditional hopes.

It was the beginning of mission that proved the turning point, and the Antioch church played a decisive role. Questions arose about what should be done pending the return of the Lord. The

Kingdom had arrived, but it was a seed that had to grow. The old hope had been fulfilled, but it had to spread now over the whole surface of the earth. The disciples felt this to be their task, under the inspiration of the Spirit. "Assemblies" were set up everywhere after the pattern of the mother-Church in Jerusalem. They had an urgent sense of mission to be accomplished before the end would come. Soon the Kingdom ceases to be something one must passively await. It is something one possesses the assurance of now: life, that is, in Christ and the Spirit. But, above all, one is called on to work for it.

The idea thus gets shorn of the sociological implications it always had (a temporal kingdom), and recovers all its eschatological dynamism, this time in a Christian context. All has been *already* accomplished, yes; but all has *still* to be accomplished gradually, by means of a partnership, in Jesus Christ, between God and men. Experience of mission by now was leading Christians more and more towards a deeper understanding of the idea of Church. They began to see that this and the Kingdom concept were closely linked. From the eschatological point of view the Church is the same as the Kingdom. Yet, on this earth, the Church is no more than the choice terrain, always ambiguous, because of sin, where the Kingdom gradually grows.

The Kingdom must not be bound within any sociological limits, even though they are religious. The Church, the body of Christ, loses all meaning if it loses the link with assemblies of believers. When Christianity became the official religion of the Roman Empire, there was a real danger that the people of the New Covenant, high with victory, would see themselves as the actual Kingdom. In our day we face the opposite danger. We could come to forget that the Church, which is not indeed the actual Kingdom, is nevertheless the earnest of the Kingdom.

Building the Kingdom in mission

We should remember first of all that terminology means nothing. The vocabulary of the Kingdom, since Christ, has nothing whatsoever to do with an earthly kingdom. What counts then is the reality, not the language that was employed.

The question we must ask ourselves is this. Is it meaningful to say that the Good News proclaimed by him, and proclaimed by us, is the advent of the Kingdom? It is a question of very great importance indeed. The gospel of the Kingdom has to be a Good News of fulfillment. Jesus himself said so. He came, not to destroy, but to accomplish the Law and the Prophets, to crown the spiritual effort of his people. The fulfillment, as we know, was accomplished by his Pasch. What was true of him is true of the Church. She comes, not to destroy, but to fulfill by repeated Paschs the spiritual effort of all peoples. This is her essential mission; everything else is secondary.

The missionary, in proclaiming the Kingdom of God, will naturally be attentive to everything in a people's way of life that prepares for its coming. Actually, what he brings is not something exterior. If he shares the pilgrimage of the people among whom he finds himself, what he does is push them beyond themselves. He helps them to see that Jesus Christ is the only possible culmination of their hope. He will be concerned with the Kingdom of God. He will realize that building it on new soil will mean the establishment of a local Church, that is truly native. But what he must proclaim above all is the advent, not of the Church, but of the Kingdom.

The dangers we have already mentioned will present themselves again. Whenever the Church becomes powerful and has human societies under her control, as has been the case in the past, the missionary is exposed to them. Unconsciously he will begin to feel that access to the Kingdom is to be identified with entry to the Church by baptism. He will often tend to ignore the positive elements in the previous religion of the people he is evangelizing. He will be concerned above all to set up the structures of the sort of Church he knows, forgetting that the Church is being implanted in a new environment and must be allowed to grow. In our world however the danger on the horizon for the missionary is the opposite one. He is usually sensitive to the religious values of the people he evangelizes. He tries to share these, but he may be all too ready to postpone indefinitely the summons to conversion, and the invitation to enter the Church. Because the Spirit is at work in the heart of every man, there is a tendency to argue that the approach to Christ may be possible without explicit attachment to the ecclesial institution.

The liturgy of the children of the Kingdom

Whatever we may say about terminology, the theme of the Kingdom is one of the richest sources of insight in the practice of Christian life. We should live from day to day in a state of expectancy, awaiting the fulfillment of the Kingdom. We realize that it has already come, but that it never ceases to be in a state of coming and actualization. We realize above all that yesterday, today and tomorrow, its coming requires a contribution from men that will be effective in Jesus Christ. Our awareness should be growing deeper all the time, and the mere passage of time will not achieve this unless we take the means.

The eucharistic celebration is our central opportunity, but we cannot expect it to be effective automatically. The liturgy we celebrate here below is that of the Church, not of the Kingdom. They are not exactly the same thing. The liturgy of the Church is that of the people of God in growth, always summoned to do their share in building the Kingdom. Every liturgical assembly, with due regard for time and place, should be made aware of the demands made upon them by this task. The celebration will only have meaning of course insofar as Jesus Christ is the principal actor and the source of all our hope. But it will not be having its full effect, unless all the members too feel impelled to put their hands to the plough.

It has happened in the past that eucharistic celebrations proceeded as if the Kingdom had been set up on earth. It was identified with the Church. Christians nowadays need more than ever to become aware that the Kingdom they are called upon by baptism to build is not of the world. But, nowadays too, it does concern the quest of all humanity.

2. The Theme of Bread for the Poor

Can we regard the Church still as the multiplier of bread for the hungry? Rather a ridiculous question, I suppose, as many people today would see it.

In our world it is undeniable that the problem of hunger is one of the most anguishing. It is far from solution. The inequality between the so-called developed nations and others continues to increase. Help contributed by richer nations to poorer nations (with unprecedented rates of increase in population) is still too thin a trickle and too badly organized to be of much help. Face to face with this colossal problem, does the Church have a contribution to make? Of course it is her duty to remind people of their grave obligations. But does it stop there? Some would say yes. The Church is a spiritual institution. The bread she procures is a heavenly bread, concerned with a Kingdom that is not of this world. Others, a much greater number, would take it for granted that, even if the Church wished to solve the hunger problem, she would be unable to do so.

In the first place, her position makes this awkward. Whether we like it or not, she is tied to the rich nations, and to the richer classes in these nations. The poor nations have made up their minds that they must depend on themselves above all in order to emerge, and that a very sharp confrontation with the rich may become necessary. Modern man anyhow has the conviction that all the great problems must be solved by human means. Any dependence on God might be merely alienating. The Church should be ignored, or even resisted.

In such a climate, can the message of today's liturgy have any meaning for us? The Church, imitating Christ, distributes to the poor the bread of abundance.

The poor of Israel await the bread of abundance

Eating is basic; the man who is hungry wants to be satisfied. Mediterranean man found bread to be indispensable to life. Natural causes, or human injustice, might create disorder and deprive him of it. Then there was famine, something felt to be abnormal. Man was not born to be in need of bread.

When the Israelites became settled in Palestine there were social disorders. Some grew rich at the expense of others. There was inequality. Members of the chosen people went hungry: the poor. It was an evil that could not be imputed to Yahweh. Only sin could explain it. When they turned to Yahweh, certain of being heard, they asked for bread. Bread was necessary for life, and Yahweh, who saves man, wants him to live. But, because of the sin of men, salvation was slow in coming. One day however it would come. Yahweh would bring all the hungry into his Kingdom: they would have the first seats, and their hunger would be satisfied.

But, as the prophets were gradually to emphasize, material poverty of itself does not convey any right of entry to the messianic Kingdom. The cry for satisfaction must be a cry of the whole being. Before Yahweh man is nothing; his poverty is absolute. Satisfaction in any domain must come from Yahweh alone. If the hungry man cries out to Yahweh for bread only, he cannot hope to be led to the eschatological banquet. But if his cry for bread wells up from a true poverty of heart, then he will be heard. One day he will receive the bread of abundance.

Jesus Christ, the bread of life

Jesus came to inaugurate the messianic Kingdom. One day, for the numerous crowd which had come to him and had not eaten, he multiplied bread. So deeply were the first disciples affected by this incident, so much did the first communities reflect about it, that the evangelists have left us several accounts. Today's liturgy gives us John's version (Gospel, 2nd cycle). More than any of the others, it elucidates the meaning.

What happened is clear. The hungry crowd was satisfied by Jesus. While the Kingdom he was proclaiming was not of this world, it was directly connected with this world. It was unthinkable that such a basic human need as the desire for bread would be left unsatisfied by it. This is something we must never forget when discussing the multiplication. Jesus actually did give food, in abundance, to people who were hungry.

Those people however had followed him in order to hear his message. That message, the Good News, could never be interpreted merely as satisfaction of a bodily need. Its essential content is of another order; the multiplication of bread is but the symbol of another bread which nourishes throughout eternity. Yet it is not altogether a symbol; it is a material thing which only discloses its full meaning when related to its true source in another order. It could be wrongly interpreted, in fact it was wrongly interpreted by the crowd. For a proper understanding of its meaning radical poverty of heart was needed, to use Matthew's phrase, poverty of spirit.

Jesus came to satisfy the poor, but the bread he provides in abundance is the bread of the Father's family. This is the only bread that will satisfy human aspirations. If man wants to be present at this banquet of eternity, he must renounce himself. He must thoroughly accept his creatural condition, and appear in poverty before God. The divine bread he will receive will lead him to love his fellow men better. It will fill him with the desire to provide bread for those who have no bread. In this sense the multiplication is more than a symbol; it gives actual body to a doctrine.

Because Jesus is the only one who corresponded perfectly with the Father's plan, he can call himself the "bread of life." He is the true bread of abundance. All the blessings of the Kingdom have been communicated to him. If we wish to share them we must be united with him.

The Church, the community of those "sated" with bread

A member of the Church is one who was hungry for the bread of the Kingdom, and has been satisfied. He is a man who realizes, following Christ, that true fidelity to the creatural condition entails self-renunciation and obedience unto death for love of God and the brethren. Believing, in answer to Christ's call, he wears the countenance of the poor. The bread he receives in the Church marks him off from those who are smug, established, entrenched in their material goods. Saint Paul calls such a man a free man, because he is liberated from all slaveries, from sin, from the law, from death. His freedom is translated into service of God and his fellow men.

He is a child born of the Spirit, a member of the heavenly Jerusalem. Christ, the first born of the new humanity, is the bread of life that alone can satisfy him. This bread is destined for those who want to do the will of the Father (cf. Jn 6). This should not lead us to think that the citizen of the heavenly Jerusalem is detached from earthly things, and insensitive to the basic needs of earthly man. The miracle (the sign that is) of multiplication is sufficient evidence to the contrary. Sharing the bread of life must inevitably be translated into passionate concerns: the desire for more justice on earth, that those hungry for bread should be satisfied, that the thirsty should drink and the naked be clothed, etc. (cf. Mt 25). The liberty of him who is born of the Spirit is a dynamic liberty. It makes a man work for that condition of humanity, where each and every person can take his place in the family of nations with dignity and pride.

Saint Paul however is careful to point out that the one born of the Spirit is persecuted by the one born of the flesh. The free man must realize that true fidelity to the creatural condition entails obedience unto death, and that universal love entails total self-renunciation. Wisdom of this kind is rejected by the world.

It is interpreted as something ineffectual, something that alienates a man and deprives him of "divine" power. Persecution of this kind will not terrify the free Christian, because he knows that is only by being loyal to the gospel he can be loyal to his fellow men.

Living bread offered to the poor

It is quite true that the first expansion of Christianity was among the insignificant folk who were devoid of wealth, and had not much instruction. It was not the great ones of the earth, but the little ones, who first welcomed the Good News. Saint Luke is the great evangelist of poverty. His infancy gospel, the contrast between the poor and the rich in supporting the Kingdom, his picture of the primitive community in Jerusalem where all goods were held in common: all this might be taken as a commentary on Jesus' words to the envoys of the Baptist "The poor have the Good News preached to them." The first Christians discerned a very close connection between "poverty of spirit," the subject of the beatitude, and actual, material poverty.

Paradoxically enough, the Church nowadays is materially rich, or comparatively so. The majority of her members belong to the rich countries, and the more active of them will often belong to the leisured classes in these countries. The ecclesial institution itself is comparatively rich: considerable sums are often needed for apostolic enterprises. Missionaries laboring in the Third World seem inevitably dependent upon sums of money collected in the Western countries. In such a situation, the proclamation of the Good News to the masses of poor throughout the universe, who are its natural recipients, presents extraordinary difficulties.

The responsibility laid upon Western Christians then is very great indeed. What is their collective duty? They must recognize as absolutely basic, at whatever cost, the right of the poor everywhere to hear the Good News. There is no more fundamental test of charity than love of the poor, and love of enemies. When we insist on the right of the poor to have the living Bread, we are obeying the last demands of love. We are continuing on a planetary scale the "multiplication of bread" which we ourselves have benefited by, in Christ. We are making our contribution to the solution of the great problem of hunger, in all its dimensions.

When Christians generally, and those responsible in the ecclesial institution, become aware of the Third World, with all that this means in terms of faith and charity, then the face of the Church will change. The nature of her association with material wealth will get clarified. She will become a sign in this world for those who hunger for bread and faith.

The liturgy of the bread of life

In the eucharistic celebration we are introduced to the new Jerusalem, the veritable city of the poor. It is a banquet where the bread that does not perish is distributed in abundance, but under modest appearances.

When we partake properly of this bread we become more and more open, because it releases us from slavery to perishable things. We become ever more free for the one task that is fulfilling: the service of God that is at the same time the service of all men.

As the liturgy of the bread of life is a constant summons to greater poverty, it is important that the actual celebration should indicate this. Dignity should be maintained, but we do not have to manifest the richness of the Kingdom by any displays of material wealth.

EIGHTEENTH SUNDAY

A. THE WORD

I. Isaiah
55:1-3
1st reading
1st cycle

This short poem is attributed to Second-Isaiah. He was a prophet who lived in a community of the poor, on whom the exile had a considerable influence. Its purpose is consolatory: eschatological hope is renewed.

For this reason the ancient theme of the *messianic repast* of the poor (Is 26:6) is taken up, and another theme of sapiental origin (cf. Pr 9:3-6; Si 24:19-22) is mingled with it. Man shall no longer live by bread alone, but by the Word of God and knowledge of it. The messianic banquet becomes a banquet of wisdom.

The poor addressed by the prophet, having based their hopes on fragile human means of salvation, are now resigned. They place all their hope in God. He will save them whenever he wills (Is 40:31; 41:10, 14, 17; 46:12-13). The faith of those destined to be assembled in the future Kingdom will be characterized by this confidence in God. We have here the picture of a group tried by poverty, whose hope nevertheless has been purged of any vengeful emphasis. They rely rather on the knowledge that comes from faith and destitution than on the material benefits of the messianic banquet.

The eucharistic assembly is an assembly of the poor insofar as its members submit themselves to the initiative of God, after the manner of Christ on the cross. Their poverty will be transformed into a witness of the salvation acquired in Jesus Christ, by contrast with any gesture by purely human means at salvation. The individual Christian, and the Church, should realize that this sign of poverty entails an obligation to confront the problem of riches, and withstand the centers of prestige and power.*

II. Exodus
16:2-4, 12-15
1st reading
2nd cycle

This account of the manna "miracle" is of fairly late compilation. It is agreed to be dependent on postexilic priestly tradition. It belongs to the literary genre of midrashic homily where traditional material is embellished. Consequently it cannot be regarded as strictly historical. We could regard the manna for instance as some sort of distillation from a tree, appearing one day in such profusion that it was thought to be a divine intervention. Probably because ancient traditions mentioned the manna as something that appeared once only, the magnification of the event and its religious significance were the result of later traditions.

The religious lesson of the account depends on the people's certainty that this was a particular intervention by God. They were undergoing a severe crisis of *discouragement* and beginning to question the liberation itself (vv. 2-3) when the phenomenon occurs (v. 4). The fact that it coincided with their discouragement led them to see it as a sign of divine presence, meant to reassure them.

Lot's wife looks back anxiously at the house she is abandoning. Peter looks jealously at the disciple whom Jesus loved. The toiler puts his hand to the plough with a backward glance. The Israelites pine for the good foods of Egypt. They are all images of the human difficulty in integrating the past with what is now happening.

But once the decision is made, we must be faithful to it; we must not take back what has been given. Only thus shall we be able to discern God's presence with us. God is with those who build the future, and he proves it by nourishing them.

*See the doctrinal theme: *poverty*, p. 263.

This is the essential lesson in the Yahwist tradition, which emphasizes the intervention of God (v. 4). Later the priestly tradition will add some other emphases. Aaron is placed at the side of Moses (vv. 2 and 6). The Sabbath legislation is mentioned (v. 5). The mediating function of the priesthood is stressed ("We, what are we ..." vv. 7 and 8). It is made clear that the heavenly nourishment is the source of the people's sustenance (v. 4).

All the emphases from both traditions combine to make a single lesson prominent. The whole desert experience has been one of *divine providence*. Faithfully, day after day, according to the needs of each, God leads his people. He does not allow man to plan his own tomorrow, and will not even let him seek his own means of subsistence. The manna event is thus a trial; it teaches the Israelite that he must become "poor."

It is doubtful whether the marvelous aspects of God's intervention in the desert convert anyone nowadays. Indeed direct intervention by God in human affairs is hardly thinkable any more.

God, I suppose we should say, only acts now through secondary causes (in this instance, possible distillation from a desert tree). In order too to perceive his presence and his intent, we have to see these causes with the eye of faith. They are not immediately evident. The atheist who sees no religious meaning in secondary causes may well force us to modify our hermeneutic, and ask the question: What is faith? We may find common ground with him, if we seek God, not in miraculous interventions, but in the ideal of human progress.

III. Ecclesiastes	Qoheleth analyzes at length what he calls the
1:2; 2:21-23	vanity of things. Today's reading applies this
1st reading	view to the meaning of man's toil.
3rd cycle	

Vanity might be described as the gulf between human aspirations and what is actually achieved. The desire for the absolute is there, but nothing satisfies it. This is not any consequence of sin, but merely the human predicament. Today we should use words like absurdity or ambiguity. A decision that can never be carried to certain resolution, a quest for absolute truth that can never be completed, working for a future that will be controlled by people who will destroy our work: these are characteristic of the human predicament.

Vanity overshadows the man who fails to see the limits and ambiguities that must circumscribe his effort. It is the lot of all who find themselves marked by death because they did not properly reckon with it.

Is there any escape from this absurdity? None lies in the direction of closing our eyes to it, certainly. Qoheleth would vigorously denounce such folly. Nor is there any by having recourse to "the other side." Our author is clearly against all messianisms and eschatologies. There is no way out of absurdity.

Unless it be absolute acceptance of all the hazards of insecurity and death itself. One man did that, and, in communion with his Father, found the way out. In death he discovered life.

IV. Romans
8:35, 37-39
2nd reading
1st cycle

The believer undergoes trials which threaten his purpose. He is imagined as defendant in a process (Rm 8:31-34) where the trials, personified, become so many sharpened barbs directed against him by the prosecution.

a) We think of Job's arraignment before the tribunal of God by Satan. Having made the accusations, Satan is allowed to use trials in order to test their validity. Likewise, for Saint Paul, the Christian's *trial* is part of the great campaign by angelic powers against humanity. God trusts man and makes an alliance with him. But the celestial powers, who have hitherto held man in thrall, try to convince God that his confidence and love are misplaced. Humanity is only capable of deception.

The catalogue of trials is the one Paul has often used to describe his own misfortunes (1 Co 4:9; 15:30-32; 2 Co 4:8-11; 6:4-5; 11:22-28; 12:10; Col 1:24). His own experience helps him to understand the plight of Christians generally. He also instances the case of Israel persecuted by the Gentiles (Ps 43/44, the vocabulary of which colors the whole account of the Maccabee martyrs: 2 M 7). "Faith is lived on the edge of death."

b) However, the attitude of the great judge of human affairs cannot be swayed by accusations from the celestial or spatial (v. 38) powers, by the forces of nature (v. 39), by trials, or by death itself. He does not rest content with showing confidence. His love enables the Christian to resist trial and liberate himself from all alienation (vv. 37 and 39b).

The Judge, so to speak, has already decided to declare the defendant innocent, and secretly gives him the weapons to resist accusations and avoid snares. God's love binds him to the defendant and gives him an *assurance* that nothing can shake. Truly man is liberated from all forces that could interfere with his destiny. If he refuses to allow sin mastery over him, the judgment for him will be a resounding victory.

The passage raises the whole question of divine providence. Paul is quite convinced that nothing, not the horror of death, the anguish of life, determinism in nature, the calamities of history, has power to disturb the Christian. However dreadfully the world be disposed, the plan of God is not jeopardized.

One must have the proper view of divine providence to make such an affirmation. It does not mean that everything is working towards harmony: many things will never be set right. Nor is there question of some happy state where the goodness of man will prevail. The providence of God is operative here and now, in the midst of contradictory and paradoxical situations. If we go on believing in providence, while tons of bombs are rained down from the sky, while people go on being divided by hate, while evil and sin continue to disfigure a miserable and suffering humanity, it is because we believe that nothing can prevent a man from plunging to the innermost recesses of his being. Here the ultimate meaning of existence can become manifest: a man always has the chance of re-creating himself. The convinced Christian will be able to generate the energy to reshape the world, because he realizes that in this area of his being he is in touch with the Christ who overcame death.

V. Ephesians 4:17, 20-24 *2nd reading 2nd cycle* — This passage is taken from the paraenetic portion of the letter (Ep 4-6). Following a fairly long discussion about Christian unity (Ep 4:1-16), Paul now passes to a series of somewhat eclectic recommendations that are introduced by a few general reflections: avoidance of paganism (vv. 17-19), adherence to the truth in Jesus (vv. 20-21), putting on the new man (vv. 22-23).

a) The initial verses remind us of the great evangelic themes. "Learning, teaching, hearing" (v. 21) imply apostolic preaching. The "manner of the Gentiles" (v. 17) suggests the *conversion* that followed evangelization. It is described by Paul in terms borrowed from Scripture, especially the Exodus episodes. Hardness of heart, religious ignorance, vanity of idols, darkening of the spirit, estrangement from God were all characteristics of Pharaoh, according to the Exodus authors.

b) The object of this preaching and the basis of conversion is the *Truth:* Jesus Christ (vv. 20-21). The theme of truth has high importance in the paraenetic section (vv. 15, 21, 24, 25; 5, 9, 6, 14), and is probably to be traced to original baptismal catechesis and apostolic kerygma (cf. Jm 1:18; Ep 1:23).

The truth, for Paul, is the revelation in Christ of God (2 Co

4:2), especially the revelation of the "mystery" (Rm 16:25; Col 1:26), the opening, that is, of salvation to all men.

It resides in "Jesus," not only in "Christ." What Paul has in mind is the gnostic teaching which distinguished the more or less celestial being, Christ, from the Jesus of the flesh who appeared in history. The truth "in Jesus" then is the message of his incarnation, death and resurrection, with all the moral requirements this entails.

c) He has the moral requirements in mind when he goes on to speak of *putting on Christ* (vv. 22-24).* Earlier, in Ephesians 2:14-16, when speaking of the unity of Jews and Gentiles in the Body of Christ, he had described the new man. This is the prototype of the new humanity recreated in the risen Jesus Christ (1 Co 15:21-22; 47-49; 2 Co 4:16; 5:17; Rm 5:18-19). If men were previously grouped about the old Adam by collective responsibility, they are grouped now, by baptism, to share divine life, around the new Adam (Rm 5:4-6).

Doubtless he is thinking about baptism (Ga 3:27-28), because he has just been talking about preaching, apostolic kerygma and conversion. The terms "stripping" and "clothing" recall the baptismal renunciation of Satan and the profession of faith. The transformation of judgment (v. 23) stands over against the darkness of Gentile thinking (vv. 17-18), as justice (v. 24) does against the dulled moral sense (v. 18) of former days. Holiness (v. 24) is contrasted with a life estranged from God.

VI. Colossians
3:1-5, 9-11
2nd reading
3rd cycle

These verses introduce the final part of the letter to the Colossians. Having affirmed the lordship of Christ over creation and over humanity (Col 2:9-15), Paul now contemplates the effect on the life of the Christian.

---

*See the doctrinal theme: *clothing*, p. 107.

a) The principal effect is *death to sin*. The passage from death to resurrection which made Christ Lord of the universe is something that takes place for the Christian basically at the moment of baptism (Col 2:12-13; 3:1-4), but goes on being deepened throughout "terrestrial" life (v. 5).

The mortification he speaks of is not connected with the body as such—Paul is not prescribing an ascetic piety (Col 2:23): it concerns "that which is of the earth." Verse 5 apparently should be translated: "Being members (of Christ), mortify that which comes from the earth." Having spoken at length about the death and resurrection of the Head of the Body (Col 1:18, 24; 2:10, 17, 19), he now deals with the members of the Body. They must become dead to the powers of the world, especially as manifested in unbridled sexuality and greed (vv. 5-6; cf. Ep 5:3-6).

Baptism has already enabled the Colossians to free themselves from sin (vv. 7-8). They must live accordingly, renouncing faults contrary to charity (vv. 8-9).

b) Demanding as it does this "denudation," baptism will lead the believer to an awareness of the transformation that has been wrought in his life. He is no longer the same. To the old man of sin a *new man* has succeeded (v. 10; cf. 1 Co 1:30, 6-11). Because of the recreative work of Christ (Ep 2:15), deepened knowledge of God, and the indwelling of the Spirit, he really has the power to be the image of God.

The state of the new man however is not something absolutely acquired once for all. The terms renewing and journeying (v. 10) indicate the necessity of ceaselessly correcting the balance of our relationship with Christ and the brethren. Everything divisive (v. 11) must be rejected: all racial, religious, cultural or social oppositions.*

---

*See also the doctrinal theme: *newness,* Lent/Easter, p. 339.

VII. Matthew
14:13-21
Gospel
1st cycle

This reading is taken from the synoptic material usually called "section of breads" (Mt 14:13 – 16:12; Mk 6:31 – 8:26; Lk 9:10-17), with the accounts of the two multiplications. Mark and Luke introduce it rather anecdotally: Matthew connects it with the death of the Baptist. However, in each case, the whole purpose of the introductory verses is to explain how Jesus comes to be in the desert (v. 13) surrounded by a crowd without food (v. 15), and to draw a parallel between him and Moses. Mark indicates the parallel by the theme of the flock without a shepherd, John by that of the mountain, Matthew by the flight and "crossing" of the water.

So, by various means, the great lesson emerges. Christ presents himself as the successor of Moses, able to nourish the people with food and lead his flock to proper pasturage. Throughout the whole section of breads the new Moses is offering manna superior to the old (Mt 14:13-21; 15:32-39), triumphing like his predecessor over the waters of the sea (Mt 14:22-33), liberating the people from the legalism into which the law of Moses had lapsed (Mt 15:1-9), opening the way to the Promised Land, not alone for members of the chosen people, but even for the Gentiles (Mt 15:21-31).

Moses' career as legislator was against the background of a society founded by Abraham on faith and the promises. This meant that his law had meaning to the extent only that it fostered the faith of Abraham, leading to the discovery of a totally other God.

One should not reduce it to a moral code without reference to the salvation events which provided its context. For Matthew, the legislator is not simply a good formulator of legal texts. He is someone who puts his hand to the plough, and positively works towards the salvation of his people in their quest for freedom (escape from Egypt, passage of the sea) and food (manna, multiplication).

Christ can be called the *new Moses,* because, in his own life, he has reinstated observance of the law to the regime of faith and attachment to the Father. He demonstrated the proper fidelity required by the true covenant, and thus could offer all humanity his example. Certain limitations of course of the old covenant had to yield under the pressure of such fidelity. It was an obedience so much more total and profound, of which death itself was the hallmark.°

Christ does not manifest himself to the world through the moral "good example" of Christians. Atheists can lay claim to ethics as well as Christians. The true sign of the presence of this new Moses in our world will be the faith with which the Christian clings to the "Totally-Other." He will show that by his attitude to daily trials, to the challenge of death, and to the massive problems of war, hunger and social injustice.

VIII. John
6:24-35
Gospel
2nd cycle

Christ has just performed the miracle of multiplication (Jn 6:1-15), and accomplished a rather signal success with the crowd.

The discourse of the bread of life is based on two considerations. The crowd has eaten a perishable food, but there is another food which lasts for life eternal (vv. 26-27). They were seeking a worker of miracles, but the personality of Jesus is of another order (vv. 26-27). Works previously accomplished by the people cannot win salvation; the only work which counts is following Christ (vv. 28-29).

The audience is taken aback by these arguments. They tend to reject the pretensions of Jesus. His miracle is ordinary; the ancients have seen greater marvels (vv. 30-31). If he wants to reveal the mystery of his person, why not give a clearer sign. He replies with the affirmation that he is the bread of life (vv. 32-35).

°See the doctrinal theme: *faith and moral law,* p. 259.

a) The early verses put forward the problem of *Jesus' person* in a manner that is enigmatic and exciting. Faith has the capacity to grasp the mystery behind the signs that manifest it. The listener is required to set himself in a proper state of inquiry so that he can grasp what follows.

b) It is somewhat astonishing to find Jesus using the vocabulary of "work" (v. 27) and "works to be done" (v. 28) in describing this quest, which is one of *faith* (v. 29) after all. The work to be done does not mean immersing oneself in the variegated requirements of the law. It is a matter of understanding Christ's activity as the work *par excellence* of the Father (cf. Jn 5:17). Men should give up worrying about the thousand and one works necessary for salvation. They must recognize that one work only is necessary. It is that which the Father accomplishes, by means of the Son marked with his seal (v. 27). It is manifested especially now in the sign of bread.

c) The signs and works wrought by Jesus are more than means of justifying his claims and his mission. It is not a matter of giving intellectual proofs; these signs are already implicated with the salvation that he brings. For this reason, he is reluctant to seem the purveyor of something better than *manna*. He does not want to prove himself greater than Moses, but to make people understand that the manna in the desert and the bread that he has multiplied imply the love the Father is extending to the world. When he passes lightly over the material significance of the manna (v. 32) he is fully in accord with the Old Testament, which frequently discerns behind this material element the Word of the life-giving God (Dt 8:2-3; Wi 16:26). Similarly, with his own miracle, he transcends material and physical life, both by his message and the mystery of his person (v. 35). His audience however fails to transcend the material level (v. 34). It only remains for him then to assert that the multiplied bread is so much involved with his spiritual message and his person that they become confused (v. 45).

d) At the very stage of revealing his personality, Jesus uses a new formula: *the bread of life,* an expression not known to the Old Testament. Doubtless we have John to thank for it, as for other comparable phrases: light of life (Jn 8:12), word of life (1 Jn 1:1), water of life (Rev 21:6; 22:1). He was probably thinking of the tree of life in Paradise, the symbol of the immortality of which man had been deprived by sin, something that manna in the desert could not restore, but which Jesus gives in response to faith (cf. Jn 6:50, 54). The notion has a paradisal and eschatological bias. Jesus is the true life of immortality towards which man has yearned from the beginning, and which is now attainable at last through faith.

John associates the eucharistic mystery with the incarnation (v. 35). The true bread is the Son of God come down from heaven, and hunger is assuaged when we come to him.

Whosoever believes in Christ and his doctrine is already nourished by him. We can never on the other hand neglect the paschal dimension. The theme of manna was perhaps suggested to Jesus by the proximity of the Pasch (Jn 6:4) and the homilies that were customary in the synagogues as the feast approached. The word "give" which occurs three times in today's reading is already an indication of the gift of Calvary, and conveys that there can be no true bread until the salvific work of the Son is fully accomplished. Faith alone is not sufficient when we eat the bread of life. We need actual bread and actual eating to attach us to the mystery of the cross.

IX. Luke 12:13-21   The parable of the foolish rich man (vv. 16-
    Gospel   21) certainly belongs to a very ancient tradi-
    3rd cycle   tion. We have it also, in a more primitive
                      form, the apocryphal gospel of Thomas (no.
63). The discussion that Luke has associated with the parable (vv. 13-14) must also, for the same reason be regarded as quite ancient; but the association with this parable, as well as verse 15,

we probably owe to Luke. He also provides the conclusion in verse 21.

a) The discussion between Jesus and the two brothers is concerned with an inheritance. The older wants to keep it undivided, following the custom. The younger on the other hand wants to withdraw his portion (cf. Lk 15:11-13). Jesus' intervention in the discussion is to the effect that he has no wish to exercise distributive justice. His reason is very clear (v. 14): he has no such mandate from the authorities.

The discussion then is to be interpreted in the context of Jesus' reflections about his own mission. He accepts the function of judge as Son of man, but this justice has nothing to do with human distributive justice. It is *justifying justice,* a symbol of gratuitous love.

There is, generally speaking, an eschatological tone. Christ is saying, at least by implication, that this matter will not be for his judgment. He refuses to allow any disciple the right to presume from earthly decisions, to sacralize that which ought not to be sacralized.

b) Luke however gives the incident a more moral emphasis. Concerned as he was with *poverty* and with the particular difficulties of the rich in living the community life of the Kingdom, he tries to convince his readers of the dangers of money. Thus he introduces verse 15, where Jesus gives a second reason for his refusal to judge. Terrestrial goods are not of sufficient importance to require the judgment of the Son of man. To reinforce this interpretation, he follows with the parable of the foolish rich man, adding a pointed conclusion in verse 21 ("for himself" . . . "with God").

We must not take it however that Luke is putting forward an ethic of poverty without eschatological reference. Jesus is not trying to frighten an insensitive audience with thoughts of a sudden death that could ruin their hopes. The death in question indeed is the eschatological catastrophe which will be followed by the judgment. The lesson then becomes clear. If one displays an attachment to goods at a time when only attachment to God can save one from the catastrophe, this is "foolishness" (in the biblical sense of the word: inability to recognize God and attach oneself to him: Ps 13/14:1).*

Luke is not condemning riches as such. Money, like electricity, is neither good nor evil; it is the use of it that makes the difference.

The mistake of the foolish rich man was to hoard his riches as if he were the only person on earth. Among the sixty-five words used to give his statements, the words "I" or "my" occur fourteen times. He is foolish in that he imagines he himself has acquired the riches, nothing inherited from his parents, no contribution by his workers. He is alone.

He is alone too in the use of his riches. His whole anxiety is to add to his capital. He does not realize that the real beneficiaries of his granaries ought to be the hungry stomachs of his brothers.

The foolishness lies in the failure to understand that all men and all nations are interdependent one on the other. It is such foolishness that has brought humanity to the brink of catastrophe: poor countries that drift further and further into famine, rich countries more and more to advertising and consumption. In such an environment of selfishness and alienation it is impossible to live with God.

*See the doctrinal theme: *poverty,* p. 263.

B. DOCTRINE

1. The Theme of Faith and Moral Law

Too many Christians make their faith simply a moral ideal. They regard the gospel as a lofty rule of life. Bearing witness to Jesus Christ means trying to live a life in conformity with the gospel ideal. It is as if Jesus had been merely a master of wisdom, as if grace simply helped one adjust one's life better to his precepts.

A view like that of Christian moral life, over-narrow and ill-balanced as it is, has many bad consequences. If we expect results from grace in an area that is not proper to it, we deceive ourselves. The consequences are most serious in missionary enterprise. An exemplary moral life is not necessarily the Good News of salvation. Christians have no monopoly in the exemplary life; men devoid of any religion often live such. Indeed the very deepest human values, like human solidarity, are often best attested among groups of people that are quite estranged from the Church.

We Christians should ask ourselves two questions. What is the meaning of the new law, revealed in Jesus Christ? And in what sense does the Christian, by his moral life, bear witness to Jesus Christ?

Moses, the legislator of the old alliance

The law of Sinai is closely linked with the regime of faith that was inaugurated with Abraham. We should be clear about this link. Moses intervened as legislator at a precise moment in the history of the chosen people, in the context of a covenant between Yahweh and Israel. He received the Law that he transmitted to the people from the hands of the Totally-Other God, when the regime of faith was at its height.

The promulgation of the decalogue becomes fully meaningful only when it is related to the first Jewish Pasch. Altogether gratuitously, Yahweh had liberated his people from Egyptian slavery. He had freely chosen them as *his* people. But he brings them to the desert before he brings them to the Promised Land, in order to show what is at stake in the regime of faith. He will save Israel, but he demands fidelity in return, fidelity of a particular kind, fidelity in the desert. There it is impossible to conceal the daily insecurities. Nothing is foreseeable; one must depend altogether on God's benevolence.

In this sense then the Law is seen to be basic in the practice of faith. It cannot be reduced to a mere moral code, divorced from the concrete events of its beginnings. It becomes an expression of Israel's true fidelity to the transcendent and unique God who leads her, and saves her, altogether gratuitously.

This close connection between the law of Sinai and the regime of faith makes Moses the first of the prophets. The old impulses of paganism will reassert themselves and seduce people from the law. It would become necessary for the prophets to read the meaning of events, and remind people who were placing illusory securities before fidelity to God of the requirements of the covenant. These are not arbitrary. The events of the people's history, of whatever kind, are their vehicle.

Once detached from the regime of faith however the law of Moses starts a downward trend towards degradation. Prescriptions are multiplied and the scribes replace the prophets. Legalism is substituted for the fidelity required by the faith.

Jesus Christ, the Moses of the definitive alliance

Where are we to place the work of Jesus in relation to that of Moses? As he himself said, he did not come to add to the law; he came to fulfill it, to bring it to its goal. The intention of the law's first legislator was that it should reveal the avenue of true fidelity to Yahweh. The first example of perfect fidelity that is found, in fact, was Jesus. What he did was to set in proper perspective, definitively, the relation between law and faith.

Because, in Jesus, it was accomplished, the law was renewed in content; but under pressure of the accomplishment the actual confines of the law were burst open. The old bottles were discarded for the actual source itself. From now on the evangelic law, based on universal love, is addressed to all men. Jesus is not slave to any exterior law; it is graven in his heart, and the Spirit is its source. The prophets had indeed foretold that a renewal of heart would introduce the new law.

The expression of his fidelity to the new law was his pilgrimage of obedience unto the death of the cross. To become the neighbor of all men implies the gift of one's life for love of them. And in that giving of life death is encountered and conquered.

The moral life of the children of the Father

The whole basis of Christian moral life is the decisive event of Christ's death and resurrection. It is not based on any theoretical wisdom however lofty; it springs from existential involvement with the Pasch of Jesus. "Love one another as I have loved you." At any and every moment we must be able to discern God's will in the event; he gives us the power in Jesus, to overcome the heavy weight of death with which the event is loaded. Our moral life is a paschal life; it has no meaning apart from a faith that is lived.

It is also a life in the Spirit. Once a man's conscience is open to the Spirit, an interior law is graven there which becomes his principle of action. If we are faithful to that law we find ourselves more and more free, because it is not something exterior to ourselves. Even when it is expressed in terms of objective precepts, the ultimate content of these is related to the action of the Spirit who transforms hearts.

And because of our dependence on Christ and the Spirit, our moral life will inevitably have an ecclesial dimension. We feel ourselves part of the salvation history that is being continuously built by the Church in the transmission of the Word. It is the

Word that beckons to the believer, and invites him to see in the Spirit of Christ the chief controller of his daily activity.

Nor does this "supernatural" ethic detach a man from his creatural condition. On the contrary it enables him to accept that more lucidly. The Christian ethic is the most rational of all, in the true sense of the Word.

The missionary significance of Christian moral life

What we have just said shows us how Christian moral life becomes a sign of the salvation acquired in Jesus Christ.

The Christian bears witness to the Risen Christ when his life manifests the fruitfulness of the paschal mystery. In evangelization, what counts is not the moral tone of Christian life, or the level of realization of the evangelic ideal. Though such a life can have profound effect, it is not necessarily Christ that it witnesses. When then does one's life witness? When it confronts in obedience the challenge of death throughout the whole texture of daily life, especially where human relationships are concerned. This requires deprivation of self, the kind of "poverty" that is open to any man.

It is said sometimes that in our actual world Christian witness is often counter-witness. In the sense that it shows blindness to the "signs of the times." We live in a world where the event that carries the will of God may have planetary dimensions. But alas, very often our eyes are closed. We fail to perceive the demands on our responsibility of actual problems like the under-developed countries, world-hunger. We cannot make the imaginative effort that will muster the charitable resources of all of us collectively. We know what is required of us if an individual hungry man crosses our path. Hunger on a planetary scale, in distant places, far from the circumstances of our daily lives, leaves us baffled.

The eucharstic event in the moral life of the Christian

Our moral lives must always draw sustenance from the eucharistic celebration, because it is here we renew the living link with the greatest event in salvation history, the death and resurrection for all of Jesus Christ. But, to ensure this, our local assembly must summon us to live God's today in total fashion. The liturgy of the Word will be of capital importance, because this proclaims Christ's presence in the actual world. The homily should always show that the forces of evil over which Christ triumphed are actually those active in our world, on the individual and collective level. It will be our business to conquer them as he did.

2. The Theme of Poverty

Material poverty has always been the lot of the human majority. Today hunger and misery bedevil two-thirds of the world. Confronted with this problem, modern man refuses to be resigned, and grows impatient about having recourse to God. He feels that he must depend upon himself, and look upon religion as altogether alienating.

We have to face the fact that, in the great world confrontation between rich and poor nations, the Church is among the rich. Yet, is she not the custodian of a Good News destined primarily for the poor? That is the main reason why it behooves us now to ask ourselves what this sacred poverty really is, and how we can truly be witnesses for it before the world.

The poor of the Old Covenant

The prophets were always denouncing Israel's infidelity to the pace of the alliance. We get the impression indeed that Yahweh is on the point of setting up a regime of vindictive justice. Yet the Covenant, because of the fidelity of a small Remnant, is preserved, these constitute the real, the choice, Israel.

From the time of the prophet Sophonias (who wrote about 640 - 630 BC) the Remnant begins to be called by a special name: "the poor" (So 3:11-13). The sociological origins of this vocabulary are clear, the precarious situation of Israel, that is, during the time of Sophonias. The prophet however spiritualizes these terms. The poverty caused by the Assyrian invader becomes the sign of that deeper poverty that a man ought to have before God. Confronted by the Totally-Other, all pride should be eliminated. A man must become humble, deprived, trusting.

After his time the theme becomes constant, always more and more nuanced. Jeremiah's handing of it destined to have considerable influence on the Babylonian exiles, whom the disasters had deprived of all former securities.

This generation of the poor, with eyes fixed on the future, will soon have their fidelity rewarded with messianic abundance. The unfaithful however will be stricken by divine vengeance. They will count for nothing any more. They are the Israel that lacks fervor, the ruling classes, those who seek after riches and the culture of the Gentiles.

Jesus, the Savior, the poor man par excellence

To this generation of the poor belonged Jesus, and he puts himself forward as their Messiah. His Good News is destined for them, the choice Israel, and the abundance of his Kingdom. Between the poor of the ancient covenant and those of the new, there is unbroken continuity.

Yet, from another angle there is discontinuity. The poor that will inherit the Kingdom must first be converted. They may even be scandalized by the nature of their Messiah.

Where messianic salvation is concerned, the poverty of the old covenant still carries vestiges of privilege. They will indeed have the place of honor, because they belong to the chosen people, in the new era; but it will be above all because of their moral stature. By one all-important modification Jesus reverses all that had been valid before. The poor he turns to are poor sinners, all mankind that is to say, of whatever provenance. All are summoned to the Kingdom. The only condition for entry is faith in Jesus as savior, and acknowledgement of one's sins.

So that, with Jesus, the core of the poverty concept is changed.

Where previously it had denoted a spiritual and moral attitude, it now denotes an ontological condition. He is poor, because the man Jesus is in exclusive relation with the Father. His poverty is salvific, because it is not a construct of human forces. It is a pilgrimage of obedience even unto the death of the cross.

But what of the poor of whom Jesus is the Messiah? They are those who, in living relationship to Christ, accept at the deepest level of their being the renewal that conforms them to the image of the Son. They are the adoptive children of the Father. Their poverty is a gift of God, not something brought about by human forces. It is not something that leads to withdrawal, it leaves a man at the disposal of God and all men. It includes awareness of the merciful fatherhood of God and the depths of human sinfulness. Quite independent of all human effort, this poverty is traceable to no one except the Son himself. He alone, the poor man *par excellence,* can give it to a man by binding him to himself.

The Church the community of the poor

The Spirit that is active in the Church conforms believers to the image of the Son. She provides the means they need to live after the example of Christ. Thus she ought to be deeply marked by poverty.

These poor of the new covenant are no longer a people apart. They have now no enemies; they are the first generation of the new humanity, and all men, without distinction, are their brothers. They know indeed better than anyone the width of the gulf between their being-in-Jesus-Christ and their daily performance. But as they owe everything to their Lord, daily more and more they await his coming. It is this constant expectation that vivifies their hope, and cleanses them even now of their faults.

Their filial adoption acquired in Jesus Christ involves them too in the enterprise of civilization. They are worlds apart from any sort of recessionist asceticism; their wisdom is based on the Scriptures, and is completely different from any brand of human wisdom. The "filial" state can measure exactly the dimensions of the "creatural" state. They know where in life lies the absolute. Because they can form a just estimate of the validity of human enterprise, they can in fact restore their original dynamism to these enterprises. Because they are concerned to keep the gospel in priority, they are the most efficient architects of civilization.

Poverty as a sign of the salvation acquired in Jesus Christ

Poverty describes the ontological state of the believer in the Church, the state of the Father's adoptive son. But, like any spiritual principle, it must penetrate all the layers of actual life, individual and collective. This will not happen automatically; every Christian must play his part. In the task of evangelizing the world men must be able to see the sign of poverty. It must then be such as they can read in the context of their own lives.

So the Church must bear witness to poverty by the action of her individual members, and also by her collective action, her institutions, the means of apostolic action she employs.

Those of us who are concerned about evangelization cannot hide our anxiety with regard to this. We may be relatively well provided, and feel the ambiguity rather deeply. Wealth begets security and nourishes the power instinct. Should fidelity to the gospel entail the voluntary renunciation of money? Not all can follow this vocation. But all should be concerned that they be not slaves to riches, that they should use their possessions (material and other) in the service of humanity. There is no doubt that we face urgent and concrete demands in this way by virtue of the sort of poverty we do profess. Today it can be said that, by and large, Christians are better off materially than the majority of human beings. It may be that in these circumstances the Spirit is urging voluntary evangelic poverty on a wider scale. Aware of the prophetic import of this, it remains for each one of us to examine his conscience.

At the institutional level, the challenges are no less great, because institutions always attract attention. If a bishop lives a life of poverty in a episcopal palace, the palace itself will still invite criticism. Accordingly we should exercise great care that all ecclesial institutions and practices (the style of liturgical celebration, procedures in mission, etc.) should never suggest prestige or power. That would require some thorough reexamination of the whole institutional facade.

The eucharistic assembly of the poor

To be poor it is not enough to be open to the initiative of grace. It is not enough to model our daily lives on that of the Poor Man *par excellence*. Careful reading of the gospels should be sufficient to lead us thus far. We must also go on being "initiated" more and more deeply into salvation history. The Christian community becomes the assembly of the poor in the Eucharist. As adoptive children of God poverty is our state, but its thorough permeation of the whole being of a man depends upon the sacramental intervention. As we emerge from the assembly of the poor, we know that everything has been given, but everything remains to be done. For these great challenges sharing the Word and the Bread will equip us.

NINETEENTH SUNDAY

A. THE WORD

I. 1 Kings
19:9, 11-13
1st reading
1st cycle

In search of Yahweh Elias departs for Horeb and Mount Sinai. For the Northern tribes God is more present there than on Mount Sion, where David had recently installed him.

He hides himself in the hollow of the rock, where Moses himself had taken refuge, to experience the theophany (Ex 33:18 — 34:9), and he too has a vision of God.

The experience shows him that God is not to be found in extraordinary natural phenomena: storm, earthquake, thunder, where the Gentiles tended to locate him (vv. 11-12). Nor is God in the fire, as the Yahwist tradition of the South had it (Ex 19:18). In his struggle for absolute monotheism Elias is concerned to desacralize nature. He wants to free the concept of God from the Baalist naturism of the Phoenicians and of Jezabel.

Finally he senses the passage of a gentle breeze, though the account does not say that Yahweh is in the breeze. Nor is the breeze (cf. Gn 3:8) a symbol of God's gentleness; there is nothing gentle about the orders God will give Elias (vv. 15-17). He is to anoint usurpers who will spread hate and violence throughout the Near-East. The breeze is actually the veil over God's hiddenness and *silence*. It is only the believer who can hear his voice.

This experience of Elias is a good image of the believer's experience in the modern world. He desacralized nature. Insofar as science now has made nature and the world "profane," it has been in fact a service to the God-concept, God has to be the Totally-Other, the Unknowable so far as human thought is concerned. The progressive deprivation was necessary if Elias was to cease searching for God in natural phenomena. But he does have the intimate encounter; he recognizes that which cannot be known; he senses the veiled presence.

So with the believer now. Living as he does in an atheist world, he knows that God is silent, yet he hears him. Like Elias he covers his face, and emerges from his retreat to accomplish his mission.

II. 1 Kings
19:4-8
1st reading
2nd cycle

Here we have the description of Elias' journey to Mount Sinai, where a vision of God is to reward his pilgrimage of forty days.

a) The first theme we notice is the *delay* of forty days (v. 8) before reaching God. It stresses the distance that divides man from God, who is always receding (Ex 24:16-18).

b) A second theme is that of *discouragement* (v. 3), the prophet's classic temptation (Gn 21:14-21; Jon 4:3-8; Nb 11:15; Jr 15:10-11; Mt 26:36-46). Elias had had a great triumph on Carmel (1 K 18), but Queen Jezabel refused to understand. She contrives a movement against the prophet, and the people who had marveled at the prodigy of Carmel, woodenly sides with the party of power. He finds himself alone, as Jesus would later. The only recourse is to turn to God.

However, to allay his discouragement, God gives him a sign. He does not abandon his chosen one, any more than he will abandon Jesus later (Lk 22:43). The appearance miraculously of the scone and the water reminds the prophet of the manna in the desert and the water from the rock (Ex 16:1-35; 17:1-7). The best medicine for discouragement is remembrance of the people's Pasch.

c) The last theme is the *Elias-Moses* association. Elias journeys to the very spot where the legislator had received the secrets of God. The association was destined to influence Christian tradition very deeply (Mt 17:3; Rev 11:1 13).

It also served as a reminder to the people that whenever a

prophet came to fulminate against institutions that issued from the covenant and the law, he was merely vindicating the original Sinai spirit. An Elias is always a living Moses who makes the prosperous dwellers in Palestine aware again of the fierce God of the desert, the God of nomads (the prolonged journey of Elias, v. 8).

We might ask ourselves whether there is really any place left for God, whenever a Christian feels smugly assured of possessing "virtue" or "truth," whenever a priest feels too sure of himself? Such states of mind are merely too human to be signs of God. It is when everything suddenly crumbles—any worthwhile life knows such moments—when the virtues we thought we had evanesce, when the truths seem all at once open to question, that God can begin to act.

His manner of action will be similar. First, a long pilgrimage by a man into the very depths of his being, long enough to have him shed all the things he thought were necessary. Then a little bread and water, to remind him of the overwhelming intervention by God once upon a time. Eating the bread and drinking the water will do more than sustain his physical life. He will find himself structuring his life around a stable center, openness to God's initiative. That is always a factor, even in a life of sin which never dies, or a life of chaos.

The bread and water bring the strong life of God into the recesses of a man's being and "transform the body of this misery." So it is that the Eucharist is meant for people who have lost their way and their certitude. It is then that it can be most fully efficacious.

III. Wisdom 18:6-9
1st reading
3rd cycle

From chapter 16 onwards, the author of Wisdom turns to a series of antitheses which show the difference between the lot of the Egyptians and that of the Jews. They were idolators and had their dark projects collapse in confusion. The Jews were chosen by God, and even their weakness and faults turned to good.

He sees history as a sort of application by God of the law of retribution. Today's passage tells how the children of the Egyptians died in the sea, because their parents had formed a plan to throw the Jewish children in the Nile (v. 5).

The *feast of the Pasch* (vv. 6 and 9) was the constant reminder for the people of the chastisement of the Egyptians and the choice of the Hebrews. Our author describes its ritual briefly, but introduces to the first Pasch some later elements that belonged to the celebration of his own time (the secret for example, and the chant of the Hallel canticles in v. 9, and particularly the celebration's sacrificial aspect).

To celebrate the Pasch is in some sense to interpret history, to realize that God goes on choosing his people among the just and chastising the unjust. We can imagine how this reading was savored by Jews who found themselves exiled once more among Egyptians. But Christ was to die during one of those Paschs, for all humanity. He was to obliterate this racist opposition and make people understand that both Egyptians and Jews could journey together along the road of election and salvation.

IV. Romans	The early chapters of the letter to the Romans
9:1-5	analyze the role of faith in human justification,
2nd reading	something that neither the Gentiles with their
1st cycle	philosophy nor the Jews with their privileges
	could allow.

By 57 Paul had already traveled the roads of the Near East sufficiently widely to realize that he could not count on an early conversion of Israel (Ga 4:29). Why had Jewry revolted against the faith and become a persecutor of the gospel? He faces the question, and our reading today indicates the pain he feels about his own nation, and his amazement that so many privileges have been conferred on the chosen people in vain.

Just as Moses would rather himself disappear than have the people destroyed (Ex 32:32), Paul is ready to become anathema if only the multiple privileges can come to full flower for his people. The privileges are enumerated, and he affirms that they cannot be ultimately in vain, characteristic as they are of the new Israel.

a) *Israel's privileges* will always remain with her, even in her situation outside the Church. For Paul there can be no doubt about this (v. 4).

The privileges are first of all those of the Word: the covenants, the legislation and the promises (v. 4). The covenants with Abraham (Gn 15:18) and David, the promises that were made, the law of Moses (Ex 20) and the commentaries of later Judaism are the Word of Yahweh (which he has never withdrawn). They are the expression of God's presence with Israel, which transcends the limits of the Law and never ceases to give indications of the Messiah through the medium of the promises.

Next come the privileges of the liturgy: the power to render cult to the true God, and the privilege of the divine presence in the temple (Ex 40:34). Cult had indeed been now transformed by the spiritual sacrifice and the glory of the resurrection; but the Jews still retained their liturgical prerogatives and would continue the quest for a cult in Spirit and in truth.

b) Finally there are the privileges of blood. Israel was of the blood of the patriarchs, Abraham in particular. This blood and strain in the body of Jesus had brought salvation, so that Israel's essential privilege lies in the fact that *from its flesh came Christ* (v. 5). Yet she refuses to recognize that her flesh could produce a divine person, a God to be blessed throughout the ages.* What an irony!

The final verse indeed is one of the most important in the

---

*Paul rarely applies the title God to Jesus. The only reason he does so here is to emphasize further the Jewish privileges.

New Testament. It affirms the fleshly reality of Christ, sprung from the race of patriarchs, but preexisting nevertheless in divine glory.*

V. Ephesians   In the final portion of this letter Paul is con-
4:30 — 5:2   cerned with weaning his audience from that
2nd reading   pagan life of which they still have vestiges to
2nd cycle   the Christian one. His argument is simple.
They are now part of the new humanity, of Christ's Body. This is the great fact that cannot be gainsaid, but there are important consequences.

a) The incontestable fact is stressed in the mention of the *seal of the Spirit* (2 Co 1:22; Ep 1:13). Not only is there the remote and mysterious divine action when we become Christian. Each one is so personally marked by this process that he becomes the property of God, carrying his seal and placed under his protection (Ex 12:13; Ez 9:4-7; Rev 7:3; 9:4). With the aid of the Spirit, baptism imposes the seal, which comes to be recognized as the gift of God, the sign of participation in divine life and the principle of brotherly communion.

b) The seal is something acquired. But it has to be lived, and it is here that the Ephesians find difficulty. Paul concentrates on one difficulty, *sins of the tongue*. Previously, in verse 25, he spoke of lies, and now, in verse 31, he turns to other sins of speech.

His contrast between the seal of the Spirit and sins of the tongue is not merely fortuitous. In Ephesians 1:13 he had associated the seal of the Spirit with the reception of the Word of truth and the gospel of salvation. It is because of his adherence in faith to the word of God that a man is saved by the Spirit. How then could any Christian give utterance to a lie or a word of malice, once he has in the Spirit heard the Word of truth?

*See the doctrinal theme: *Israel*, p. 283.

c) To mention the Spirit of God in man is to speak of inter-personal *communion* in the Body of Christ. But actual practice does not correspond to this. Paul is referring to a situation that is fairly distressing. Irritations have multiplied to the point of expression in reproaches and insults (v. 31). Obviously such behavior should be discontinued in a Christian community, which is ánimated by a "Spirit" altogether different. People dem-onstrate what they are by the exercise of kindness and compas-sion (v. 32), above all pardon. The seed of all these virtues is in them and is called the Spirit.

d) *Mutual pardon* has special importance for Paul: it will make his correspondents imitators of God (v. 1) and Christ. It is less a matter of imitating Christ's outward behavior than of bear-ing public witness to the pardon one has received oneself (v. 2; cf. Mt 18:23-35). If some deprivation be necessary in doing this, we should remember that this is imitation of him who delivered himself for us (v. 2). Simple logic demands that his gift should reproduce itself in our lives, not as obedience to some exterior commandment, but as the echo of an experience from which we ourselves have been the first to benefit. We ourselves cannot love until we have experienced the love of God.

Even on the human level sin brings about a cleavage in the person, a clash between what one is and what one ought to be. It is similar with the new humanity. In the Christian the Spirit is as much a part of the person as the faculties of intelligence and will.

This new faculty in a man is at once witness to an event and seed of a real experience. Salvation has touched him at his roots and he must henceforth live in harmony with this state. He must pardon, deliver himself for others, and extend to his brother the benefits he has derived from his own salvation.

The Christian moral code then is above all God-centered. It is based on contemplation and on experience of salvation events.

VI. Hebrews   The author is addressing himself to Christians
11:1-2, 8-12   of Jewish origin whom persecution has driven
2nd reading   from Jerusalem. They are disturbed and dis-
3rd cycle   couraged. They fear that their exile from the
Holy City may disassociate them from the inauguration of the Kingdom. He recommends a spirit of faith that
is concentrated only on the invisible and sustained by the certainty of possessing here and now the earnest of heavenly things
(v. 1). He encourages them with reminders of their ancestors'
faith. Today's reading is concerned with Abraham.

Like these Jews of the first century, Abraham knew exile, the
severance of family and national ties (v. 8), all the insecurity of
the "displaced person." He made all this the basis for an act of
faith in God's promise (v. 9).

The believer must always be a pilgrim. He is in the world, but
not attached to it, because he has opted for the invisible goods.
Abraham's wanderings did not lead him to a terrestrial city (this
Jerusalem which this Jewish audience yearns to regain), or a
material promised land, but to an invisible city (v. 10), the city
of life with God. Faith is not fulfilled by tangible goods or immediate hopes. It is characterized by waiting, by the goal which
is not material, which seems always to recede.

Furthermore Abraham had to endure the barrenness of Sarah
and the hopelessness of progeny (Gn 15:1-6) (v. 11). This was
his greatest trial. He had to face death (vv. 12-13) without fulfillment of the promise. This is the final test of faith, the encounter with death in the conviction that it cannot nullify
God's plan.

In the eyes of the author, the faith of Abraham in offering his
son Isaac is faith in the resurrection. He was ready to give over
to death his hope for progeny, because he was entrusting to God
the task of raising him up again. His confrontation of death then
was similar to that of Christ on the cross. There was a total com-

mission of his fate to God, and absolute confidence in the abundance of Yahweh's life.*

More than suffering then, the sign *par excellence* of faith, of the total gift of self to God, is death. Abraham believed in "something beyond death." He believed that even to his worn out body a progeny would be given because it had been promised. This is essentially the attitude of Christ himself on the cross. He had given himself completely to the Father for the realization of the salvation plan. But he had to endure the agony of total failure in his enterprise. He who was sent to reassemble all humanity is absolutely alone. He trusts in the something beyond death that the resurrection will manifest.

It is the Eucharist that enables Christians to share this faith and learn to triumph over their own failures.

VII. Matthew   In both Mark and Matthew this episode fol-
     14:22-33   lows immediately the multiplication of the
     Gospel   loaves. The first two verses (22-23) still reflect
     1st cycle   the atmosphere of the miracle. Realizing that
     the crowd continues to regard him as a conquering and vengeful Messiah, Jesus takes his leave to devote himself to the training of his disciples. We might regard this storm episode as their first lesson. His particular concern with Peter is noteworthy (cf. Mt 16:16-21; 17:24-27).

a) The *victory of God over the waters* is a highly important theme in Jewish cosmogony.

Following ancient Semitic traditions the Bible describes the creation of the world as God's victory over the sea and the monsters of evil that dwell in it (Pss 103/104:5-9; 105/106:9; 73/74:13-14; 88/89:9-11; Ha 3:8-15; Is 51:9-10). The victory over the Red Sea (Ps 105/106:9), like the eschatological victory over

---

*See the doctrinal theme: *the promise,* p. 289.

the Lake (Rev 20:9-13), are regarded as decisive stages in salvation history.

Primitive Christians accordingly interpreted the stilling of the tempest (Mt 8:23-27) and walking on the water as a manifestation of the one who is bringing to fulfillment the work of creation. It was a sign of the dawning of the day of Yahweh (Ha 3:8-15; Is 51:9-10; cf. v. 33). Walking on the water was an epiphany of the divine power that resided in Christ.

b) The triumph however took place at a decisive turning point in the life of Jesus. The role of itinerant rabbi, idol of the crowds, no longer corresponds to the Father's salvific will (cf. the prayer of v. 23). He decides to give himself exclusively to the task of *intensive training for the apostles,* Peter in particular. He will reveal to them his messianic power and teach them to have confidence in him. The walking on the waters is directed to this end. He convinces Peter that he does possess the power to conquer evil (symbolized by the waters on which Peter treads: vv. 28-29). And he makes him realize that this is due not to any magical faculty, but to his fidelity (vv. 30-31).

The apostles thus have power over the forces of evil insofar as they have confidence, and remain attached to, the person of Christ.

When one affirms that Christ has vanquished the powers of evil, one is proclaiming the cosmic dimensions of his achievement. Prior to him all creation was involved in the solidarity of sin. By his fidelity he smashed the yoke.

So it is that the Christian's victory has a cosmic dimension as well as being a victory over himself. He really has overcome the world; he dominates the elements of the world just as Christ and Peter mastered the sea. It is his destiny to topple the forces of evil wherever they still emerge, the manifestations, that is, of death above all.

Our best weapon for this combat is the Eucharist. It makes us sharers in Christ's victory over Satan and death.

VIII. John   From the very beginning of his discourse on
     6:41-51   the bread of life, Jesus is concerned to turn
     Gospel   the thoughts of his audience from the marvels
     2nd cycle   wrought by Moses to what he himself has just
done. He then passes to the second stage: the
transition from his marvels to the mystery of his person and
his mission.

Now comes the decisive moment for those who listen. Either
they "come to him" (vv. 44-45) or murmur against the pretensions he makes (v. 41).

a) "Seeing the Son" (v. 40) or "coming to him" (vv. 37 and
44) is equivalent to recognizing the relation between Christ and
the Father. The moment the *disciple* enters into proper relationship with Jesus is the moment when he sees the relationship
between Jesus and the Father, and consequently the mystery of
Jesus' person.

We shall understand the importance of this text more fully if
we see it in the context of the rabbinic schools that were contemporary with Christ. In the Old Testament God was wont to
instruct his own (Is 2:2-4; 54:13 cited in Jn 6:45; Jr 31:31-34;
Ps 50/51:8, etc.). Whenever the sages grouped about them
disciples or "sons" (Pr 1:8-10), they claimed to present, not a
particular doctrine, but God's own law. At a later stage, masters
would set themselves up independently so to speak, and gather
schools of disciples where they gave particular interpretations of
the law (reference in Mt 23:8-12).

Apparently Jesus began his public life with the intention of
being a rabbi of this sort, with disciples of his own (Lk 6:17;
Mt 12:15; Jn 6:60). Like the contemporary rabbis he frequently
imposed austere and difficult tasks on his disciples: the renunciation of family ties (Lk 9:59-62; 14:33); the carrying of the cross
(Lk 14:27; 9:23) — the acceptance, that is, of the death which
was the promised lot of the messianic revolutionary, and which

excluded any romanticism in discipleship of Jesus; the service of the master in daily needs (Lk 8:3; Jn 4:8), etc.

Gradually however his relationship with his disciples deepened. Saint John will present a new view of the meaning of this relationship. Jesus is actually restoring the old tradition of disciples who are taught by God, of whom the rabbis are but the messengers. This is his attitude in our Gospel of today (cf. also Jn 6:37-40). He will have no disciples except such as recognize his basic unity with the Father, and come to him for the sake of his mission in the name of God, not because of a particular doctrine. Those moved by mere attraction or enthusiasm he rejects. It is God himself who chooses his disciples, "gives" them to him and begets their vocation (v. 37; Jn 6:43-44; 15:16). For Saint John it is always essential, before the link of discipleship with Jesus is formed, that one recognize the link binding Jesus to the Father. It is not because of what Jesus says that the disciple comes, but over and above all because of what he is. Where the synoptics speak of "following Christ," he speaks of "seeing" Christ (v. 44).*

b) By contrast with the disciple, the one who "murmurs" (v. 41) fails to see Christ's relation with the Father, and refuses to recognize that the son of Joseph is someone come down from heaven (vv. 42-43).

Christ responds to the murmurers by proclaiming himself "the bread of life come down from heaven" (vv. 48-49), repeating what he had said earlier (Jn 6:31-33). The phrase indicates his personal relation with the Father as bearer of the divine life in the mystery of the incarnation. Then, abruptly, the discourse changes from Bread-as-person to the *eucharistic Bread* (v. 51).

It is the Eucharist then which forges the deepest relation between the disciple and the Master. In this sacrament we can best "see" the link between Jesus and the Father. It is rightly called the "mystery of faith."

---

*See the doctrinal theme: *discipleship*, p. 134.

In celebrating the Eucharist the Church is bearing witness to the love and knowledge that bind the Son to the Father and us to the Son. It is the decisive sign, because it expresses the perfect response of the man-God to his Father, and the Church's response to the requirements of fidelity and love.

In counterpoint to the descent of the bread of life in the incarnation and the eucharist, we have the upward movement of the disciples toward Christ. God who sends Jesus among his own assures him at the same time of the disciples' faith.

IX. Luke
12:31-38
Gospel
3rd cycle

This piece is made up of three texts that were originally independent. The first concludes the preceding narrative. The second and third illustrate the Christian virtue of vigilance. Luke combines them because of their common eschatological import.

a) In verses 33-34 we have a theme which the evangelist found doubtless in his sources and uses as conclusion to the ensemble concerning the foolish rich man and the troubled poor man (Lk 12:22-23). It need not detain us here. We should note however that Luke's version is rather different to Matthew's (6:20-21). He introduces the theme of *almsgiving*, a favorite one with him (cf. Lk 12-21; 16:9; 11:41; 6:34-35; Ac 9:36; 10:2, 4, 31), and is more intransigent than Matthew about the choice between heavenly and earthly treasures. Matthew does not make the choice exclusive. He does, because he takes a more eschatological view.

b) Verses 35-38 give us the parable of the porter opening to the master, but Luke's version does not seem to be the primitive one. Like most of Jesus' parables this one too underwent some allegorization among early Christians. Instead of accepting the stories as simple illustrations of moral teaching, they tended to read into them allusions to the life of Jesus himself, and his return. The very profusion of variants that we find for this parable in the three synoptics indicates how profoundly important it seemed to the primitive communities (cf. Mt 24:42-44; Ac 13:33-37).

Verse 37b appears to be an addition. It is too similar to Luke 17:7; 22:27 and John 13:4-5, and it breaks the continuity between verse 37a and verse 38 by introducing the theme of the messianic banquet. This contributes nothing to the understanding of the parable. Furthermore all the servants are recommended to watch, whereas in Mark it is the porter only, whose duty it is. Luke is modifying the parable to include all members of the community.

The oncoming event is a cataclysm (cf. Lk 17:26-29), which will separate the good from the bad and open to them the gates of the Kingdom. There is going to be a "trial" which will be inaugurated by the Passion, and which can only be withstood by prayer (Mk 14:38; Lk 11:4c) and *viligance*.

Understood thus, the parable was probably directed at the scribes, who were sleeping through the moment of crisis though their mission was one of guiding the people. It proclaimed the hollowness of a theology that failed to discern God in the event.

The early communities however allegorized this by discerning themselves in the servants, by representing Jesus as having gone on a long journey (Mk 13:34), and seeing the Lord himself as the server of the messianic banquet (v. 37b).

c) Verses 39-40 belong to another parable which we might call that of the burglar. The aorist tense in the Greek version suggest that Jesus was alluding to a recent incident. He takes advantage of this to give a warning about the approaching trial: "you too must be careful that you be not surprised."

There was no attempt to allegorize the terms of this parable (it would have been difficult to see the Son of man as a burglar), which simply describes the suddenness of the trial to be (cf. 1 Th 5:2-4; 2 P 3:10) and recommends people to be *vigilant*.

Both parables indicate that Jesus, and subsequently the first Christians, were expecting a trial that would usher in the last times. It would unmask the forces of evil and their partisans, and divide off the small remnant of the "saved" who would share the Kingdom. Jesus however is stressing the suddenness of this oncoming event, and the unpreparedness of the leaders whose duty it is to announce it. The first Christians allegorize, and turn their gaze towards the end of time where they understood their happiness to lie.

B. DOCTRINE

1. The Theme of Israel

In the declaration on non-Christian religions the Second Vatican Council devotes a special section to the Jews. The horrible Calvary which had been the lot of the Jewish people under the Nazi regime made it imperative that the Church should state unequivocally what were the relations between Christianity and Jewry, and above all that she should formally condemn anti-semitism, rejecting those arguments on which it had frequently, even in Christian circles, been based. Her statement on the Jews very opportunely reminds us of the close links that bind the Church to Israel.

Today's formulary (2nd reading, 1st cycle) invites us to analyze the problem of Israel in all its deepest implications. Christians are not always aware of the importance this has for the correct understanding of what faith in Jesus Christ means. Though the Church itself has always held the Old and New Testaments in equal reverence, some Christians are inclined to think the Old was canceled once for all with the coming of Jesus. They fail to appreciate the significance of that historic spiritual pilgrimage that leads from Abraham to Jesus. And, even though Paul in his letter to the Romans devotes several chapters to the destiny of Israel, they do not see that the continuance of the Jewish people throughout the centuries becomes a challenge for the Church. She has to demonstrate her authenticity. A question arises that may not be disregarded. Why has anti-semitism been prevalent among Christians? Is it just another manifestation of racism?

Obviously one cannot, in a few pages, deal thoroughly with so complex a problem. We shall have to be satisfied with indicating the avenues of reflection that will enable our readers to see for themselves how important the Jewish question is in the actual practice of the faith. The fact of Israel is immensely relevant if we are to have a balanced view of the Christian doctrine of salvation.

Israel, the People of Yahweh, the God of Faith

Often we tend to see the religious history of Israel as that of a people whom God set up in special authority as witnesses of faith. He revealed himself to them and made with them the covenant of Sinai. They were a people to whom God sent prophets in order to prepare them gradually for the fullness of revelation in Jesus. Apart from the fact that this is an inadequate view historically, it does not help us at all towards a proper appreciation of the remarkable spiritual quest of Israel.

We must go back of course to the patriarchal period to discern the origins, but, as a people, Israel was really born in the exodus from Egypt. Through the hazards of the desert they lived the liberating event, and were led by Moses to the regime of faith. This was when the Covenant was made, the Law given, and the Promised Land was seen as the gift of Yahweh. The collective history of faith begins. Despite all their pagan impulses, this people, led by prophets of whom Moses was the first, embarks on an unparalleled spiritual quest, the encounter with God in the event. Previously, like all other peoples, they had sought security in rites that celebrated the recurring cycle in events. Now we see them turn to a reading of events that is unprecedented. The vicissitudes of their own history, the ups and the downs, are seen as epiphanies of the living God. They do not escape the insecurities of the human predicament. It is in this human context, challenged always by uncertainty and by death, that they are drawn to poverty of heart. God seems now the Totally-Other, the Creator of the universe, the unchallenged Master of their own history and that of all peoples, the God on whom no man can lay hand, the God who gratuitously reveals himself and saves.

Corresponding with this insight about Yahweh, we have the

passionate Jewish quest for the man who could respond with sufficient fidelity to the God of the Covenant to bring about the definitive regime of salvation. Paradoxically, in a negative way, the conditions for such fidelity became clear through experience of sin. Man has been created in the image and semblance of God: it is only in God that he can be fulfilled. Sin however is some sort of illusory gesture at self-divinization. What sort of man could ever reach from the depths of the creatural condition to meet God's initiative? This is the question which burgeoned, with more or less obscurity, into messianic hope. People waited for the Savior, the man who could save men.

Israel's great achievement was to clarify the essential polarities of salvation in the regime of faith. The people of the old Covenant might have been content with their recognition of the Totally-Other God, and the radical dependence of the creature on God. They might have seen God as the exclusive architect of salvation. This would indeed have been easier. But they did not see it that way. Throughout their spiritual pilgrimage, though Yahweh was always seen as the great Initiator of salvation, they turned more and more to messianic hope. This indeed, as has been remarked, becomes the "back bone" of the Old Testament. And it is because this expectation of the Messiah-Savior never ceases to recur that Israel gradually came to discern the secret of God's salvation plan. He is the God of love, the God who gives himself and awaits the man who will respond perfectly in kind.

Jesus of Nazareth, child of Israel, the awaited Messiah

One is liable to be wrong about the mystery of Christ unless one remembers always that he belonged to the Jewish people. We sometimes talk of the Incarnate Word as if the fact that his mother was the Jewish girl, Mary, were not of real consequence. There is a school of theology which is unconcerned with the history of Christianity, and concentrates on the assumption by the Son of human nature as a salvific fact, as if time, place and circumstances of the Incarnation did not matter. This kind of thinking tends to make salvation extrinsic. It does not indicate how Jesus' intervention in history fulfilled beyond all expectation man's secular hope, as it was expressed in Israel. Most of all it fails to make people understand how the human life of Jesus culminating in the death on the cross was the great sign of salvation, in that men were called on to affirm his divinity. For such insights we have to see the incarnation in its exact historical context.

Jesus was a typical Jew of his time, distinguished in no way from the others unless by his awareness of Messiahship. When his public ministry began he put himself forward as Savior. The real nature of salvation and the true character of the Messiah would gradually be clarified by the concrete manner in which he did this, by his behavior and his teaching. He takes up one of the great messianic titles, Son of man, but radically modifies its connotation. From the prophet Daniel onwards the title celebrated the grandeur and exceptional character of the awaited Savior. He would arrive on the clouds, and intervene spectacularly. Jesus however was an ordinary Jew, the son of a Nazareth carpenter. There could not be a greater contrast. He made no attempt to hide his origins, but put himself forward as one who shared the human lot in every detail. He performed his saving mission by absolute and ceaseless acceptance of creaturehood. This entailed on the one hand complete renunciation of self, because man never drew salvation from his own resources. It entailed, on the other, fraternal love for everyone regardless of the person. The Son of man on this earth would be the suffering Servant. His Saviorhood, the fact that he was able to respond adequately to the divine initiative, was due to an origin other than his human origin. This Son of man is the Son of God. In him all men are called to become children of the Father in absolute acceptance of the creatural condition until death, if necessary the death of the Cross.

The importance in salvation history of national churches

As we have seen, Jesus revealed the nature of salvation and his own identity as Son of God by bringing to accomplishment in his person, but in an unexpected manner, the great hope of his people. His people however recoiled from this sort of accomplishment which, while offering men sonship with God, required total conversion and love without limits. They chose to condemn their Messiah to death on the Cross. What he did for Israel, it becomes the Church's mission to do for all peoples. She is the Body of Christ, the actual presence of the Risen Lord among men. She must reveal the nature of salvation and the identity of the Savior to everyone. It is a task that she can only accomplish by making her own the circumstances of Jesus' incarnation. All peoples must undergo their own spiritual pilgrimage, in search of a solution to the human predicament. They are constantly seeking salvation, and deceiving themselves with the hope that it is attainable by their own resources. This is where the Church must intervene, to bring about salvation in Jesus Christ, always again in an unexpected manner. It will cause "scandal," and make people recoil. The Church can never hope to evade the mystery of the Cross. Indeed it is by living this, as Jesus did, that she will clarify for people the nature of the salvation they are seeking.

There are however some differences between what Jesus did for Israel, and what he does not through the Church for other peoples. They deserve our attention. The spiritual quest of other peoples does not have the particular intensity that the Jewish one had. Most often it will be arrested at a point antecedent to the regime of faith. It will be the Church's task to march side by side with such a people. She will travel with them the road that leads from Abraham to Jesus, marking all the stages that bring men finally to him. Again, Jesus was a Jew who followed naturally a tradition of messianic hope. The Church, however Jewish her beginnings were, is always under the necessity of becoming Greek with the Greeks, Indian with the Indians,

Chinese with the Chinese, African with the Africans, and so on. Before a native church can get set up among any people, there is always that crucial stage where their spiritual quest must be turned to the person of Jesus Christ. In a way there is less real difference here than appears at first glance. The message of love that Jesus conveyed to his own people entailed renunciation of their privileges so that they could become open to the whole world. Saint Paul, while always remaining a simple Jew among Jews just as Jesus had been before him, could become Greek with the Greeks, and found native churches throughout the Greek world. He did so by initiating the sort of brotherly dialogue that knows no frontiers. All our churches everywhere, if they are to provide answers to the spiritual quest of peoples, must be centers where the cooperation of all men, in love, becomes ever more rooted.

The Church of Jesus Christ and the Jewish people

Though the Church can rightly be described as the "Israel of the final times," though all the apostles and the majority in the primitive communities were Jews, it is nevertheless true that, as a people, Israel officially rejected the salvation offered by Jesus Christ. Why? Because she did not accept the total sort of conversion that he demanded if she were to become the instrument of his universal mission. She did not renounce the "privileges," or more accurately the defective interpretation of those privileges she had made her own. Her election was in fact only because of Jesus of Nazareth, the unique mediator of human salvation; but she made this the basis of a claim from God to a special place in the coming Kingdom. Faithful observance of the law was made to seem a title of merit to salvation, whereas, as such, all that it could lead to was death. The noble biblical doctrine of poverty was not brought to the point of absolute dependence on the saving God, who would meet in the Incarnate Word finally the perfect response.

This said however, it remains true that the endurance of the historic Jewish people throughout the ages poses a fundamental problem for the Church. Saint Paul in his letter to the Romans ponders the problem of his people's destiny, and expresses the conviction that they will be converted after all the Nations have entered the Church. In attempting to probe the meaning of all this, what can one say. We might say perhaps that the inclusion of all Nations within the fold of the Church will present an ecclesial sign so overwhelming that even a people as proud as the Jewish one is of its own indefectibility will be forced to acknowledge it. Pride will yield to the all-encompassing divine benevolence. The Church however must always strive to remain faithful to her own destiny, which Saint Paul has described as the reconciliation in the blood of Christ of the Jews and the Nations. She will find in the endurance of the Jewish people a challenge to constant fidelity to the law of universal charity. She will be open for true dialogue with the Jewish people to the extent that she wears the true visage of catholicity, that she represents both diversity and unity at once. On the other hand insofar as she becomes recessionist, or narrows her horizons to any one particular culture or enclave, she will be closed to dialogue. The seed of antisemitism may burgeon again, because in such a climate the only way of dealing with an embarrassing witness is to remove him.

2. The Theme of the Promise

Christians are generally aware that mere religious practice is not an adequate fulfillment of the faith's requirements. It must be woven into the texture of daily life by following the essential norms of the gospel. But when we remember the rich horizons opened up by the Bible, it must be admitted that the general understanding of what the faith means is rather poor. Where it should be experienced as a dynamism that summons our deepest energies for a great spiritual adventure, it is often understood as conformity to some moral principles for living. Biblical faith is not like this: it speaks the language of love. It brings about deep personal relationship and builds fidelity.

Faith in the promises is an integral theme of both Old and New Testaments. It is perhaps, of all biblical themes, the best key to an understanding of what faith means. It recurs at every stage in Israel's history: Yahweh is always the God of the promises. But it was not until the intervention of Christ that it came to definitive culmination. Human salvation was accomplished when the man-God continued the tradition of promise. He promised the Spirit. From then on an order of love was set up between God and humanity.

Yahweh, the God of the Promises

The vocabulary of promise has nothing to do with man's quest for salvation in a pagan context. It always springs from a desire for security and a thirst for possession. Salvation is seen in terms of divinization: what man wants is communication with this divine world which is stable and unchangeable. The gods do not make promises because they do not intervene. Nothing new can happen, because there is a fixed order established for all time. Man's problem is to find adequate means of grafting himself into this.

Israel's quest was different. Jewish man's realism as he confronted the event gradually led him to the insight that salvation is not within human capacity, that it must come by God's altogether gratuitous initiative. Yahweh is the Totally-Other God, the only architect of salvation. But, discerned in the event, he is the living God, the God who intervenes, the God who reveals himself. Seen with the eyes of faith, he is above all a personal God. When he intervenes in Jewish history, he does so in order to set up personal relations with the people he has chosen gratuitously.

It is easy then to see how he became the God of the promises. People who have encountered the living God, who depend upon his power and fidelity, readily see salvation as something in the order of promise. It hinges on the delicate exchange of love. When Yahweh promises, he binds himself as only God can with the bonds of love. He makes man realize that the human quest can only reach fulfillment at the end of a long pilgrimage. The bonds of love take a considerable time to forge, and those who love know that the time is never measurable.

Israel of course always questioned herself about the content of the promises. As faith deepened we can see the trend of these reflections. In the beginning people looked to Yahweh for favors and blessings: a fruitful soil, numerous progeny, prestige among nations, in a word, tangible goods. But by the end the object of the promise had become Yahweh himself, his favor and his grace, because God alone was sufficient. This was the moment when the content of the promise became clear: it could only be understood in the context of love.

Jesus Christ, the answer to God's promises

When we affirm that Jesus of Nazareth fulfilled God's promises, we are clarifying at once the mystery of Jesus himself and the nature of the promise. Jesus is the man-God. He is the greatest gift of love that God could make to humanity; but simultaneously he is that man among men who is capable of the perfect response to God's antecedent initiative. His way is that of double love, love for God and love for all men. He saves men because in him the perfect encounter between God and man took place.

The promise thus becomes meaningful as communion between persons. God's promise is the gift of himself in his incarnate Son. It offers no easy security, no tangible good; the gift itself is everything. Such a gift cannot be merited; observance of a law does not lead to it; it is absolutely gratuitous and open to all. The hesitations of the Old Testament in this context are at an end; with the advent of Jesus Christ Israel's spiritual quest, as Saint Paul clearly perceived, comes to an end in the manifestation of the God of the promise. But the promise was accomplished in reciprocity. The Incarnate Word was the man capable of saying the "yes" of accomplishment, and it is clear that for the promise two polarities of fidelity cooperate. In salvation the sovereign initiative always remains with God, but man's active response is an essential element. That God does not save man without man is a fundamental principle in the religion of love.

And, to understand the full implications of the promise, we must go further still. It is as if with Jesus Christ the whole tradition of promise suddenly, in answer to the demands of love, takes a new direction. Throughout his public ministry, Jesus himself did not cease to make promises. Saint John, with his profound insight, makes all these coalesce in one: the promise of the Spirit. It is in the Spirit that the love between God and humanity is brought to consummation. Two things become clear: that human salvation depends altogether on Christ, the unique mediator; but that salvation is inaugurated only, and destined to develop in a history where each one of us is summoned to respond personally to God's initiative.

The ecclesial heritage of the promise

The Church is the heir to the promises. She had her origins in the sending of the Spirit, who was the fulfillment of the Father's promise and that of the Incarnate Word. When he descended on the apostles, he bore witness to the real presence with his own of the Risen Lord, and the fact that the Church is really the Body of Christ. He is sent to all those who, by baptism, receive the gift of filial adoption.

What does this sending mean? It clarifies the state of the Christian, who is heir to the promise. He is a person possessed by the Trinitarian God, who has given himself personally in Jesus Christ. In his link with Christ he becomes capable of responding actively to God, and meeting the divine initiative of love. Possessing the Spirit, he can say the filial "yes" that is pleasing to the Father. Because the Spirit has been sent, the members of the Body know that they now have a genuine relation of reciprocity with God, according to the order of love.

Why then do we have the New Testament references to the earnest of the promise only? They indicate that it is only after death that the plenitude of the Spirit comes, while here below the history of the promise continues to expand. The Christian who has received the Spirit in baptism and confirmation is confronted by a task. He must bring his stone to the building of the Kingdom. His faith must grow and grow towards fuller obedience and love. Inheriting the promise is more than the reception of a gift: it is above all the assumption of new responsibilities. There is a period of waiting before definitive accomplishment comes, but it is filled with the progressive growth of the Kingdom here below.

Those for whom the promise is destined are Gentiles as well as Jews; they are, that is to say, all humanity. But the promise will only be received by those with faith; the only communion that the Spirit can set up between God and men is one of love; the only man that God can give himself to is the one who welcomes him in absolute poverty. Where this promise is concerned, there are no privileges and no prior claims; it is genuinely open to all.

The history of the Promise and its realization in mission

The Spirit's coming kindles a missionary zest in those with proper insight. Revealing as it does the meaning of the Church as the Body of Christ, the Temple of the love — dialogue between God and humanity, it is always in process until the Body grows to the required stature. It is not an event that terminated on Pentecost day.

Mission is the actualization of the Spirit's coming. It aims at increase in the Church, and wherever the Church is implanted the Spirit is sent. He is sent to the Church so that the Church in turn may send him wherever she brings Christ. So high then is the dignity of the Christian who is conscious of his missionary responsibility. He is a sharer in the promise, an agent as a member of the ecclesial Body in the sending of the Spirit that is constantly in progress. The Church's mission can only be comprehended in terms of the great mystery of the Trinity.

This link however with the mission of the Church does not mean that the Spirit's action is limited to the physical frontiers of the Church. Since the first day of creation the Spirit of God has filled the universe. The grace of God is at work in the hearts of all men and all peoples. It leads them to the encounter with Jesus Christ in the fold of the Church. It is constantly with them in their spiritual quest. But there is a special sending of the Spirit that can only come with mission and the foundation of a church. That is the moment when a non-Christian people will enter the Temple of dialogue with the living God.

If we appreciate the importance of this link between mission and the sending of the Spirit we shall realize the true character of missionary witness. One cannot be a missionary unless one has oneself encountered the living God of Jesus Christ, unless one is personally involved in a reciprocal relationship of love. Missionary witness is the highest expression of a faith that goes to the limit in self-renunciation. It is a work of love.

The sending of the Spirit on the eucharistic community

On Pentecost Day the Spirit came down on the assembled apostles, and at once they bore witness to the Risen Lord present among them. Every eucharistic celebration is a new Pentecost. It is the great focus in ecclesial life of the coming of the Spirit, and of sharing in the promise. Christ is most fully present there among his own, and he breathes his Spirit.

When Christians come together at this sacred moment they are being initiated into an ever deeper encounter with God. Joined with the Risen Lord, they chant the praises of God, and give thanks for his marvels and his salvation, in the realization that through their adoptive sonship in Jesus they can reach the Father. When they say the Our Father all together the Spirit is at work in them. After the Mass they return to their daily lives more than ever strengthened in their conviction that the one important task is this. They must bear witness to what they have become through the action of the Spirit, and they must contribute to the Church's missionary dynamism, so that the history of the promise will go on.

TWENTIETH SUNDAY

A. THE WORD

I. Isaiah
56:1, 6-7
1st reading
1st cycle

This is the beginning of the third portion of the book of Isaiah, which is dated a century later than the exile. The author is describing the conditions for admission of Gentiles to the temple worship.

Third-Isaiah takes up once more the question of *universalism*. First-Isaiah had envisaged the reassembly of all nations in a spiritual Jerusalem, transcending any physical location, with foundations laid not now on Mount Sion, but on the very person of the Messiah. Faith would be the only title to citizenship here (Is 4:2-6; 26:1-6; 28:5-6, 16-17). Even the conversion of the Gentiles is envisaged, and the establishment of a cult independent of the temple (Is 19:18-22). Second-Isaiah however in the meantime had considerably narrowed these horizons, by concentrating on the hope of restoring the historic Jerusalem. Universalism is seen as a kind of making amends and complete submission to Israel by the nations (Is 33:17-24; 51:9-11; 52:1-2).

Third-Isaiah, though perfectly aware of failure in the attempt to restore Jerusalem, and conscious that dreams of eventual domination over the great contemporary powers were illusory, remains concerned about the role of the holy city and its temple. He opens the gates more fully to the Gentiles. The uncleanness of the eunuch or the stranger is no longer reason for excommunication. Whoever accepts the provisions of the covenant, in particular ritual laws like that of the sabbath (vv. 2, 4), can be part of the liturgical assembly and offer valid sacrifice there (v. 7). Then the temple will really be fulfilling God's purpose. It will be a "house of prayer for all the peoples" (v. 7). Because the conditions for reassembly there are essentially religious, God will gather there not alone the dispersed of Israel, but many others with them (v. 8).

Thus his universalist outlook is clearly wider than his predecessor's; but it still falls far short of that of Isaiah himself.*

The failure of this prophecy was stressed by Jesus, in a temple of watertight compartments and rigid tabus (Mt 21:12-17). We might well question ourselves about how open our eucharistic assemblies are. Are they really signs of that universal reassembly we struggle to implement in our daily lives. How do we welcome the stranger and the traveler? Do we positively try to involve people of another class or another culture?

II. Proverbs 9:1-6
1st reading
2nd cycle

This passage is taken from the latest portion of the book of Proverbs (chap. 1-9; 5th century?). The author is concerned not only with the achievement of God's Wisdom in creation, but with its intellectual influence, and mysterious influence generally. He chooses to personify the notion, not to make it a divine person, but to make its appeal to humanity more striking, and its desire to communicate more evident.

In our reading Wisdom is represented as eager to communicate itself to men. Though he is transcendent, God does not cease to animate all things in the universe and thus prepare his incarnation. To be prepared for this man must be poor in spirit and acknowledge his ignorance (v. 4; cf. Lk 6:21; 1 K 17:1-15; Is 55:1-3).

The image of a *banquet* best expresses the communion between host (v. 3) and banqueters (v. 5), the riches and abundance of God who invites, and the spiritual poverty of those hungry for divine life.**

*See the doctrinal theme: *catholicity*, Advent/Christmas, p. 257.
**See the doctrinal theme: *eucharistic banquet*, p. 308.

It seems thus very understandable that it was during the course of a repast that Jesus brought the justice of God to sinners (Lk 5:29-32), revealed to the poor the bread that comes from heaven (Jn 6:56-59), and gave his own life to his disciples (Lk 22:14-20).

**III. Jeremiah
38:4-6,8-10**
*1st reading
3rd cycle*

The passion of Jeremiah is a brief episode and need not detain us long. He had been imprisoned for a considerable time when it was decided to throw him in a cistern and let him die of hunger or suffocation. The prompt intervention of a black servant of the king saves him, in symbol of the salvation that God reserves for those who "fall in the trench" but do not cease to hope in him.

The prophets of the past, and the prophets of today, all come to realize, to their cost, that the truth hurts. Given a pretext, unrelated to their message, the mob, or the authority, will seek to be rid of them. They will not hesitate to write a new installment in that long series of *passions,* the heart and center of which is Christ's own cross.*

Jeremiah was particularly sensitive. Everything in his temperament turned him towards indulgence. He would have made an excellent prophet of well-being. As it was he had to be a prophet of doom, the lesson being that God's scale of values and choices is not the human one. This may actually have to be turned awry.

Sensitive and depressed as he was, he would have been happy surrounded by peace and tranquility. Faced with the context of his time, he had to encounter persecution and seek sustenance in sources that lay beyond himself, in the faith and abandonment that single out the witness of God.

Being true to oneself always means going beyond oneself, and it is to God that one has to go.

---

*See the doctrinal theme: *persecution,* p. 102.

IV. Romans The Church is the new Israel, because in her
11:13-15, 29-32 the promises are accomplished and the spirit-
2nd reading ual privileges of the chosen people given real-
1st cycle ity. She is however largely made up of former
Gentiles; the Jews are only a small minority,
a very little "remnant" (Rm 11:4-5; cf. 9:27-29). She now has
the patrimony of Israel. Yet why should she, not the Jews, enjoy
this. In salvation-history what is the meaning of the rupture between the Church and Israel?

a) Paul's first observation is that it is not God who took the
initiative in the rupture. He remains faithful always to the people
he has chosen (v. 2), and the Jewish people will continue to be
the object of the promise even in their sundered stage because
God is present with them. He will reiterate this in different language in verse 16. The first fruits offered in the temple sanctify
the whole harvest. Likewise the first fruits of the people, the
patriarchs who lived according to the promise (cf. Rm 4:13-25),
continue to give the people a special *cachet*. The Jew who does
not believe in Jesus is still superior to the Gentile. Yet prece-
dences of this nature ought not to absorb our attention.

The *continuity* of God's presence with his people, and the sanc-
tifying influence of the promise, indicate that the rupture is not a
complete disaster, but a mistake (v. 11). Furthermore, even outside the Church, the chosen people still have a positive *raison
d'etre*. They bear witness dramatically to the failure of human
attempts to achieve salvation. As such they are a reminder to the
Church that she must remain faithful to the promise and to the
grace of reconciliation (vv. 12 and 15a).

Paul goes on to hope (this is a hope, we should note, not a
prophecy: v. 14) that Israel's negative role outside the Church
will one day become a positive and vitalizing role within her fold.

b) Verse 12, at first glance, is rather astonishing. How could
a mistake by Israel enrich the Gentiles? The observation could
not have been made by Paul were it not for his experience in all

the towns he has traveled, where his expulsion from the synagogue forced him to turn to the Gentiles (Ac 13:44-52; 17:1-9). Nor could he have made it in any context other than that of his own eschatological thinking. The Lord is about to come. But he delays his coming through *mercy*. He waits for all men to be converted (1 Tm 2:4). Jewish unbelief prolongs this delay, and enables a greater number of Gentiles to enter the Kingdom. Conversely, the witness of converted Gentiles ought to bring about the conversion of the Jews (through "jealousy": vv. 11 and 14). If it fails to do so, perhaps it is because the witness is not pure. So that in fact the salvation of both Jew and Gentile is not dissimilar. They can only be saved through mercy (Rm 11:30-32).

When Israel is converted to Christ it will bring to that moment something the Gentile could never bring. It will welcome Christ as the fulfillment of a history that the Jews were the only ones to live. It will demonstrate, as nothing else could, that salvation is the gift of God's mercy. This people, who had their origins in an initiative of love, are pursued by that love even in withdrawal. They live because God is faithful to his Word. The Christian can hasten the return of Israel by laboring to build a Church that will be worthy to welcome her, a church, that is, which derives all its strength from the divine initiative.*

V. Ephesians 5:15-20
2nd reading
2nd cycle

This passage can be regarded as the conclusion to Paul's teaching about the new life of the believer in Christ, in particular about the tension between the flesh and the spirit. It is a tension that has to be resolved in the life of every person.

We can distinguish two portions. Verses 15-17 develop the theme of wisdom, and recommend us not to lose the time we

---

*See the doctrinal theme: *Israel*, p. 283.

have been allotted. Verses 18-20 mention the plenitude of life in the Spirit and its expression in the liturgy.

a) A number of New Testament texts associate Wisdom with an awareness of *time*. To be wise is to watch at the "appointed time" (Mt 24:45-46), to await the moment of the Spouse's coming (Mt 25:1-2), to make the best of the actual moment (Col 4:5; Rm 13:11) even if one is in difficulty. The "last times" are really the proper combination of the two times: the eschatological era which has been inaugurated since Christ fulfilled the will of his Father, and secular time, sometimes so ambiguous and equivocal. The danger lies in opting for one or other of these times to the exclusion of the other. We can seek escape in a premature, disincarnate eschatology, or give ourselves to secular time as if that were the only reality. Making the most of the actual moment consists in blending our involvement with eschatology with the time we are living. We refuse any value to the latter that does not correspond with the former. This is the secret of divine will and human wisdom.

b) The juxtaposition of eschatology and secular time sets up a tension between the *Spirit and the flesh* (vv. 18-20). It is only by the Spirit that we can live with eschatological dynamism, and this necessarily entails a break with the world of the flesh (cf. 1 Th 4:3-8). Paul contents himself with one example: drunkenness. To this he opposes the religious atmosphere of the Christian banquets and the spiritual intoxication they engender. Perhaps he is remembering what he had to say earlier in this regard to the Corinthians (1 Co 11:17-34). Or he may wish to stress that it is not through the trances and orgies of the pagan mysteries that one reaches God, but through prayer, and in the Spirit.*

Whether we live in the Spirit or in the flesh is always influenced by our concept of time. Certain trends among today's youth (the hippie movement, for instance) are very revealing in

*See the doctrinal theme: *flesh and spirit*, p. 154.

this regard. Young people reject the society of their elders as one of the over-consumption and immediacy, and have recourse to styles that shock, but are logical. They refuse to be part of a society that makes an object of a man, and spurn a wealth that makes them feel alienated. There is certainly wisdom in this attitude. However there is a lack of realism in the concept such people have of the transcendent, or of time. One does not react the transcendent by using devices such as drugs, LSD, or sex to evade time. The wisdom of Saint Paul is still valid, and there must be a lucid view of the meaning of time.

VI. Hebrews The author has earlier reminded his Judaeo-
12:1-4 Christian readers, who were exiled from
2nd reading Jerusalem and yearning to return, of the pil-
3rd cycle grimage their ancestors had to undergo (He
11). He now applies this lesson to Christians.
They will always be nomads in this world.

a) With the imagery of nomadism is combined that of the athletic stadium (as in 1 Co 9:24 – 10:5). Christians are envisaged as runners in the stadium, and the spectators' seats are occupied by their ancestors (v. 1). These encourage their descendants to endure. The course is long and runners must lose weight ("throw off everything": v. 1) in order to sustain the trial to the end.

Not all spectators are "supporters." There is a hostile group, the "sinners" (v. 3) who have in the past subjected Christ to many insults and have others still in store for Christians.

b) The image however of a pilgrim people remains the predominant one, and is especially evident in the recommendation to Christians (v. 2) to keep their gaze constantly on the one who leads them, Jesus Christ, as the pillar of fire guided the people in the desert. The pillar in the desert led to material blessing. Christ is leading his people to *perfection* and to the throne of glory. Perfection describes the state of humanity that is faithful to the term of the pilgrimage. Christ is the "perfectioner," if one may coin a word that represents the Greek text more accurately. He will, that is to say, provide a culmination for the earthly pilgrimage of his people in the sanctuary of glory.

Although we have no specifically liturgical term in the passage, it can be taken as a description of the *priestly* function of Jesus. Previously the author had used the ritual of the feast of expiation to show his readers that Christ had gone from earth to the very throne of God (He 9; 11:10-17), just as the high-priest leaves the outer sanctuary for the Holy of Holies. The high-priest enters alone. Jesus, on the other hand, brings all the people with him (He 9:14). The means he gives them is none other than his flesh delivered for us (He 10:20) on Calvary, and, symbolically, in the Eucharist.

VII. Matthew 15:21-28 Gospel 1st cycle   We continue with the section of breads. Jesus has offered bread to all who wished to partake of it, but there were not sufficient people to exhaust the food (Mt 14:13-21). Twelve baskets of fragments were taken up.

We are later told why so few had eaten, leaving so many fragments. There were two reasons. The Pharisees, because of their regulations about ablutions (Mt 15:1-20), placed considerable obstacles in the way of those desirous to eat. Secondly, the Gentiles were refused access to the crumbs (v. 24). Our passage today is concerned with this second reason.

The account of the miracle at Tyre is given by Matthew (15:21-28) and Mark (7:24-30) only. The differences between the two versions are a good indication of their different approaches to the episode. Matthew has the Syro-Phoenician woman come to Jewish territory in order to get heard (Mt 15:22; like Naaman the Syrian; 2 K 5:12-14). Mark has the itinerant rabbi Jesus go into Gentile territory to proclaim salvation (Mk 8:24; cf. Mk 5:1 and Mk 6:53). He avoids reproducing the extremely harsh remark that Matthew puts in Jesus' mouth (v. 24). Nor does he have the Gentile woman confer the Messiahship of the Son of David, as Matthew does (v. 22). They both however give the exchange about the crumbs (vv. 24-26; Mk 8:28-29), because they see here a possible allusion to the fragments after the multiplication.

The intention in both accounts becomes clear. *Gentiles* too share the bread of salvation, because they too share the Lord's pity (cf. Mt 14:20; 15:32). One day the table of the disciples should be accessible to them.*

A celebration of the Eucharist on this day will be worthy of the name if it despatches its members with the purpose of gathering in those who are still far removed from the banquet table.

Jesus made no distinction between persons, between Jew or stranger, man or woman, child or adult, poor or rich. In so doing he was following one of the most explicit trends in later Jewish thinking, and he was setting the tone for Christian practice. When we share the same eucharistic table, with our diverse sociological backgrounds, we are bearing witness to Christ's sacrifice "for the many." We are hastening the advent of the moment when all humanity will be gathered together in the glorious Body of Christ.

VIII. John
6:51-59
Gospel
2nd cycle

This is the conclusion of Christ's discourse about the bread of life. He has made a gradual revelation of his person. He has spoken of bread, then of the bread of life. Then he has likened himself to the manna come down from heaven, and shown how this bread expresses his obedience to the

---

*See the doctrinal theme: *Gentiles*, p. 340.

Father and is a sign of the great sacrifice he has "given for men."
His blood will be shed for them in like fashion.

a) A stronger term than "body," the word "flesh" sets the
eucharistic event in the same context as that of the incarnation,
where the Word becomes "flesh" (Jn 1:14). This new sign henceforth will be weighted with divinity, the *flesh* of the Son of man
becoming the reality of the Son of God.

Exegetes are never quite agreed about the exact significance
of this bread which is Christ's flesh. The listeners at least got the
message about the reality of the man-God's incarnation and his
sacrifice. They were already on the point of rejecting such a
mysterious affirmation. Doubtless it was after the resurrection
that Saint John and the first Christians discerned in these words
the proclamation of the eucharistic mystery.

b) John goes on to stress the link established by Jesus between
this bread (which is sometimes his person, sometimes the eucharistic bread) and *Trinitarian* life. As the Son lives by the Father,
who is the "Living One," so the Christian lives by the Son
through the medium of "bread." This enables him to have with
the Son those bonds of dependence and communion that the Son
has with the Father. The bread is the Christian's passport to
Trinitarian life.

The last verse directs attention again to the manna. If this new
bread is in very truth a continuance of the incarnation, and an
introduction to Trinitarian life, the manna has been no more than
an inadequate symbol.

The eucharistic bread follows the pattern of all bread offered
by a father to his children. In itself it is nothing. The significance
lies in the toil and effort that produce it, and in the fact that it
is going to be eaten by persons. When parents offer this bread
that represents their life and their toil there is a sense in which
they can say: "This bread is my flesh given for my children" (v.
51). And the children who partake of it share in some sense the

very life of those who give (v. 54). If parents and children, each time they break bread, can give it this profound significance, it seems fitting that Jesus should act so. He is the perfect man among men, and gives the bread he offers an altogether new meaning, raised to the level of the life that he lives. He makes it a sharing of his life with the Father (v. 57), the sustenance of a new humanity, charged with eternal life (v. 54).

IX. Luke 12:49-53
Gospel
3rd cycle

This passage combines two sayings of Jesus that present some difficulty in interpretation. The first we have only in Luke's version (vv. 49-50). The second appears in Matthew too (10:34-36) in a form on which Luke's text appears to depend.

a) Verses 49-50 follow the rules of Hebrew parallelism:
   — fire and water (baptism)
   — Jesus' yearning and distress
   — kindling the fire and consuming the baptism

The association of fire and water is characteristic of the description of the *judgment* in Jewish apocalyptic literature. This is when God will bring the old, corrupt world to an end and substitute for it a new world that will remain faithful to him (cf. 2 P 3:5-7). Doubtless Jesus is referring to this belief, but he stresses the fact that it is he himself who will be the object of this judgment. He will be consumed with fire and plunged into water. It is then in his person that the ancient world will be purified to become the new world. This is what he yearns for most ardently, with the greatest distress: the passion. The Son of man does not come to judge and condemn, but to take on himself the judgment of the world and enable the universe to be transformed.

The transformation was wrought in his person when it was given up to death. But this has repercussions on every member of humanity. Each one must be converted and substitute new attitudes for his ancient ways. Some will accept *conversion*, others reject it. Through the very center of Jewish families themselves the line of division will run between those who remain loyal to Judaism and those who become loyal to the Lord.*

*See the doctrinal theme: *division*, p. 313.

B. DOCTRINE

1. The Theme of the Eucharistic Banquet

Vatican II, in promulgating the constitution *De Sacra Liturgia*, brought to completion the movement of fifty years duration to restore the eucharistic celebration to its proper place. Reforms introduced since the Council have made it clear that changes in depth were very necessary. Not everything has been solved, but at least the essential problems have been raised.

Where the Mass is concerned many Christians have a real malaise. Among apostolic groups there is no doubt at all about its importance, but it is poorly understood. The better Christians are centered more on "life" than on "rite" and do not take religious practice for granted. They consider the witness given by the exercise of charity to be much more important. A man today is liable to think that it is with his brothers, above all the poorest, that the encounter with Jesus Christ takes place. Not in the eucharastic celebration, however important that may be.

The failure to integrate the Mass into the texture of daily existence arises from a generally poor understanding of the link that ought to unite the two. Too often the homily seems set at some abstract level. The scriptural readings seem indecipherable, without relevance to the realities of living. Even the well-conducted celebration is open to such criticisms.

We should often ask ourselves about the place occupied by the Eucharist in our Christian lives and the meaning that it has. The stake is a considerable one. The whole balance of our apostolic life depends in large part on our understanding of this mystery.

The paschal banquet in Israel

In all "traditional" civilizations the meal has a religious import. Most religions have had sacred banquets. To share the same table and eat in common creates sacred bonds among the banqueters with which the gods are associated. When the food is an immolated victim, the meal is often regarded as an infallible means of winning divine benevolence. However, in pagan religions, the sacred banquet did not purport to set up a covenant or establish communion with the divine world. It simply maintained the bonds that had been forged.

In Israel, under the regime of faith, the pagan concept of the sacred banquet was changed, though the temptation to revert to it always remained strong because it was more reassuring. Yahweh's covenant with his people is not something in the cosmic order; it is an event in history, in the fullest sense of the term. He, the Totally-Other, concludes on Sinai an alliance with the people he has chosen, altogether freely and gratuitously. From now on Israel is launched upon the unpredictable path of faith. Yahweh brings his people out of Egyptian slavery to lead them to the Promised Land. But they must undergo the trial of the desert. Between the Exodus, the Covenant and the faith there is an indissoluble link.

So that among the chosen people the sacred banquet takes on a particular significance. It maintains the Covenant as a memorial of the marvels wrought by Yahweh in delivering his people. But on the other hand the communion with Yahweh springs from his own free initiative, and there is no question of appropriating divine energy. The annual paschal meal in particular commemorated the Exodus, the liberating event *par excellence*. It was a privileged Jewish occasion which gave actuality to their hope for salvation as a "memorial" of ancient marvels. The meal followed the immolation of the lamb. And the spilt blood of the lamb recalled at once the first Pasch in Egypt (when the exterminating angel "spared" the Hebrew first-born) and the Covenant itself that was concluded on Sinai.

There were developments in the paschal meal as Jewish religious insight deepened. The prophets reacted against overly material concepts of the sacrifice, insisting on conversion of heart. This led to emphasis on "celebration" and the "sacrifice of praise" during the meal. The material dimension becomes less and less important.

The supper and the sacrifice of the cross

Jesus shared the traditional paschal meal with his disciples on the night before he gave his life for love on the cross. Because it was presided over by him, this particular meal acquired a new meaning. The memorial, the "anamnesis," took on here a new dimension.

Previously the major event in salvation history that was commemorated was the Exodus, and the covenant associated with it. At this Supper something new and tremendous was taking place. On the following day the new and definitive covenant, sealed in the blood of the man-God, would be concluded by the death on the cross. At once the Sinai covenant would be seen as void. It was in the cross of Jesus that human salvation was acquired once for all.

Henceforward the event to be commemorated at the paschal meal would be, not the Exodus, but the cross. This becomes the true Pasch of Israel, and of humanity. Jesus' words "Do this in memory of me" (in memory, that is, of my death and resurrection) simply ratify what this Supper now is. The shared bread and the cup of blessing derive their "sacramental" value exclusively from the "body that will be delivered" (Lk 22:19), and the "blood of the covenant that will be shed for many for the remission of sins" (Mt 26:28).

So that the Supper is the true fulfillment of the Jewish paschal meal. Messianic hope has reached its culmination: Jesus, the mediator of the definitive covenant, has established in his person communion between God and humanity. The communion is possible because the Father's salvific initiative received the perfect response from the man-God. The paschal meal has all its essentials in the spiritual sacrifice of Jesus, his obedience unto the death of the cross for love of God and all men. The Supper inaugurates the sacramental economy properly understood. Centered on the sacrifice of the cross, it brings the banqueters into a true relationship with God. The rite of the definitive covenant is already determined.

Because the death of Jesus opens the way to the true life of the definitive era, eschatological tension mounts to its highest point at the Supper. "I have longed to eat this passover with you before I suffer because, I tell you, I shall not eat it again until it is fulfilled in the Kingdom of God" (Lk 22:15b-16). And again: "I tell you solemnly, I shall not drink any more wine until the day I drink the new wine in the Kingdom of God" (Mk 14:25).

The Eucharist, the heart of the mystery of the Church

In Christian usage the word "Eucharist" has come to designate the paschal meal of the disciples of Jesus. Gathered together, as they commemorate the death of Christ, they join in their communion meal in the one act of thinksgiving that is agreeable to the Father, that of the man-God. The eucharistic memorial is not just a simple remembrance of a past event; it is a summons to the eternal sacrifice of the one and only High Priest.

Sharing the Eucharist is not just a celebration of the greatest of all marvels: the Father's initiative in giving us his Son. It means that we enter as active *partners* into the salvific act of the *man*-God. We make our own, through the living link of communion, that which he did once for all on the cross.

The eucharistic assembly also takes place under the aegis of charity, of mutual service that knows no limits. The washing of the feet, which John includes in his account of the institution, is a clear indication that there is a close link between the eucharistic meal and sacrifice for love of God and men. The first fruit of the Eucharist is the establishment of a community bound by real ties of brotherhood. Any eucharistic theology that neglects the aspect of brotherhood is inadequate. It is not sufficient for worthy reception of the sacrament that one be "well disposed."

It is also very clear that these ties of brotherhood established in the Eucharist should reach into the texture of our daily lives. What has been "already accomplished" in the rite must be implemented in "life." Ecclesial existence is made up of this: the continuity between "rite" and "life" is absolutely essential for the life of faith. There can be no proper participation in rite without constant exercise of charity.

Eucharist and mission

Christians assemble for the Eucharist in a specified place. But they are answering a summons which is, of its nature, universal. The aim of every eucharistic celebration is that all men should be gathered in brotherly unity around the First-Born of the new humanity. For Christians there can be no exclusivism. Wherever they are gathered for the eucharist they are being initiated into the sort of communion from which no one can be excluded. They should not alone be aware of their relationship to all the other members of the Body throughout the world who celebrate the same eucharist; but they should be open to absent brethren, to all those throughout the world who have not yet heard the Good News of salvation. These are the dimensions of the mystery of the cross: we cannot make the "anamnesis" of Christ's death without involvement in universal fraternity.

Such is our rite of thanksgiving, which must penetrate every corner of our lives. We must make our fundamental attitude the one which colors all the life of Jesus: obedience to God's plan until death. The inspiration, the integrating element in all our daily activities, our fidelity in love, must be modelled on his. Then we shall be rendering to Christ, who died and rose again for all, a witness before God and men. Our apostolic lives and our eucharistic lives will be interwoven. Mission in the Church has always a "religious" (something that binds to God) emphasis, and the eucharistic rite always emphasizes absolute openness. If he shares the Eucharist properly, the Christian cannot but be an apostle, and he cannot evangelize or witness properly without giving glory to the Father through Jesus Christ.

The eucharistic reassembly under the sign of charity

Theological reflection in the past was a good deal concerned with sacramental objectivity, altogether dependent on the action of Christ. "It is Christ who baptizes and Christ who performs the Eucharist." There was less concern with the development of a theology of the eucharistic celebration itself. Vatican II did something to redress the balance by extending the dimension of sacramentality to the bonds of union that ought to be developed between the members of Christ's Body in the ecclesial Institution. The doctrine of collegiality for instance is only comprehensible in the context of the law of charity. In actual fact it has set up among the episcopacy a brotherliness that is unprecedented.

It is something like this that should be manifested in the eucharistic celebration itself. Collegiality concerns bishops, true, but it also concerns priests and all members of the Church. All eucharistic assemblies, and indeed all ecclesial assemblies of any kind, ought to exhibit the note of catholicity. The Church brings people together as they are and where they are, but such gatherings, once there, have a being of their own. They should be a visible sign of catholicity. Thus the eucharistic assembly which is presided over by the bishop serves as a norm for all others. The number of different people that we find here responding to the summons to salvation under a single head indicates both unity and diversity. The unifying influence is not destructive, but purifying.

We should beware above all of allowing purely administrative criteria to dominate in the ecclesial Institution. In our time indeed the whole Institution should be directed towards Mission, because it is imperative that we recover a sense of catholicity in every eucharistic assembly.

2. The Theme of Division

To use the term division, in a doctrinal sense, may seem at first sight somewhat extraordinary. Surely nothing is more contrary to the idea of Christianity. We do not find it in the indexes of works on biblical theology, whereas terms like unity and communion will have many references.

We are convinced, none the less, that this theme should receive special attention, particularly now. Too often Christians are unrealistic about it; their attitude shows that they do no want to look it in the face. Because it is obviously something bad, there is a tendency to minimize it as much as possible. It receives cursory and perfunctory attention, and consequently the means we take of dealing with it are in general disproportionate to the magnitude of the challenge. Nowadays it is becoming more and more impossible to ignore the existence of division. Indeed in our world it assumes gigantic proportions, and because of the media of communication everyone knows about it. We have division between cultures, between races, between peoples, between classes, between generations. In the fold of the Church likewise there is manifest division. Of course the great fissions in Christianity extend back for several centuries, but up to now Christians were living as if there weren't any. At the moment the majority is beginning to perceive that this situation is quite critical for the Church's essential mission. Furthermore, even within the various Christian confessions, division is so pronounced that sociologists tend to query the very notion of a single catholicism.

What is one to say about it all? A saying of Jesus that we have in today's readings (Gospel, 3rd cycle) throws light on the matter, we believe. It is indeed an arresting remark: "Do you suppose that I am here to bring peace on earth? No, I tell you, but rather division."

The faith of Israel and division

Pagan man, in search of security, tends to affirm the unity of the human race, a unity however that is preestablished and static. The differences between men seem accidental only; one man is like another. This attitude makes for security, because it is a blanket justification for all unifying enterprises. It enables any people to feel themselves to be the center and provides ground for instance for projects of universal empire. Division is just an evil that must be eradicated.

Israel, under the regime of faith, was more realistic. Facts ran counter to the pagan view. Unceasingly men were divided against one another, and there was little point in wondering whether or not, by nature, they should form a single unity. What was important, and fundamental, was the knowledge that Yahweh is the God of all nations and that his plan for humanity must be one. This unity however is connected with the covenant. It is a gift of the Creator, which will be accorded men in proportion to their fidelity. If men are in fact divided it is because they have sinned. Division is a divine chastisement.

Sin is as old as humanity. Adam and Eve were unfaithful to the first covenant, and their descendants became divided. After the deluge, Noah again tried to realize the divine project of unity, but pride led men once more into infidelity. Yahweh punished them by dispersing them over the surface of the earth and multiplying their languages (the tower of Babel episode). Then came the covenant with Abraham, in which all the nations are to be blessed. Israel however is stiffnecked, and is herself dispersed among the nations.

But Yahweh is faithful. The day of the definitive covenant will come. Israel will have the favored position, but all nations will take the road to Jerusalem. This will be the reign of peace. All peoples will be gathered together and will understand one another. There will be no more confusion of tongues and no more differences.

The realism of Jesus about division

It was the Jewish expectation that, with the advent of the Messiah, a new Kingdom would be inaugurated where there would be no division and no death, and where the Jewish privileges would be confirmed. But actually, when Jesus came, things happened otherwise. The Kingdom that he proclaimed did not substitute a new world for the old one. He did not eradicate death and division. He confronted them and emerged victorious.

So that Israel's hope is altogether changed from now on. What is the explanation? Could it be that Jesus did not consider peace among men as essentially a divine gift? On the contrary: no one affirmed so resolutely as he the gratuitous initiative of the Savior-God. Could it be that he did not regard division as a divine punishment? It is here that we must be precise. For Israel one of the greatest symptoms of division among men was diversity of tongues. This in itself was a divine punishment, a retort to man's pride. For Jesus, the consequence of sin was division itself, opposition, hatred. But not human diversity, however pronounced, and the multiplicity of languages indicates how diverse people are. Division is what diversity becomes once human pride enters the scene.

The originality of the gospel consists altogether in the commandment of brotherly love without limits. The earthly state is not a fallen state; it is simply the human one. It is in this state that men are summoned by God to make their contribution to the building of the Kingdom. Loving all men means loving them in their diversity, as they are. Man is always other to his fellow man and love requires that one accept his otherness. Such love will entail absolute self-renunciation, because one cannot really love without being free from sin. This is the moment when we can see properly the meaning of diversity, that it is part of the human condition, and indeed a constitutive element. When we confront it realistically we feel the urge to make this the area of our accomplishment.

In this sense Jesus was realistic about division. He knew that in the context, because of human sin, his project of love would inevitably arouse hatred. This is the sense in which he said he came to bring division, not peace.

The Church's task in a divided world

The disciple is not greater than his master. The victory of Jesus over division had all the appearance of failure, because its sign was the cross. For the Church, the Body of Christ, the situation must be similar. Her triumph over division will never seem to be a success. Hate will always seem to overshadow love. To the end of time the spectre of division will haunt the human race.

What then is the task of the Church, of small local assemblies in particular? Simply fidelity to the new commandment. Wherever human diversity has hardened into division, the disciples of the Risen Lord have a mission to make this the theater for the exercise of their charity. Such a love will not be blind to the walls of separation that men continue to erect between themselves. It will not minimize the obstacles that have to be surmounted. It will realize how very vulnerable it is. It will be a love that builds unity at the price of self-renunciation, a love that triumphs over, but does not suppress, hate. It will even be prepared to allow hate a seeming victory.

One final question presents itself. In a divided world, is it incumbent upon the witnesses of true love to show that, at least where they themselves are concerned, the walls of separation have been razed? In other words, must the Church exhibit to the world the signs of genuine communion among its members? The answer to this question is yes, given that there is a proper understanding of what these signs are. Christians are sinners like other men. The sort of communion they achieve would be a mere travesty were it to be understood flatly as something material and palpable. It is an effective communion, but it depends on the always actual initiative of Christ. It may at times indeed appear to be compromised, but there always arise those spirits who bear testimony again to the hope acquired in Christ.

We must guard against the concept of Christian unity which has not the gospel realism regarding division. Christian unity is a unity of communion, and may give the appearance of failure. A unity of communion seems always inchoate and unrealized, but it always holds the promise of fulfillment. That is why division and sin are not destined to have the last word in human history.

Missionary activity a source of division?

Should the missionary say, like Jesus, that he has come to

create division on earth? Is there any point indeed in raising the question, if mission is the work of peace *par excellence?* Of course all missionaries know very well from experience the grave dissensions that can sometimes be set up in pagan families by conversion of a member. They have reason to recall the words of Jesus that follow the saying we mentioned. "For from now on a househeld of five will be divided: three against two and two against three; the father divided against the son, son against father, mother against daughter, daughter against mother, mother-in-law against daughter-in-law, daughter-in-law against mother-in-law" (Lk 12:52-53). Yet, surely this falls short of an affirmation that all missionary activity is necessarily divisive.

The more closely we examine the matter, the more we see that there is not a real contradiction between the two statements: that mission is a work of peace and that it brings division. They are actually complementary. Activity in mission is the highest form of fidelity that the people of God can show to the new commandment of universal love. Yet a first requisite in love is lucidity. This sort of love does not disguise the differences between men. On the contrary it stresses them, accepts them. It insists that they be recognized, and creates as it were insecurity by forcing each person back to the bedrock of his dignity as a human person, so inviolable, yet so daunting. The recipient of this love is startled from complacency and must opt either for or against the witness of Christ. If, through pride, he opts against, he becomes more than ever an architect of division. If he opts for, and chooses himself to follow Christ, then he will become an architect of peace. He will realize that peace can only be built on the basis of love for the other. To love one's neighbor only, the person who is like oneself, is not true love. We must learn to love every man as other than ourselves, in his otherness. We must learn, over all the hazards of insecurity, to become the neighbor of those divided from us.

Missionaries have always striven to be builders of peace and unity, but sometimes they have failed to realize the depth of diversity between men. As a result, it is not surprising that many Asian and African Christians in our day find themselves torn between their own cultural allegiance and their Church membership.

Celebrating the victory of faith over division

The Eucharist should be celebrated by an assembly of believers as the proclamation of the death of Christ on the cross. Saint Paul tells us this. It is a victory that is celebrated, that of Christ and, in him, of the people of God, a victory over division and hate. Division and hate however continue to exercise sway, even among Christians, who are like other men sinners.

Throughout all the Christian centuries, in eucharistic assemblies, everything went on as if the victory being celebrated were already visibly accomplished. Everywhere, including African and Asian churches, the liturgy presented the same aspect. The ecclesial Institution was mainly occupied in making all Christians fit an identical mold. Wherever they gathered for a eucharistic celebration they found themselves among their counterparts. Unity seemed an accomplished fact, and no hint of division was allowed to show itself in the celebration.

Today however Christians are becoming more and more aware of differences. At the very moment when they stand shoulder to shoulder with their non-Christian brethren in the same cultural or social environment, the same intellectual climate, they realize that the seed of division is at work in the people of God. The question is raised how people who are engaged in such harsh conflict can join one another at the communion table. The very fact that the question gets asked shows how much the heritage of the past is still with us. In fact nothing could be more consonant with a realistic faith than the expression in the eucharistic liturgy of everything that makes for division in actual living. The kind of unity this is meant to celebrate does not cloak differences or even divisions; the assembled faithful know they are sinners.

But they are sinners with a certitude: that division can never have the last word. Christ conquered it once for all on the cross. Until the end of time he is offering a share in that victory to all those who do penance, and attempt to go one step further along the road of evangelic love.

TWENTY-FIRST SUNDAY

A. THE WORD

I. Isaiah 22:19-23
1st reading
1st cycle

This oracle refers to the quarrels between the officers of King Ezechias' court and Isaiah, which are described at length in Isaiah 36-39. One of these functionaries, Shebna, had been disgraced by the king, and the prophet sees this as a punishment for his luxurious living (Is 22:15-18). His successor receives congratulations. This was one Eliakim, who during the Assyrian invasion, applied with success the political dexterity recommended by the prophet.

The only interest of the passage is the detailed description of the investiture of a royal functionary. The robe, the sash, and above all the *keys,* are the insignia of office. The keys symbolize the extent of the power that is entrusted (cf. v. 22 where the "opening-closing" formula foreshadows the "binding-loosing" one in Mt 16:19).

The one who is entrusted with the keys becomes a sort of plenipotentiary. That is the intention of Jesus in entrusting this power to Peter, and God in giving the keys to Christ (Rev 3:7-8) makes him messianic plenipotentiary of the Kingdom.

II. Joshua 24:1-2, 15-17, 18b
1st reading
2nd cycle

Chapter 24 is a sort of appendix to the Book of Joshua, added a century or two after the deuteronomic recasting of the chronicle. Its lateness however does not alter the fact that it is based on a very ancient tradition concerning the Sichem alliance, anterior to the traditions of Joshua 8:30-35 and Deuteronomy 27:1-26. It described the Sichem alliance in terms of the pact, customary at the time, between a suzerain and his vassals. We have a preamble (v. 1), a passage recalling the previous associations between the parties (vv. 1-15), the stipulations of the contract (vv. 16-18), an enumeration of the maledictions and penalties which will be the sanction for any breach (vv. 19-24; cf. especially Dt 27), and finally a reference to the rite of alliance and the inscription of the contract on a stone (vv. 25-28). This primitive tradition certainly inspired the formulation of the Sinai alliance in Exodus. The code, which was promulgated on Sinai according to Exodus, was in fact promulgated at Sichem.

Sichem was indeed for a time the sanctuary of the covenant with Yahweh. The final redactor of Joshua 24 modified the account rather considerably in order to transfer to Sinai the importance that had been originally that of Sichem.

a) The tribes which gathered at Sichem were those who had been installed in Palestine since the time of the patriarchs and had never left it; those who had returned to Palestine before Joshua after a foreign sojourn; and finally "the house of Joseph," those who were the last to return, under the successive leadership of Moses and Joshua. The final group doubtless rapidly became the most important, in any case the best organized and most cultivated, no doubt because of the Egyptian sojourn. This enabled them to group the other tribes around them, and involve the people as a whole in their own proper history, that of exodus and alliance.

It is then at Sichem that the God of the house of Joseph becomes the God of all tribes, and the traditions of each tribe are fused to become the law of the *covenant*.

b) The passage of dialogue between the people and God retains some elements of the primitive tradition (vv. 14-15 and 18), but the remainder was added after the exile. The sign of true acceptance by the tribes of the terms of the covenant will be their rejection of false idols. Every alliance then presupposes a *conversion*. This entails rejection of the ancient gods of Mesopotamia, worshiped by the ancestors of Abraham, and those Canaanite gods known to the tribes who had stayed in Palestine.

c) The purpose of the alliance between the tribes is religious not political: the *service* of God (vv. 14-15). What we have doubtless is the organization of a Yahweh-cult on the amphyctionic pattern. Twelve tribes agree to ensure the "service" of a common sanctuary (perhaps the high place of Sichem), each one serving for a month. By the time of our redaction of the tradition, "service" of God has taken on a more spiritual meaning. The author was aware of the infidelity of preceding centuries. For him, service of God lies particularly in fidelity to the precepts of the law, as a vassal fulfills the will of his suzerain.

This account of the Sichem gathering is enlightening with regard to the covenant itself. Basically this is not recognition of a people by God, or recognition of their God by an already established people. It is rather the constitution of a people on the basis of a common faith and a common cult. In other words, it was at the moment when all recognized their God that Israel was born as a people, culturally and politically. Nationality and religion are inseparable. The Jews are "chosen" in their capacity as a people; the whole religious covenant has a collective dimension.

This is an important consideration whether one belongs to the old or new covenant. The contract is not just a charter of relations between God and the individual. More exactly, it denotes the solidarity set up between men themselves because they serve the same God. This solidarity can have wider horizons than the nationalistic ones of Sichem, and will have, overwhelmingly, with Jesus Christ. But the notion of covenant will always imply this living together, because God lives with us.

III. Isaiah 66:18-21 *1st reading* *3rd cycle*   This poem, which was compiled during the first century after the return from exile, is one of the most daring in the whole Old Testament on the theme of universalism.

Like his predecessors, the author still thinks that a colossal struggle, from which Israel will miraculously emerge as victor over enemy nations, will characterize the end of time. When he speaks of "survivors" (v. 19) he is referring to this belief. But he has no restrictions where these are concerned. However far away, the Jewish mission will seek them out. Jarshish could be in Spain, Put in Somalia, Yavan in Ionia, Jubal in Asia Minor and Lud in Lybia. Apart from Mesopotamia (doubtless annihilated completely after the eschatological conflict), *missionary enterprise* will embrace the whole world known at the time.

The "uncleanness" which denied Gentiles access to the temple is altogether abolished. They will join the traditional pilgrimages. Their offerings will be acceptable (v. 20), and some among them will even become priests, thus ending the aaronid monopoly (v. 21). Liturgical ferment seems to go with missionary fervor. When there is question of gathering in the Gentiles, rubrics and tabus disappear. The worship of God cannot be restricted to any caste or culture, however "chosen," if it is to be the expression of a gathering of all humanity before God.

Israel however refused to destroy the barriers erected against Gentiles (Mk 11:15-19), and Jesus forfeited his life in attempting to make the temple worship universal.

The poem speaks of a mysterious *sign* that will be offered the nations in order to include them in the new liturgy. The nature of this sign will have to await the eschatological discourse of Christ for clarification (Mk 13:4, and especially Mt 24:30). It is the "sign of the Son of man," the sign that is of the Risen Christ, who takes humanity to himself and gives it his "glory." Thus the assembly of the nations foreseen by Third-Isaiah around the temple is henceforward an assembly in the person of the Risen Christ. This is the new sign of gathering because in him all humanity is restored, and because in his sacrifice all humanity is presented to the Father in an obedience that they have only to ratify.

The Eucharist brings together people who have made their own the obedience of Christ. It builds the new temple that is open to all nations. It can only do this properly if those who are gathered together accept their mission to the nations, so that in spite of diversity and division they may become a sign of the reassembly of all in Jesus Christ.

IV. Romans Paul concludes his analysis of Israel's destiny
   11:33-36 by recapitulating, rather hesitantly, his argu-
   2nd reading ment (vv. 30-32), and rendering thanks to
   1st cycle God (vv. 33-36) for his mercy and his plan of
   universal salvation. This concludes too the
doctrinal portion of the letter. There can be no doubt that he has had in mind the salvation history of all humanity from the fall of Adam and the promise to Abraham right up to justification in Christ, and the final gesture by God that will save Israel.

a) Paul sees all human history as a sort of counterpoint between Jews and Gentiles. The Jews were the first to obey, but they disobeyed afterwards. The Gentiles, who disobeyed to begin with, obeyed when the time came (vv. 30-31; cf. Mt 21:28-32). But, over-arching this ebb and flow and providing the key, is the *mercy* of God (v. 32). It enables every man to learn by sin the vanity of his own will, and to open himself to God's gratuitous love, which is the only solution to the human predicament.

b) The *thanksgiving* for God's mercy and human conversion is principally inspired by Psalm 138/139 (vv. 6, 17, 18), which celebrates the immense knowledge of God that baffles human comprehension. He goes on to allude to Isaiah 40:13, one of those oracles that gave people hope about God's salvific plan for his people at the time of return from exile. Finally he quotes Job 41:3, but according to a version that differs from the original, and celebrates the faith of the poor man who is undaunted by events, however incomprehensible.

All through these avowals of ignorance and humility Paul is using terms (wisdom, gnosis, depth) that were current at the time. He is thinking of the gnostic effort to destroy the idea of God, and he is confining this to its proper limits.

He is concerned with the destiny of Israel, but does not find basis for hope in this unfaithful people. He turns to God, a God who is faithful to his promises, even when he is countered, and only refrains from anger to give opportunity for repentance. One day Israel will repent for her unbelief, not because she decides herself, but because God will no longer endure estrangement from the people he has joined to himself in everlasting covenant.*

V. Ephesians 5:21-32
2nd reading
2nd cycle

This passage is taken from a section where the apostle is describing the new life "in Christ." He has shown the influence of this in the texture of moral life (Ep 4:17; 5:20). How he illustrates in some specific institutions: conjugal life (Ep 5:21-33), the family (Ep 6:1-4), social intercourse (Ep 6:5-9). It is natural that Paul should think of marriage "in the love of Christ," and tell Christian spouses that genuine love for one another is a reflection of Christ's love. The Christian is always a witness of that love of the brethren and of God of which Christ was the perfect exponent, and which each member of his body is called upon to manifest (v. 30). This will sometimes be difficult, and it will be often good to have recourse to the memory and the Spirit of Christ in order to love as he did (vv. 25-28). In any case married couples are asked to provide an extension in their conjugal lives of his relationship with the Church.

a) Christian marriage, as he sees it, reflects the love of Christ for the Church. We should realize that there is nothing new in

---

*See the doctrinal theme: *Israel*, p. 283.

this doctrine. Paul was too familiar with Old Testament imagery about the *espousals* of God and his people not to make good use of it when the occasion arose.

A marriage between God and his people mirrors something very deep indeed, a love of God for man that is a love of sharing. There is nothing here to suggest those gnostic hierogamies where love is practically nonexistent. And if Paul passes from the image of marriage between God and Israel to that of marriage between Christ and the Church, it is to emphasize that the love of God for humanity achieves its plentitude in Christ, something that was decisive for the history of humanity.

The trend then of his thinking becomes clear. To begin with he situates Christian marriage "in Christ," who is always for him the concrete center we must all seek. He then invokes the espousals of Christ and the Church to describe the type of love that ought to characterize Christian unions. The little ecclesial cell which is set up in every Christian household ought to be shaped by the love of Christ and the universal Church.

b) It is *baptism* that bring about the association between the Christian household and the espousals between Christ and the Church. Christ's union with the Church is achieved by his redemptive death (v. 25); and baptism which makes us members of Christ (v. 30) is our avenue of entry to the mystery of Christ and the Church.

The word which accompanies the baptismal rite (v. 26) is none other than the Word of God made manifest in the Christ event, and the word with which this event is proclaimed in kerygma and catechesis. The faith which joins us to the paschal event of Christ automatically associates us with his work of love for his Church, which is the "great mystery" (v. 32) of God's salvific plan for humanity.

c) He goes on to push the similitude very far indeed. Within. the Christian household, the characteristic roles of the Christ-Church espousal are paralleled. So, the husband has the prerogative of *Christ-Head,* a confusion between the symbolic role

(Ep 1:18-20; 2:19; Col 2:10) and the husband's juridical title of head.

This strains the comparison considerably. It is true that the love of the Christian couple is a sign of the love of God (manifested in the Christ-Church espousal). But because of this image too much should not be made of particular roles, as if the husband alone were fitted to play the role of Christ (mediator, head: cf. v. 23; cf. 1 Co 11:3) and the wife that of the Church (warmth, receptivity, cf. v. 27). No comparison, however apt, should be extended that far. The important thing is that the love which binds Christ and the Church should be evident in conjugal love, not that mutual roles should be paralleled.

Paul is in fact too influenced by his Judaism and by the juridical structure of the household with which he was familiar. He could not see the female spouse in the role of Christ exercising the mediation for her husband, or the husband in the warm receptive role of the Church.

His wish to see the love of Christ for humanity in the love of a Christian couple is perfectly valid: that is the whole meaning of the sacrament. However, he lived at a time when the man was always the mediator in the family. The mutual roles then seemed to follow as a matter of course. But we should be straining the applications unduly and running the risk of obscuring the message, by insisting on details that really vary according to culture, or history.

VI. Hebrews 12:5-7, 11-13
2nd reading
3rd cycle

The author continues his argument as begun in Hebrews 12:1-4. It is designed to encourage his readers to endure the trial of separation from Jerusalem, the holy city. Here he brings up another point. Trial is a correction such as every child gets from his father.

This idea of *paternal correction* is rather novel in the New Testament. The author simply appeals to ordinary experience. Everyone has had a father who was sometimes very angry. His correction seemed at the moment harsh and unjust, but later it was seen to be benevolent and just (vv. 9-11). So it is with God's correction of his children.

He relies on a sapiental argument too (vv. 5-7). Rabbis were wont to correct their disciples very severely (Si 4:17; 23:2; Pr 3:11-12; 13:24; 23:12-14) and generally called them "sons."

The two examples illustrate a more profound truth. If God corrects his "sons" (v. 8), according them a treatment that would be denied to illegitimates, it is because he sees in them his own son raised up on the cross (v. 10: "to share the holiness" acquired by Christ). God is no monster; he does not chastise through harshness, but in the name of the highest form of love: agape (v. 6).

VII. Matthew
16:13-20
Gospel
1st cycle

This is the account of what has come to be called in the synoptic tradition the "confession of Caesarea." It is a fairly homogeneous section which comprises Peter's profession of messianic faith, the first prediction of the passion, a moral application (the apostles too must carry their cross), and finally the transfiguration. Very probably the ensemble is as old as the primitive catechesis, even though the episodes recounted took place independently.

There are many indications that Matthew's version is the best, but its redaction appears to be the work of the primitive community, concerned to date a post-paschal mission prior to the resurrection.

To understand Matthew's text properly the reading should be extended as far as verse 23. We shall then have the following structure:

A	B
v. 13 Christ's question	v. 21 Christ's question
v. 16 Peter's intervention	v. 22 Peter's intervention
v. 17 Thoughts of God, not of men	v. 23 Thoughts of man, not of God
v. 18 You are the rock of the Church	v. 24 You are a rock of scandal

a) The account then is built around the double *exchange of titles* between Jesus and Peter. Peter gives Jesus the title of Messiah, and Jesus responds by calling him the Rock and giving him the messianic power of the keys. Peter refuses to give Jesus the title of suffering Servant, and Jesus responds by calling him the Rock of scandal.

b) The title given to Jesus is essentially *messianic:* "you are the Christ." Matthew however adds to it the phrase "the Son of the living God." It does not appear that this indicates divinity strictly speaking. It is often used in the Old Testament to describe angels (Gn 6:1-4; Jb 1:6), judges (Ps 81/82:6-7) and the king (2 S 7:14; Ps 88/89:27-28). What we have then is simply a doublet of the title Christ, which affirms the heavenly origin of Jesus' Messiahship. To be recognized as Messiah means recognition as the man of all men who can give meaning to life and make it succeed.

c) No sooner is his Messiahship recognized than Jesus, in Matthew's version at least, hastens to share it with Simon. First of all he gives him the messianic title of *Rock* (v. 18) which is destined to be his personal name. He is then communicating to him the prerogatives of invulnerability and firmness that were attributed to David, Sion and the Messiah (theme of the gates of hell: v. 18; cf. Is 28:16).

Then he gives him the power of the keys (v. 19). The symbolism here is highly biblical. The Christ has the keys of David's dwelling (Is 22:22). He is the high steward of the house of the Father (Mt 16:19) and he entrusts this charge to Peter.

Finally there is the power of "binding and loosing" which he is to exercise in collegiality with the others (Mt 18:18; cf. Jn 20:22-23). The force of the phrase lies in the combination of two contraries, thus expressing totality of power. Peter is really a plenipotentiary.*

VIII. John 6:61-70 John is always interested in giving us the
      Gospel   reaction of listeners to Jesus. Earlier he has
    2nd cycle   analyzed the attitudes of a doctor of the law
                (Jn 3), a woman of the people (Jn 4) and
an official (Jn 4:43-53). Now he gives us the reaction of the crowd to the bread of live discourse.

a) The Jews, as John stresses throughout the discourse, were adamant in opposition and "murmuring" (Jn 6:30-31, 41-42, 52). They even win over the group of disciples, who are scandalized by the vigor of the language that reverses their traditional idea of relations between disciples and master (cf. Jn 6:37-40). The apostles on the other hand seem to have an attitude of *faith*, which is clearly expressed in Peter's profession. It seems to be limited however to Jesus' Messiahship (vv. 67-70).

b) From the whole confrontation John draws two important lessons. In the first place, the desertion by the crowd and the disciples demonstrates that one cannot have faith unless by gift of the Spirit. Human means ("flesh," v. 63) cannot reach to it. Secondly, the dispersion of the disciples is the prelude to the *paschal mystery*. The repeated reference to betrayal by Judas (vv. 64 and 71), and the reference to Jesus' ascension (v. 62) show that here at Capharnaum the mystery is already at work, in the dimensions of humiliation and glorification.

In the Church, which is the Body of Christ, the discourse on the bread of life must always go on reverberating, explicitly sometimes, sometimes as an undertone. The Christian is in

*See the doctrinal theme: *primacy and collegiality*, p. 335.

variably a person who takes the measure of existence and realizes that he can give faith to none but Jesus. He is called to seek the will of the Father, and his best avenue to that is the eucharistic bread, the sign of the perfect intimacy between Jesus and his Father.

IX. Luke 13:21-30 Circumstances that Matthew (7:13-14 and 22-
   Gospel   23) passes over in silence, in order not to
   3rd cycle   break the altogether artificial continuity of
                     the sermon on the mount, are preserved by
Luke (13:22-23). In Luke 13-24 the image of the narrow gate is not combined with any other, whereas Matthew (17:13-14) rather confuses it with the theme of the two ways. The gate in Luke is that of the eschatological banquet (a primitive note, very likely) while Matthew seems to envisage the gate of a city which comes at the term of a moral "road." He is replacing the primitive eschatological emphasis with a moralizing and catechetical one. In Luke 13:26-28 Jesus alludes to the attitude of his listeners (v. 26), while Matthew has in mind the charismatic Christians of the primitive communities (Mt 7:22). This suggests a later redaction for Matthew. In verses 28-29 of Luke we seem to have the original context. There is a reference to the eschatological banquet predicted at verses 24-25, and the whole ambience is typically Jewish.

a) Thus the basic theme in the passage is the *eschatological banquet* of Isaiah 25:6. The crowd will press for entry, but the door will be too narrow to admit all. The less vigilant will remain outside (v. 28; cf. Mt 25:10-12), and appeal in vain to their previous association with the master of the house (v. 26).

The sifting process at the door is not a separation of Israel from the nations, but a choice of the more deserving from both groups. Those united at the table are Jewish patriarchs and prophets (v. 28), together with the more deserving from all nations (v. 29). So that the banquet will reassemble both Jews and Gentiles, with equal rights, in the new Kingdom. The Gentile uncleanness, which prevented Jews from sharing meals with them, is no more (cf. Ga 2:11-14).

b) With Luke 13:22-30 should be compared those other passages where Jesus speaks of the *convocation* of *the Gentiles* to the Kingdom, always set in an eschatological context. We have the themes of banquet (Mt 25:1-12), the regathering of the flock (Mt 25:31-32), the building of the temple to include the nations (Jn 4:21-23, 12:20-23), and the return in power of the Son of man (Mt 24:29-31).

For Jesus the conversion of the Gentiles was an eschatological initiative of his Father. Thus he was not concerned to call them during his public life (Mk 7:24-30; Mt 10:5-6), remaining in this faithful to the economy of salvation that is "first for the Jews" (Rm 1:16).

c) The first lesson would seem to be that Jesus' saying (vv. 28-29) is a warning to listeners who do not read the signs of the times (cf. Lk 12:54-56; 14:16-24), and fail to grasp the decisive nature of his ministry. Their *exclusion* is imminent. Not even fidelity to Moses will avail them, if they do not recognize his message. However, this will not prevent fulfillment of the ancient prophecies about eschatological assembly of the nations. The Gentiles will enter, and the Jews will find themselves outside (cf. Mt 10:15; Lk 10:13-14; 11:31-32).

d) Matthew actually affirms that it is because of their faith (Mt 8:11-12) that the Gentiles will replace the Jews at the banquet. But Luke seeks another explanation. It is works and the practice of *justice* that will admit Gentiles to the banquet (vv. 23-27; cf. Lk 8:21; 11:28). As he sees it, God is not an accepter of persons. The decisive factor will not be membership of the chosen people, but the practice of justice. The two evangelists are not at one in their interpretation of Jesus' saying. Matthew is endeavoring to explain why the first Christian communities are more Gentile than Jewish. Luke has a more universal outlook. Salvation is attainable by all men: there will be no automatic salvation on the basis of membership of the chosen people.*

The Christian also is included in Jesus' warning. Membership of the people of God does not make him a missionary and a sign of salvation. But salvation itself will altogether depend on personal justice. He is a "savior," but is not himself automatically saved.

*See the doctrinal theme: *Gentiles*, p. 340.

B. DOCTRINE

1. Primacy and Collegiality

Vatican II inaugurated a new era for the Catholic Church. It is rich in promise, but none the less beset by dangers and difficulties. All over the world, Christians in local churches are rediscovering the importance of the prophetic ministry, and new projects are multiplied. That law of uniformity which hitherto governed the whole of Christian life is gradually yielding place to another principle of unity, something that depends on mutual exchange of life and energy.

The importance of episcopal collegiality, which was fully stressed at the Council, is becoming more and more evident. Facts are forcing us to develop a new structure of relationship between the center and the peripheries, between Rome and regional Churches. The episcopal synod of October 1969 can be regarded as an important step forward that augurs well for the future. But we shall have a long way to go before all the practical implications of the conciliar doctrine are implemented.

When we recall the exchanges at the Council, it is evident that the reasons which swayed the fathers towards collegiality were practical rather than theological. That was to be expected. The bishops are pastors, and expressed the practical needs of their mission. Two main considerations urged collegiality. It was no longer practical for the pope to govern the whole Church personally. During the course of a century it had become very extended and very complex. On the other hand it was evident that pastoral problems confronting bishops in their own dioceses extended beyond the boundaries of these dioceses, and required collective action on a regional, national, or continental basis. These reasons though, however compelling, were not theological. Thus, if it is correct to say that collegiality is something of divine institution, then it was always with us, and its doctrinal basis should be examined.

We hope to show that primacy and collegiality are essential structural elements in the Church that concern our life of faith. The "confession of Caesarea" (Gospel, 1st cycle) is a reminder to us, where Peter's primacy is concerned. We should like to examine the matter more thoroughly.

Collegiality an expression of Christ's charity

We know that Jesus entrusted his Church not just to one man. He made a simultaneous commission, in similar terms, to the Twelve as a group, and to one in particular, Peter. This corresponds to the plan of that salvation that had been acquired in his person. In founding the Church he affirmed his intention of remaining with his own all through history. As unique mediator of salvation, in his resurrection, he could only be present to men through envoys, ordained for that purpose. One single person could not take upon himself the communication of Christ's mediatorship to men, because that would be a duplication of something that is essentially unique. That a group together could do this is the basic meaning of the sacrament of orders. They were established by grace in those bonds of charity of which Christ alone possesses the secret. Salvation was wrought by the superabundance of his charity on the cross.

Apostolic or episcopal ministry is rendered authentic by the *brotherly accord* of the members of the college as they fulfill their charge. Through the grace received by the imposition of hands, this accord becomes an adequate expression of the law of charity, which makes the Church the Body of Christ.

Church history indicates that, while the realization of this truth was never lost, it was not always present to the same degree. Saint Paul, so that he should not have run in vain, was concerned to have the approval of the other apostles for his missionary projects. Throughout the first Christian centuries, the successors of the apostles, who were not residential bishops, maintained frequent contact with one another in order to strengthen the ties of brotherhood, which was the guarantee of

their individual efforts. After the 4th century begins the long
series of ecumenical councils. All bishops are brought together
to seek solutions for the problems which beset the Church of
their time. Soon the ecumenical council becomes the normal
vehicle of episcopal collegiality. The Church grows more and
more established. Different historical developments, in the East
and in the West, lead her to seek unity by legislation that
promotes uniformity. Brotherly accord among the bishops yields
place as the principle of unity to edicts issued by Rome or Con-
stantinople. Communication between bishops is no longer necessary, because all are required to follow the same pattern. There
is unity, but the image presented by the Church is an im-
poverished one. Schism comes about between East and West.
Worst of all, missionary enterprise is hardened into stereo-type.
It is simply the extension to outside territories of an "order" that
has been set up in Christian countries.

The twentieth century has brought a profound change. We
have the growth in native episcopacy, the decline of Europe in
the concert of nations, the challenge to Catholicity by modern
atheism, the disestablishment of the Church and her reversion to
a state of mission everywhere, the increased communication
between peoples on a really planetary side. These and other
factors have brought about a situation where Church unity can
no longer be assured by uniformity. It has become imperative
that the essential organ of Catholicity and of missionary dynamism be strengthened. That is the episcopal college. It was the
great achievement of John XXIII that he recognized this urgency
and summoned Vatican II.

The primacy of Peter, the living standard of collegiality

Jesus entrusted the destiny of his Church simultaneously to
the Twelve, and to Peter as head of the college: "You are Peter
and upon this rock I will build my Church" (Mt 16:18). The
basic reason for setting up the apostolic college, we have said,
is the law of charity which makes the Church the Body of Christ.

This law is also the basis for primacy. If the authenticity of apostolic or episcopal ministry is to be assured by fraternal accord, that accord should have some sort of verifying norm. The norm is the presence of a visible head, of whose role it would be hard to find a better definition than that of Irenaeus. He tells us that the successor of Peter "presides" over charity.

Whether the pope acts by himself, or in concert with the bishops (which is the case in an ecumenical council), he is always acting as head of the college, in order to assure the fraternal accord which makes the ministry authentic. His primacy is necessary for episcopal collegiality. It is the living standard of that fraternity which builds up the Church in the charity of Christ. Bishops realize that their communion is truly edifying when it is exercised in union with Peter's successor.

It is a grave error then to see the Church as having two centers of supreme power, the pope and the episcopal college. The pope himself is a member of the college; when he acts it is as head of that college. Conversely the college is not complete without a head; unless there is communion with the pope the bishops alone do not constitute the college.

Since the conclusion of the Council, various measures have been taken to ensure effective exercise of collegiality in the government of the universal Church. Adjustments in this domain are indubitably delicate, in that everyone's position must be fully respected. But adjustment is imperative; the renewal of the Church is at stake.

Universal mission, the dynamic principle of collegiality

Some fifteen years after Pentecost, as the apostolic community of Jerusalem increased day by day, and the Hellenist members had been despatched to evangelize the neighboring territories, the Risen Lord appeared to Saul of Tarsus on the road to Damascus. To this persecutor of Christians he gave the mission of evangelizing the Gentiles.

The conversion of this man, who took the name of Paul, is

certainly the most important event in primitive Church history. His ministry was destined to implant Christianity firmly in the Greek world and throw the gates of the Church open to the uncircumcised. The foundation of the Antioch Church and the efforts of Barnabas had indeed broached the project before his intervention, but it was his missionary journeys which really marked the stages of Christian expansion through the Mediterranean world. So determining was his career for the future of the Church, that we can describe the Christianity of the following centuries as largely Pauline in origin.

It is important to note that throughout the long years of his ministry Paul was concerned to maintain his equality with the apostles, the members of the first apostolic college. When he began his mission, he was conscious of being an evangelist, but he was far from being a member of the apostolic college. Gradually he began to realize the ecclesial importance of what he was doing, and he pressed for the endorsement of this by the highest Church authority. That the great apostles should admit him to their college was a matter for him of first consequence. The missionary enterprise could never display its proper dynamism until the apostolic college was completely involved and responsible.

The Pauline history conveys a great lesson. In that first apostolic college it was not one of the Twelve, but an unexpected outsider, a member of the Diaspora, whom the Risen Lord himself had called from nowhere, who fostered missionary enterprise with the greatest vigor. The achievement of the Twelve was that they added to their ranks a man of such quality.

Subsequent Church history was similar. The Risen Lord raises up the people he wants to foster missionary enterprise according to the needs of the time. Any member of Christ's Body, or even a non-Christian, may be summoned to the task. It is the business of the apostolic college to be always ready for the co-option of such men, whose lives are dominated by missionary zeal, laity and priests.

On those occasions when the episcopal college failed in this responsibility, enterprises that were very daring, but very necessary, finally failed too. A case in point is the Jesuit enterprise in China at the end of the 16th century. Evangelization in China called for a new approach. There was a challenge to be met, that of a great sophisticated nation who had nothing to gain, culturally, from acceptance of the faith. There could be no question of attempting to implant here the Christian "order" of the West; the proclamation of the Good News would have to be its own justification. The Jesuits gave themselves resolutely to the task. Pope after pope recognized the quality of their contribution. Yet, in the event, they failed. The fundamental reason for the failure, in our opinion, was that the enterprise was never really endorsed by the apostolic college itself, and consequently by the Church as a whole. In all essential domains, Western Christianity, the pope, the bishops and the laity, remained uninvolved in this task of Pauline dimensions.

There are many reasons for regarding our ecclesial situation today as a Pauline one. The challenges Catholicism has to meet are certainly comparable. It will not be sufficient that the successor of Peter play his normal structural role, and the episcopal college follow its normal course of action. That college will have to have in its ranks men of Pauline quality, who will force the whole body towards those daring measures that are called for by the actual situation.

2. Theme of the Gentiles

The notion entertained by Christians about non-Christians is always a good index of their grasp of the basic realities of their faith, in particular of their missionary responsibility.

Up to modern times it was normal to classify men according to their religious allegiance. In any sacral regime the obvious center of gravity for human existence is religion, because men seek happiness through communication with the sacral world. It is in these terms easily understandable that a Christian living under a sacral regime will tend to set up a barrier between himself and the non-believer. He worships the true God, the other is an idolator. His mission is to convert the other, so that everyone can be saved, for that is the will of the Father. Yet it should be said that not everyone was content with such a flat view of the difference between Christian and non-Christian. At all times there were missionaries who were very keenly sensible of the fact that the Spirit was at work among all peoples, preparing them for the reception of the gospel.

Today of course religious allegiance does not have the same importance. If it is ever given as a reason for keeping people separate, everyone realizes that the real reasons are different. Men are classified according to geography or culture, according to social status or profession. That which divides them, or sometimes sets them in opposition, is their view of human prospects, their manner of confronting the great human challenges; war, injustice, under-development, etc. In our scientific and technological world the center of gravity has gradually shifted from the "religious" to the "profane." The paramount problem has become that of making the earth more habitable for men, and the matter of religion is considered only in this context. Christians themselves have become so preoccupied with the problem that their view of the task confronting the people of God has taken on new dimensions. The non-Christian is not viewed as someone who must be brought to a true knowledge of God as soon as possible. Mission in the traditional sense does not have the same appeal. We should ask ourselves frankly what *is* the meaning of non-Christian in our sort of world, and how the enterprise of mission should be conducted in this new environment.

Israel and the Gentile nations

The destiny of the Gentile nations, and the meaning of their religious pilgrimage, was a constant worry to Israel. It could hardly have been otherwise. She was never an isolated nation. She had numerous contacts not only with neighboring tribes, but with the great civilizations of the time (Egypt, Assyria, Babylon, etc.). After the fall of Samaria and Jerusalem, she herself was dispersed, and practically everywhere, in and among foreign peoples, there were Jewish communities.

Her attitude in all these associations was determined by religion. She was, by virtue of the Sinai Covenant, the chosen people of Yahweh. She worshiped the true God, and was bound by all the spiritual and moral requirements that flowed from the Covenant. The first result of this was very obvious. She had to defend her right to existence, and above all to preserve her religious identity. The danger of religious perversion would always be for her more serious than that of political servitude. There was always the temptation to revert to paganism.

At no time was there question of according any value to the religions of the Gentile nations the Jews encountered, still less of allowing these to share the adventure of faith. But the Gentile nations are not excluded from the Jewish visions of the future that were constantly being elaborated. The God of faith is the absolute Master of all creation, and his mercy is infinite. He chooses Israel, but is not disinterested in the other nations. The prophetic visions of the future would, with varying degrees of emphasis, picture the Gentile nations as the recipients of salvation as well as judgment. On the Day of Yahweh there will be opportunity for universal conversion. Some authors actually assert that the response will be more pronounced outside the frontiers of Israel than among the chosen people. They did not hesitate, at least in the realm of imagination, to have a Gentile play the role of Job, which is so revealing about the meaning of faith. And to Jonah's preaching the Ninevites have an unprecedented reaction.

Thus, in Jewish estimate, the religious experience of the Gentiles is worthless because they do not know the true God. The day will come however when Yahweh will manifest himself to them too, and they will have their place in the definitive city, though Israel, of course, will be the principal beneficiary.

Jesus of Nazareth, brother to all

With the Messiah's intervention in history, the pilgrimage of Israel reaches its goal. The ultimate implications of a recognition of the Totally-Other God become clear. God's creative initiative is concerned with all humanity, and all men are brothers because of their basic dependence on God as Father. The choice of Israel does not of itself entail any privilege. It simply marks out this people for a unique role in the realization of the universal plan. The concept of the Gentile which Jesus had is set against this background.

His ministry is revealing. He does not seek out Gentiles. His mission is to Israel, and as Messiah he endeavors to mobilize all the energies of Israel for her great task as witness among the peoples of the earth. But when he does encounter the occasional Gentile, he does not hesitate, if that is the case, to marvel at their faith, very often to the astonishment of Jewish witnesses. He is clearly convinced that, before God, all men are brothers; that the Spirit is at work among the Gentiles, that their religious experience has a meaning. As time goes on, Israel's refusal as a people to accept the thinking of the Messiah throws his universalism into higher relief. The mission reserved for the chosen people will henceforward be entrusted to any man who follows Jesus, and agrees to obey his new commandment of love without limits.

In this view, worship of the Father in spirit and in truth is bound up inextricably with the practice of fraternal charity, and the double love is brought to perfection in his own person. The Spirit, at work in all men, is already leading them towards this ideal. Religion and life are one. Insofar as he devotes his life to the least of his brethren, any man, whether he realizes this or not (note the last judgment scene in Mt 25), is on the way to encounter with Jesus. The opposition between Jew and Gentile now becomes the opposition between hate and love, and here there can be no reconciliation.

The people of God and all humanity

The very first years of the Christian religion made its unique character unmistakeable. The story unfolded from the Cornelius episode through the foundation of the Antioch Church up to the Council of Jerusalem (see first readings of this Sunday) has one major lesson. Faith in the living Christ requires a radical breach in Jewish particularism. Every man is summoned to be a disciple of the Risen Lord, and in order to become that it is not necessary to follow the road of Judaism and mosaic observance. As we read the Acts of the Apostles we are struck by the fact that all incidents indicative of this major preoccupation are presented in terms of the first Pentecost. The discovery that is being made by the apostles and the first Christians, all of Jewish origin, is that the Holy Spirit is at work outside the confines of Judaism. Despite the hesitancy and opposition of some at the beginning, Christian experience itself is leading to this conclusion. It is a thoroughly disconcerting conclusion for anyone with a Jewish habit of thinking.

The Second Vatican Council was voicing this same conviction when it offered a dynamic concept of the Church which had no juridical limits except those of humanity itself. The constitution on the Church tells us that every man is "ordained" to the people of God. That is to say that every man's spiritual pilgrimage, under the influence of the Spirit, leads him towards the fulfillment that Christ, through the Church which is his Body, can provide.

A dynamic concept of the people of God suggests a dynamic concept of the non-Christian as well. The non-Christian is a man journeying towards Christ. However tentative his pilgrimage, it has meaning in the eyes of God and will be fulfilled in Christ. One day he should find himself at home in the Church, as a brother among his own, because he is already virtually part of it. The mission of the people of God is to encounter all men, as they are and where they are, bearing witness to genuine love. It is a mission of dialogue: the non-Christian is always being invited to take one step more, perhaps the decisive step, along the road he has been traveling.

Evangelizing non-Christians now

We repeat. Our basic responsibility as people of God is to engraft the mystery of Christ into the spiritual consciousness of all peoples. We want them all, under the inspiration of the Holy Spirit, to find the answer to their most profound and secret yearning.

That being so, why is it that Christians have been so slow to discern the influence of the Spirit in the religious experience of non-Christian peoples? The answer is very obvious. Whenever Christianity takes root in a non-Christian environment, it takes time, on some points a great deal of time, before its full implications are discerned. The world in which Christianity first spread was a sacral world, as the history of Western Christianity shows. The language of rite and religion was vastly more important than the language of life, so much so that Christians during the early centuries had to meet the accusation of atheism. From the 4th century onwards, when the Empire become officially Christian, its sacral structure as well became part of Christianity. Once more there was great emphasis on religious expression, and liturgies were multiplied. Unwittingly for the most part, there was a regression to Old Testament attitudes about unbelievers. The Jewish mentality rather than that of the apostolic Church, grew prevalent. Mission itself took on the characteristics of Jewish proselytism under the Diaspora.

Yet, as time went on, the missionary ferment in the Western Church led to the eradication of such attitudes. By inviting men to accept fully the human predicament under the aegis of the new commandment of love, Christians were really countering the natural tendency to sacralize. Gradually, in the West, the center of gravity shifted from religious expression to actual living. Once set in proper perspective, man could form a clearer view of what his liberty meant, and what the actual practice of love without limits demanded. The analysis of the whole development would require much space, and it is a development that is far from being completed. Since the 13th century, when Thomas Aquinas formulated accurately the distinction between supernatural and natural, we have its theological justification.

So that, at the point where we find ourselves today in this development, the normal Christian concept of the non-Christian is already vastly different from the one that prevailed for centuries. It is also much closer to the gospel concept. The man who does not know Christ belongs already to the order of salvation accomplished in Christ. He is on his way towards Christ, insofar as he is involved in the service of his fellow men. In the conduct of mission the people of God, since Vatican II, are fully aware that proselytism must be definitively replaced by dialogue.

Welcoming non-Christians to the eucharistic assembly

The picture presented by the ecclesial Institution and the groupings that it sponsors, will depend on the concept that prevails in the Church of the non-Christian. Should it be altogether negative, the exchange between Institution and non-Christian will be a one-way exchange. He will not be thought of as having any contribution to make to those who possess the truth. But if he is regarded as someone whom God loves, with whom the Spirit works, someone who is needed by the Christian in order that he himself be realized, someone who is already a brother in the people of God, he will find his natural place in the institution. At the point where he finds himself in his spiritual search, he will be welcomed, and he will have something to bring.

Apart from formal catechumenates, the only ecclesial assemblies we know are those composed exclusively of Christians. Our heritage from the past has made us too prone to regard baptism as the essential gate of entry. It could of course be conceivably postponed, and made the term of a long series of associations where Christians and non-Christians would come to know one another deeply. Happily there are indications of such association. Christians who have explored avenues of reflection with non-Christians know how enriching this can be for their own understanding of the mystery of Christ. Even the atheist must be regarded as a brother, who shares the human condition. His questionings are very relevant to Christian problems.

All our assemblies should be assemblies for all people; and this is particularly true of the assembly *par excellence*, the breaking of the Bread. Every eucharistic celebration should reach out to all humanity, and exhibit to the full the note of catholicity. When Christ gives us his body and his blood, he is giving us all men as brothers in faith. Believing this, we are fitted to engage in dialogue with all for the furtherance, under God, of all humanity.

TABLE OF READINGS